➢ 2018-2019 EDITION ◄

A COMPLETE GUIDE TO GUN LAW IN FLORIDA

FLORIDA GUN LAW

Armed And Educated

By Attorneys
David S. Katz, and James D. Phillips, Jr.

Written by David S. Katz, James D. Phillips, Jr. and published in the United States of America
By U.S. Law Shield, LLP
ISBN 978-0-692-68021-6

To order additional books by phone or for wholesale orders call (877) 448-6839.

TABLE OF CONTENTS

PREFACE

As the independent program lawyers for U.S. Law Shield in the State of Florida we have had the opportunity to lecture to thousands of gun owners throughout the State of Florida at hundreds of workshops and seminars over the last six years. We have been surprised, and often times shocked at the misinformation about the law that circulates in this State on social media, the press and in the form of urban myths and legends. We have attended conceal carry classes and listened to the instructors do a great job informing their classes about firearms law in the limited amount of time they have. We have decided to do our part in assisting these intructors and other firearm professionals in eradicating rumors, folk lore, and mistaken beliefs about Florida Gun law and the right of self-defense.

The right to bear arms is a fundamental right found in the Second Amendment to the U.S. Constitution. Our passion is helping to protect Second Amendment rights for all legal gun owners. Equally important is our desire to protect those legal gun owners forced to defend themselves. As lawyers with years of experience representing law-abiding gun owners in cases all over the State of Florida, we have seen what can happen to those exercising their Second Amendment rights when they get mixed up in the legal system. Sometimes they are wrongly accused. Other times, they simply were poorly trained, and improperly educated about the requirements and responsibilities of Florida law that come with firearm ownership.

The law can be complicated, overlapping, and difficult to understand. In some cases, Florida law and federal law seem to contradict each other. There are also times when the state law seems to contradict itself. These contradicting and confusing laws often lead attorneys and judges with years of experience to disagree about what is required to comply with the law. How then are those not trained in the law to figure this out for themselves?

After years of legal work in the arena of firearms law, and speaking to gun owning Floridians at hundreds of gun law seminars throughout the State of Florida, we found there did not exist a resource that explained gun law in a manner that was easy for everyone to understand. Because understanding the law goes far beyond just reading it, we decided to produce this work. If you do not know either the process by which the law is being administered or how the courts are interpreting the meaning of the law, then you don't understand the full legal story.

That is why we wrote Florida Gun Law: Armed And Educated. Whenever appropriate, we tried to present useful analysis and real-world applications. Our goal was to explain the "law" so gun owners who wanted to could inform and educate themselves. Thousands of attorney hours have gone into producing this book, always with education as the goal. Many people firmly believe that "it" can't happen to them. However, even people that have never been in trouble before can find themselves in the world of law, lawyers, and law enforcement through ignorance of the law.

In this, the second edition, we have expanded the topics covered, updated sections on the recent changes in Florida law, and added three new chapters on the law of search and seizure.

We want people to know the law; because only through eternal vigilance will we protect our cherished right to bear arms. If you own a gun, the laws concerning firearms and their use apply to you. Ignorance of the law is not a valid legal excuse. Therefore, if you want to stay legal, know the law; be ARMED and EDUCATED.

- David S. Katz, Esquire
- James D. Phillips, Jr., Esquire

"Laws that forbid the carrying of arms…only disarm those who are neither inclined nor determined to commit crimes…Such laws make things worse for the assaulted and better for the assailants; they serve rather to encourage than to prevent homicides, for an unarmed man may be attacked with greater confidence than an armed man."

- Thomas Jefferson quoting Cesare Beccaria's Essay on Crime and Punishment.

CHAPTER ONE

BRIEF LEGAL HISTORY OF
THE RIGHT TO BEAR ARMS
And The Laws Regulating Firearms

I. INTRODUCTION AND OVERVIEW

To fully understand gun rights today in Florida or the United States, one should start first at the beginning: the formation document for our federal government, the United States Constitution. The Constitution was written without any enumerated guaranteed individual rights. The founding fathers thought it obvious and apparent that individuals had rights; therefore, there was no reason to write them in a document that was supposed to control the government. James Madison also thought that by naming certain rights, it would imply that those were the only rights an individual possessed. After much discussion, and a complete change of opinion by Madison, the lack of enumerated rights was remedied in the first Congressional session and the state ratification process. When the dust settled, ten amendments were added to the Constitution; these ten amendments are the Bill of Rights. It is the Second Amendment that concerns firearms specifically, though throughout this book we will reference many others, including the Fourth and Fifth Amendments that both affect your right to bear arms and other fundamental rights we all share.

II. DO I HAVE A CONSTITUTIONAL RIGHT AS AN INDIVIDUAL TO KEEP AND BEAR ARMS?

Yes; the United States Supreme Court has decided that an individual has a constitutionally given right to keep and bear arms that flows from the Second Amendment, which states simply:

> A well-regulated Militia, being necessary to the security of a free State, the right of the people to keep and bear Arms, shall not be infringed.

From a plain reading, there are two important parts to this amendment: first, that a well-regulated militia is necessary to the security of a free state, and second, that there is a right of the people to keep and bear arms. For years, before the issue was decided, anti-gun activists have tried to argue that the Second Amendment only applied to "militias" and not to individuals. Luckily, this argument is not the law. Nevertheless, despite the Supreme Court rulings stating otherwise, this myth seems to persist. What do these parts of the Second Amendment mean? Are they the same, or are they different?

A. What is a "Well-Regulated Militia?"

As we discussed earlier, the first part of the Second Amendment references a "well-regulated militia." What is a well-regulated militia? The U.S. Supreme Court has held what this phrase does and does not mean. In 1939, in the case of *United States v. Miller*, 307 U.S. 174 (1939) (ironically, a ruling that upheld firearms regulation), the court defined a Militia as comprising "all males physically capable of acting in concert for the common defense." Based on how the amendment was drafted, the Court stated, it was clear that the Militia pre-dated Article I of the Constitution, because unlike armies and navies, it did not have to be created by Congress. What then is "well-regulated" per the court? It is exactly what it sounds like: the imposition of discipline and training. So, is this just the National Guard? No.

In the case of *D.C. v. Heller*, 554 U.S. 570 (2008), the Supreme Court stated that the well-regulated militia is not the state's military forces, but a separate entity altogether. The Supreme Court stated that the word "militia" referred to the body of the people, and they—the people—were required to keep a centralized government in check. The Supreme Court considered and rejected the position that the National Guard is the current militia under the Second Amendment.

B. How has the phrase "right to keep and bear arms" been interpreted by the courts?

One of the first cases to directly deal with the Second Amendment was *United States v. Miller*, 307 U.S. 174 (1939). In Miller, the Supreme Court found that the National Firearms Act ("NFA"), which imposed registration requirements on machine guns, short-barreled weapons, destructive devices, and other similarly unique firearms, did not violate the Second Amendment. The Court used the reasoning that possession of weapons regulated by the NFA did not reasonably relate to the preservation or efficiency of a well-regulated militia, therefore, the NFA was held constitutional.

UNITED STATES V. MILLER, 307 U.S. 174 (1939)

THE FACTS

Defendants, Miller and Layton, transported a double barrel 12-gauge shotgun with a barrel length of less than 18 inches from Oklahoma to Arkansas, and were being prosecuted under the National Firearms Act (which required certain types of firearms to be registered and a tax to be paid). Defendants challenged the NFA as an unconstitutional violation of the Second Amendment.

THE LEGAL HOLDINGS

Upheld the National Firearms Act as Constitutional and not a violation of the 2nd Amendment.

An interesting quirk of history in the Miller case (and not a shining moment for the legal system) is that Miller's attorney never appeared at the arguments before the U.S. Supreme Court because he was court-appointed and had not been paid. There was no written brief and no legal representation at oral arguments by the party arguing that the law was unconstitutional. The Court only heard the government's side. To make matters worse, Miller was shot to death before the decision was rendered.

C. 69 years later, the U.S. Supreme Court interprets the Second Amendment again: *D.C. v. Heller*

It would be 69 years after Miller until the U.S. Supreme Court addressed the Second Amendment directly again, except this time the Court would hear both the government's and the defendant's arguments. Fortunately, freedom and Second Amendment rights prevailed in court that day. The Court held that individuals have a right to keep and bear arms.

DISTRICT OF COLUMBIA V. HELLER, 554 U.S. 570 (2008)

THE FACTS

Heller had applied for a handgun ownership permit and was denied; without such a permit, D.C. required that all firearms (including rifles and shotguns) be kept unloaded and disassembled, or bound by a trigger lock, even in a person's own home.

THE LEGAL HOLDINGS

1. The Supreme Court found that the Second Amendment protects an individual right of firearms ownership for purposes of self-defense, not connected with any militia or military purposes; it further elaborated that individual self-defense is "the central component" of the Second Amendment. Further, handguns are the primary defensive weapon of choice and are protected by the Second Amendment.

2. A well-regulated militia is not the state's military forces.

3. The Court also discussed what the phrase "bear arms" meant: "wear, bear, or carry... upon the person or in clothing or in a pocket, for the purpose... of being armed and ready for offensive or defensive action in a case of conflict with another person."

4. The D.C. regulation was held to be unconstitutional.

5. The Court concluded that like other rights, the right to bear arms is not completely absolute. Reasonable provisions and restrictions have been upheld.

Keep in mind *D.C. v. Heller* was a split 5-4 decision; only one justice away from a completely different outcome, where the Second Amendment (according to the dissent) had "outlived its usefulness and should be ignored."

D. Can states ignore the Second Amendment? *McDonald v. City of Chicago*

D.C. v. Heller was fantastic, but there was a slight quirk: The District of Columbia is under the exclusive jurisdiction of Congress and is not part of any state. Therefore, the case shed no light on the question of what states can do when it comes to regulating or banning firearms. How do state constitutions interact with the Second Amendment and can states ban guns outright?

McDonald v. City of Chicago sought to answer these questions.

MCDONALD V. CITY OF CHICAGO, 561 U.S. 742 (2010)

THE FACTS

McDonald v. City of Chicago was decided in 2010; a Chicago ordinance banned handgun possession (among other gun regulations). McDonald was a 76-year-old retired maintenance engineer who wanted a handgun for self-defense. Chicago required that all handguns had to be registered, but refused all handgun registration after a 1982 citywide handgun ban.

THE LEGAL HOLDINGS

The Supreme Court held that the Second Amendment is fully applicable to the States and that individual self-defense is "the central component" of the Second Amendment. Therefore, the Second Amendment prohibits states from enacting bans on handguns for self-protection in the home.

E. Legal limitations of the right to keep and bear arms

The U.S. Supreme Court has stated: "Of course the right [to keep and bear arms] was not unlimited, just as the First Amendment's right of free speech was not." Courts may have struggled over the years with what the Second Amendment means, but they have been resolute that there is an element of self-defense. The Heller Court stated that, "The Second Amendment does not protect the right to carry arms for any sort of confrontation," focusing their decision on self-defense. Further, the Miller Court stated that the weapons protected were those "in common use at the time" of the decision. This is supported by historical traditions of prohibiting the carry of "dangerous and unusual weapons" that are commonly used by criminals offensively, as opposed to by law-abiding citizens for defensive purposes.

The Second Amendment does not protect against prohibitions on firearm possession by felons and the mentally ill; Heller made this point in its decision, and many circuit court cases such as *U.S. v. Everist* follow the same reasoning. The Court of Appeals in *U.S. v. Everist* states that the Second Amendment is subject to, "limited narrowly tailored specific exceptions or restrictions for particular cases that are reasonable; it is clear that felons, infants and those of unsound mind may be prohibited from possessing firearms." *U.S. v. Everist*, 368 F.3d 517, 519 (5th Cir. 2004). Along this same train of thought, the Heller Court did not want to eliminate laws that imposed conditions and qualifications on the commercial sales of firearms.

PRACTICAL LEGAL TIP

Currently, the two most important court decisions fortifying our gun rights are Heller and McDonald. But those cases were very, very close to going the other way! Both were decided by a 5-4 majority, meaning that if only one other Supreme Court Justice had decided differently, our individual right to possess and carry firearms could have been severely limited. -David

III. MAJOR FIREARMS STATUTES
EVERY GUN OWNER NEEDS TO KNOW

At the Federal level, there are plenty of laws and regulations that concern firearms, but this section will focus on some of the more major legislative actions that all gun owners need to know.

A. Gun Control Act of 1968

The Gun Control Act of 1968 ("GCA") was enacted by Congress to "provide for better control of the interstate traffic of firearms." This law is primarily focused on regulating interstate commerce in firearms by generally prohibiting interstate firearms transfers except among licensed manufacturers, dealers, and importers; however, interstate commerce has been held by the courts to include nearly everything. It also contains classes of individuals to whom firearms should not be sold. For the specifics of who can and can't purchase a firearm, please refer to Chapter Three. Among other things, the GCA created the Federal Firearms License ("FFL") system, imposed importation restrictions on military surplus rifles (adding a "sporting purpose test" and a "points system" for handguns), and marking requirements.

B. The Brady Handgun Violence Prevention Act

The Brady Handgun Violence Prevention Act, commonly referred to as the Brady Law, instituted federal background checks (the National Instant Criminal Background Check System or NICS) for firearm purchasers in the United States. It also prohibited certain persons from purchasing firearms; for more information on who can or can't purchase a firearm, see Chapter Three.

C. The Firearm Owners' Protection Act

The Firearm Owners' Protection Act ("FOPA") revised many

provisions of the original Gun Control Act, including "reforms" on the inspection of FFLs. This same Act updated the list of individuals prohibited from purchasing firearms that was introduced by the GCA. The FOPA also banned the ownership by civilians of any machine gun that was not registered under the NFA as of May 19, 1986. FOPA created what is called a "safe passage" provision of the law, which allows for traveling across states with a firearm. Finally, FOPA prohibited a registry for non-NFA items that directly linked firearms to their owners.

D. The Public Safety and Recreational Firearms Use Protection Act

The Public Safety and Recreational Firearms Use Protection Act, commonly referred to as the Federal Assault Weapons Ban, was a subsection of the Violent Crime Control and Law Enforcement Act of 1994. It banned outright the manufacture and transfer of certain semi-automatic firearms and magazines. This ban grandfathered-in previously legally owned weapons, but no prohibited firearm could be acquired or manufactured after September 13, 1994. With great foresight, the drafters of this law included a so-called "sunset provision," that stated the ban would expire ten years later unless renewed. The ban expired in 2004, and all attempts to renew have been unsuccessful.

E. The National Firearms Act

The National Firearms Act ("NFA") regulates and imposes a statutory excise tax on the manufacture and transfer of certain types of firearms and weapons: machine guns, short-barreled weapons, suppressors, explosive devices, and "any other weapons" (AOWs can range from everyday objects that are actually firearms, such as an umbrella that can fire a round, to other weapons the ATF decides to place in this category). The tax is $200 if you make or transfer an item (other than for the transfer of AOWs); the tax for transferring AOWs is $5. The NFA is also referred to as Title II of the federal firearms laws. For more information on how to navigate the NFA while remaining legal, please see Chapter Fourteen.

IV. DO FLORIDIANS HAVE A RIGHT TO KEEP AND BEAR ARMS IN THE FLORIDA CONSTITUTION?

Yes. The Florida Constitution acknowledges the right to keep and bear arms in Article I, Section 8. This provision of the Florida Constitution has been amended several times. Article I, Section 8 currently reads:

a. The right of the people to keep and bear arms in defense of themselves and of the lawful authority of the state shall not be infringed, except that the manner of bearing arms may be regulated by law.

b. There shall be a mandatory period of three days, excluding weekends and legal holidays, between the purchase and delivery at retail of any handgun. For the purposes of this section, "purchase" means the transfer of money or other valuable consideration to the retailer, and "handgun" means a firearm capable of being carried and used by one hand, such as a pistol or revolver. Holders of a concealed weapon permit as prescribed in Florida law shall not be subject to the provisions of this paragraph.

c. The legislature shall enact legislation implementing subsection (b) of this section, effective no later than December 31, 1991, which shall provide that anyone violating the provisions of subsection (b) shall be guilty of a felony.

d. This restriction shall not apply to a trade in of another handgun.

The more observant will notice that, as opposed to the Second Amendment of the United States Constitution, this provision specifically allows for legislation. Article I, Section 8 of the Florida Constitution actually requires the regulation of the purchase of handguns and allows for further restrictions to be put on the method of carrying firearms within this state.

A. Can Florida prohibit local municipalities from making certain gun laws?

Yes. The Florida Legislature can and does prohibit local municipalities from making certain gun laws by the legal doctrine known as "preemption." A preemption statute is a mechanism by which the Florida legislature sets certain areas off limits to local governments, which helps ensure the uniformity of law across the state, in this case, firearms law.

B. What local governments may not regulate

The Florida preemption law can be found in Florida Statutes §790.33. It reads:

1. PREEMPTION.—Except as expressly provided by the State Constitution or general law, the Legislature hereby declares that it is occupying the whole field of regulation of firearms and ammunition, including the purchase, sale, transfer, taxation, manufacture, ownership, possession, storage, and transportation thereof, to the exclusion of all existing and future county, city, town, or municipal ordinances or any administrative regulations or rules adopted by local or state government relating thereto. Any such existing ordinances, rules, or regulations are hereby declared null and void.

This statute's intent is to provide uniform firearms laws in the state by prohibiting the enactment or enforcement of any local ordinances or regulations relating to firearms, ammunition, or components thereof and to prohibit the enactment of any future ordinances or regulations relating to firearms, ammunition, or components thereof unless specifically authorized.

C. What local governments may regulate

In the area of firearms, the Florida Legislature is very serious that local governments may not interfere with the rights of citizens of this state. In fact, Florida Statutes §790.33 specifies that elected officials or agents of the Government who attempt to enter the area of firearm regulation may be personally liable for penalties up to $5,000 and may not use public funds in defense of themselves or the laws, even when enacted in good faith. Further, individuals and organizations adversely effected by these illegally enacted laws may be entitled to damages up to $100,000. However, there are a few very limited areas that the State Legislature has left to the local governments that may affect a firearm owner's rights. These include:

a. Zoning ordinances that encompass firearms businesses along with other businesses, except that zoning ordinances cannot be designed to regulate firearms in conflict with the statute;

b. A law enforcement agency may enact and enforce regulations pertaining to firearms, ammunition, or firearm accessories issued to or used by its officers in the course of their official duties;

c. The ability to enact and enforce regulations of an employee of the entity during and in the course of the employee's official duties;

d. A court or administrative law judge from hearing and resolving any case or controversy or issuing any opinion or order on a matter within the jurisdiction of that court or judge; or

e. The Florida Fish and Wildlife Conservation Commission may regulate the use of firearms or ammunition as a method of taking wildlife and regulate the shooting ranges managed by the commission.

CHAPTER TWO

THE FOURTH AMENDMENT
KNOW YOUR RIGHTS
Understanding Police Power
Some Basic Legal Concepts

I. INTRODUCTION AND OVERVIEW

It's 3:00 am, the police barge into your home with a search warrant…they're at the wrong address, your family is terrorized, what are your rights? An officer approaches you on the street and asks to pat you down for weapons, what are your rights? The government listens to your private telephone calls or looks through your private documents, what are your rights? An officer wants to search your vehicle during a traffic stop, what are your rights? The answers to all these questions are found in the jurisprudence of the Fourth Amendment to the U.S. Constitution. The court cases and legislation coming out of this area are some of the fastest changing and most hotly contested in the country right now. Everything from when the government can take your DNA, to what parts of your house the police can look in, the use of "no knock warrants," to searching a smartphone are disputed topics. Commonly known as the law of "search and seizure," this is the most crucial protection we have from the government prying into our private lives and property. Let's take a closer look at Fourth Amendment rights.

II. WHAT IS THE FOURTH AMENDMENT?

The American Constitutional restriction on governmental searches and seizures is one of the first attempts by any society to protect the people from the government itself. Simply put, the Fourth Amendment stops government agents (usually the police, but applicable to any person acting under government authority) from interfering with, searching, or seizing a person or their property without first establishing "probable cause" and securing a warrant. The actual text of the Fourth Amendment reads:

> The right of the people to be secure in their persons, houses, papers, and effects, against unreasonable searches and seizures, shall not be violated, and no Warrants shall issue, but upon probable cause, supported by Oath or affirmation, and particularly describing the place to be searched, and the persons or things to be seized.

A. Why was this protection included in the Bill of Rights?

The men who drafted the U.S. Constitution and its first ten amendments, the Bill of Rights, wanted to keep the government from gaining overarching power to abuse its citizens. The Fourth Amendment, specifically, is a result of these founding fathers' disgust and concern with the British "writ of assistance." These writs were widely used by Great Britain in the American colonies and functioned as general search and seizure warrants with no requirement they state what locations to search or what items to seize. To make matters even worse, they never expired and could be transferred from person to person. The result was a blanket authorization by the British government to interfere with the private affairs of the colonists, with no real restrictions, checks or balances. The goal of the Fourth Amendment was to restrict the police and provide "security" to Americans against a snooping, abusive government.

B. How is the government limited today?

Today's driving force in Fourth Amendment law is called the "reasonable expectation of privacy." This concept recognizes that private affairs follow the person, and are not necessarily confined to a particular location (such as a home or car). When an individual is guaranteed a reasonable expectation of privacy, the government must obtain a warrant from a neutral magistrate (or satisfy an exception as discussed in Chapter 4) before conducting a lawful search or seizure. This reasonable expectation of privacy is what we think of as our "right to privacy." While it is not a right specifically guaranteed in the Bill of Rights, it is a principle that comes from courts interpreting the Fourth Amendment over the decades.

III. LEGAL LEVELS OF PROOF

Officers must meet certain standards of proof before engaging in many police encounters with citizens. To lawfully detain, search, or arrest, the police must obtain certain levels of proof to believe that a person is connected to some criminal activity. What are these levels of proof and how are they defined in Florida?

A. Reasonable suspicion

Reasonable suspicion is the legal standard that a police officer must have to legally stop and detain a person or "pat down" a person for weapons or contraband (a Terry Stop, discussed below). What does this murky concept mean? It is a very low standard of proof and requires a minimal level of objective evidence. Reasonable suspicion occurs when a police officer has "a reasonable suspicion that a person has committed, is committing, or is about to commit a crime. § 901.151 Fla.Stat. (1991). In order not to violate a citizen's Fourth Amendment rights, an investigatory stop requires a well-founded, articulable suspicion of criminal activity. Mere suspicion is not enough to support a stop. *Carter v. State*, 454 So.2d 739 (Fla. 2d DCA 1984)." *Popple v. State*, 626 So.2d 185, 62 USLW 230818 Fla. L. Weekly S533 (1993). Reasonable suspicion cannot be based on a mere hunch or guess. Unfortunately, the facts and reasons can be subject to interpretation, and the U.S. Supreme Court and Florida Supreme Court have found reasonable suspicion from conduct that is as consistent with innocent activity as it is with criminal activity. For example, reasonable suspicion can come from your car being too clean, being too dirty, driving under the speed limit, or driving the exact speed limit, depending on the situational factors.

TERRY V. OHIO, 392 U.S. 1 (1968)

THE FACTS

John Terry was stopped and frisked by a veteran police officer when the officer spotted Terry and another man repeatedly walking up and down a street and peering into store windows. During the search, the officer found a concealed handgun in Terry's possession, which was a violation of Ohio law. The officer testified that he conducted the frisk because he suspected the men were "casing" a store for a potential robbery.

THE LEGAL HOLDINGS

The Supreme Court held that an officer may stop a suspect and perform a brief search for weapons when he has a reasonable belief that the person may be engaging in criminal activity and is potentially armed. This ruling made history by providing the government an avenue to search on a standard less than probable cause.

As you can see, Mr. Terry did nothing more than lawfully walk up and down the street and look in some store windows; an activity that is done by millions on a daily basis.

B. Probable cause

Probable cause is the minimum legal standard of proof required by law before a police officer may lawfully arrest someone or search a vehicle without a warrant, or, for a judge or magistrate to issue a search warrant or arrest warrant. This relatively low level of proof is defined by the U.S. Supreme Court as available trustworthy facts that would lead a reasonable person to believe that the person under investigation had committed or is committing an offense. *See Beck v. Ohio*, 379 U.S. 89, 91 (1964). Probable cause is evaluated on a case by case basis and has no precise formula. Sometimes, a person is eligible for certain defenses or exceptions to shield him from criminal responsibility. Unfortunately, an officer does not need to investigate and rule out all possible defenses and exceptions before developing probable cause that an offense is being committed.

C. Preponderance of the evidence/clear and convincing evidence

Preponderance of the evidence and clear and convincing evidence are standards of proof that predominantly apply to civil causes of action. For more information on these terms, and civil liability generally, see Chapter 15.

D. Beyond a reasonable doubt

This is the highest level of legal proof and is the standard of proof that must be established in trial before a person can be convicted of a criminal act. How is it defined? In Florida, the definition of reasonable doubt can be found in the standard jury instruction for criminal cases, which reads, "A reasonable doubt is not a mere possible doubt, a speculative, imaginary or forced doubt. Such a doubt must not influence you to return a verdict of not guilty if you have an abiding conviction of guilt. On the other hand, if, after carefully considering, comparing and weighing all the evidence, there is not an abiding conviction of guilt, or, if, having a conviction, it is one which is not stable but one which wavers and vacillates, then the charge is not proved beyond every reasonable doubt and you must find the defendant not guilty because the doubt is reasonable." In general, it has been described as the level of certainty that a reasonable person should have before unplugging the life support system for a loved one, or the certainty that a person would need in packing their parachute before jumping out of a perfectly good aircraft. The government must provide this level of evidence before a conviction may occur. In short, the State needs reasonable suspicion to detain a person, probable cause to arrest a person, and proof beyond a reasonable doubt to convict a person.

IV. WHAT IS A SEARCH?

What definition do courts give to the term "search" under the Fourth Amendment? A search must be 1) an intrusion into an individual's reasonable expectation of privacy; 2) by a government agent. If the examination or investigation of a person, place, or property does not violate someone's reasonable expectation of privacy, or, was not done by a government agent, it is not subject to the restrictions of the Fourth Amendment.

The most common searches are of the home, vehicle, and person. However, the Fourth Amendment is not limited to these areas. As stated above, a search can occur anywhere a person has a reasonable expectation of privacy. For example, searches often include private documents, bank records, electronic communications, DNA samples, and countless other intrusions into private affairs.

V. WHAT IS A SEIZURE?
If the government demonstrates the appropriate level of proof, they may make a seizure of either a person or property.

A. What is a seizure of a person?
Someone is "seized" when a reasonable person would understand from the conduct of a police officer and the circumstances surrounding the encounter that he or she was not free to terminate the encounter and leave the interaction. Two elements must be satisfied for an act to constitute a seizure of a person: 1) there is a show of authority by the officer, and 2) the citizen submits to that authority. This kind of seizure occurs during investigatory stops, detentions, and arrests (see police encounters, below).

B. What is a seizure of property?
The government has "seized" property under the Fourth Amendment anytime a government agent creates a meaningful interference with a person's possessory right in property. To seize, the government must show probable cause that the property was 1) illegal; 2) evidence of a crime, or 3) "fruit" or property acquired as a result of a crime.

VI. POLICE POWER
The power of police is bestowed through legislation and affects the rights of individuals when the balance of interests favors the health, safety, and maintenance of the general public over the individual's rights to act as he or she pleases free from government interruption, intrusion, or prohibition.

A. What is the role of police?

There are many different police organizations. Most often, we encounter police employed by the State of Florida, individual counties, municipalities, etc. There is no general federal police power. However, there are law enforcement bodies controlled by the U.S. government that enforce laws in areas specifically under federal control. Federal law enforcement bodies (often referred to as "bureaus") include the Federal Bureau of Investigation, the Bureau of Alcohol, Tobacco, Firearms, and Explosives, United States Immigration and Customs Enforcement, United States Park Police, and many others.

Though it's hard to generalize the day to day routines of these vastly different agencies, law enforcement functions performed by police can be broken down into three broad areas: 1) maintaining order through general patrols and surveillance, particularly with high visibility policing; 2) enforcing the laws against violators and apprehending and arresting those suspected of breaking the law; and 3) providing services unrelated to criminal activity, such as rendering first aid, helping distressed citizens, etc. For example, a patrol officer on a usual day can patrol streets, investigate a burglary, and help get a cat out of a tree all before lunchtime.

It's the "law enforcement" function that we are most concerned about in this chapter. This is where the police commit the most intrusion and are most likely to run up against (or through!) the rights of individuals.

B. Limits on police power

The Florida and U.S. Constitutions serve as the greatest restraint on police power. Specifically, the Fourth, Fifth, and Sixth Amendments to the U.S. Constitution, and the case law that has flowed from these amendments, function to keep the government in check with strict consequences for violations. *See* Section IX below for a detailed explanation of what happens when the police violate your rights.

VII. ENCOUNTERS WITH THE POLICE

A. When do my Fourth Amendment rights matter?

The Fourth Amendment is designed to protect citizens during encounters with the police and other government agents. These encounters take several different forms. The Fourth Amendment does not cover a private citizen interacting with other private citizens.

B. Voluntary encounter

AA police officer can approach any person who is located in a "public place" and engage them in ordinary conversation, just as any other person could do. The approach can be very casual; "lovely weather," or "nice boots." A person who finds themselves in a voluntary encounter with a police officer is fully within their rights to not engage in conversation or to walk away.

Courts have decided that the act of walking away from a police officer during a voluntary encounter does not create a reasonable suspicion that they are involved in criminal activity. However, any statements given or observations made during a voluntary encounter may establish reasonable suspicion to detain or probable cause to search and/or arrest a person. Any evidence found during the voluntary encounter may be used in court based on the person's consent in talking with the police officer. (See Chapter 4 for more issues on consent.)

Jim is walking at a bus stop when the police approach and ask where he is going. Jim ignores them just as the bus pulls up. Jim has a legal right to get on the bus without being detained by the police.

C. Temporary detention

A temporary detention occurs when a police officer stops and holds a person, restricting their right to walk away. A police officer is legally justified in conducting a temporary detention when the officer has "reasonable suspicion" based on specific articulable facts that a person has broken, is breaking or will break the law. While lawfully detained, a police officer may check arrest warrants, frisk the outside of clothing, and/or remove weapons.

Typically, there is no requirement for a police officer to read a person their Miranda Rights warning (*see* discussion of *Miranda v. Arizona*, below) during a temporary detention. What a person says to the police and the surrounding circumstances of the detention may give rise to probable cause to arrest even if the detention was based on completely different suspicion. Any evidence obtained during the temporary detention may be used against that person in court.

Police receive a call about a man wearing a red shirt who is causing a commotion at the park. Upon arrival, the police observe a man matching the description who appears intoxicated. The police have reasonable suspicion to detain this man for criminal investigation.

D. Arrest

Police may arrest a person if they have probable cause to believe a crime has been or is being committed. In Florida, a formal arrest occurs when someone is placed into custody in a manner such that a reasonable person would believe they have been deprived of their freedom. At the point of arrest, most of the person's legal rights and protections are triggered, including the right to remain silent, the right to counsel, etc. Remember: Don't waive your rights without talking to your lawyer!

EXAMPLE

Police are called to the scene of a convenience store robbery. While talking to the clerk, he says "There he is!" and points to Gordon walking down the street. The police lawfully detain Gordon, pat him down and find a 10-inch chef's knife in his jacket. Gordon can now be lawfully arrested.

E. "COMMUNITY CARETAKING"

This encounter doesn't fit nicely into the categories of police interactions. An officer may approach a citizen if he "reasonably believes" the citizen is in need of assistance. It was expressly allowed in Florida by the Fourth District Court of Appeals in the Court of Criminal Appeals in the 2007 case of *Castella v. State*, 959 So.2d 1285, 1292 (Fla. 4th DCA), relying on the U.S. Supreme Court case of *Cody v. Dombrowski*, 413 U.S. 433 (1978). Courts will determine whether the officer was reasonable by looking to the level and nature of distress exhibited, the location of the individual, the ability to receive assistance from others, and the extent to which the individual posed a danger to himself or others. A community caretaking encounter does not provide the right to search absent independent reasonable suspicion or probable cause, and generally only applies to public property. However, the incriminating information an officer gets from this encounter can give him reasonable suspicion for an investigation or probable cause for an additional detention or arrest.

A police officer observes Michele sleeping in a car outside of a bar. The officer can lawfully approach her against her will to determine whether she needs medical attention. After waking her, if he determines that she is intoxicated he can arrests her for DUI, even though he had no initial indication of a crime.

VIII. THE FIFTH AMENDMENT

A. What are my rights against self-incrimination?

The Fifth Amendment to the U.S. Constitution protects an individual from being compelled to be a "witness against himself," among other rights. This means the state cannot force a person to make statements or testify in court, especially when they are against their own self-interest or are incriminating.

B. Do the police have to read the Miranda Rights warning after every arrest?

No! The Miranda Rights warning is not required simply because a person is placed into handcuffs and charged with a crime. This warning is only required when the police 1) place a person into custody, and 2) wish to interrogate that person. Whether or not someone is in "custody" for the purposes of Miranda Rights is determined by analyzing the facts and circumstances to determine if his or her freedom of action has been deprived in a significant way. Generally, an arrest will equate to "custody." However, there are some circumstances in which a person has not been arrested, but is in "custody" for the purposes of the Miranda Rights warning. If the police do not wish to interrogate the person in custody, there is no need for a Miranda Rights warning to be read. However, if the police wish to ask questions of the individual in custody to further their own investigation or to obtain a confession, they must administer this warning.

MIRANDA V. ARIZONA, 384 U.S. 436 (1966)

THE FACTS

The decision of *Miranda v. Arizona* actually addressed four different cases. In each case, the criminal suspect was questioned by law enforcement for many hours, isolated in an interrogation room with no outside communication, and ultimately each suspect gave a confession to law enforcement. None of the four defendants were advised of their Fifth Amendment rights during the interrogation process.

THE LEGAL HOLDINGS

The Court held that "there can be no doubt that the Fifth Amendment privilege is available outside of criminal court proceedings and serves to protect persons in all settings in which their freedom of action is curtailed in any significant way from being compelled to incriminate themselves." They concluded that, "the prosecution may not use statements, whether exculpatory or inculpatory, stemming from custodial interrogation of the defendant unless it demonstrates the use of procedural safeguards effective to secure the privilege against self-incrimination. By custodial interrogation, we mean questioning initiated by law enforcement officers after a person has been taken into custody or otherwise deprived of his freedom of action in any significant way." The result of this holding is the "Miranda Warning" we are familiar with today. When a suspect is subjected to custodial interrogation by law enforcement officials, the resulting statements are not admissible unless the suspect first knowingly waived his or her rights.

IX. WHAT HAPPENS IF THE POLICE VIOLATE MY RIGHTS?

A. Exclusionary rule

What can you do when the government has overstepped its limits and violated your Fourth or Fifth Amendment rights? If a person is found to be in possession of criminal evidence or contraband, or have made statements that are against their interest and they are successful in persuading the judge that the police officer's search, seizure, or interrogation was unconstitutional, their recourse is found in a legal principle called the exclusionary rule. The exclusionary rule states that illegally obtained evidence or evidence obtained as a result of or consequence of the violation of an individual's rights are "fruit of the poisonous tree" and cannot be used as evidence in the criminal trial of the person, even if this results in a guilty person going free. The exclusionary rule exists at both the federal level and the state level.

B. The federal exclusionary rule

There are a few judicially recognized exceptions to the exclusionary rule where the "illegally obtained" evidence may still be admissible against the accused. This includes evidence found in "good faith" reliance on a search warrant later determined to be legally defective, or pursuant to a statute later declared to be unconstitutional. Evidence may also be admitted if it has become sufficiently disassociated with the illegal police action, it was legally obtained from an independent source, or it would have been inevitably discovered through other legal means. The U.S Supreme Court has also ruled that the government may use illegally obtained evidence if the police officer made a "reasonable" mistake of fact or of law. Further, any evidence excluded during the prosecution phase of a criminal trial can later be admissible if the defendant "opens the door" to the issue by referring to it in the testimony at trial.

In order to take advantage of the exclusionary rule, the person charged with the crime has to have "standing" to make the evidentiary challenge. What does this mean? Simply that the person making the challenge had an expectation of privacy, was wronged by the police action, and their personal Fourth or Fifth Amendment rights were violated.

EXAMPLE

George and Mary go out to a bar. Mary drives her car to the bar but gets drunk, so she asks George to drive home. On the way home, George is pulled over and arrested for DUI. After his arrest, the police search the car and find a bag under the driver's seat that contains cocaine and stolen firearms. George denies that the bag is his, but the police charge him with possession of cocaine and possession of stolen property among other crimes. George does not have standing to challenge the search of the bag since he denies it was his, he cannot claim any expectation of privacy in it.

C. The Florida exclusionary rule

Florida has its own version of the Exclusionary Rule found in the Florida Constitution. Article 1, Section 12 of the Florida Constitution reads, "Searches and seizures.—The right of the people to be secure in their persons, houses, papers and effects against unreasonable searches and seizures, and against the unreasonable interception of private communications by any means, shall not be violated. No warrant shall be issued except upon probable cause, supported by affidavit, particularly describing the place or places to be searched, the person or persons, thing or things to be seized, the communication to be intercepted, and the nature of evidence to be obtained. Articles or information obtained in violation of this right shall not be admissible in evidence." The last sentence of this section mandates the exclusion of any evidence obtained unconstitutionally.

D. Section 1983 claim

When a person's civil rights, including their rights against illegal searches, are violated by a police officer, a person may file a civil lawsuit under Title 42 United State Code Section 1983, which is commonly referred to as a "1983 Claim." The United States Supreme Court has ruled that a police officer and his or her department may be liable for monetary damages if a person's civil rights are violated. However, there is a huge exception to this rule: If the court finds a reasonable police officer could have believed a search or seizure was lawful, a police officer will be cloaked with qualified immunity, legally excusing the officer from civil liability. This means a plaintiff will have to show that a police officer knew his or her conduct was against the law. This will make a 1983 Claim an uphill battle for any aggrieved person.

To bring a successful Section 1983 Claim, a person must show 1) A person acting under the color of law (for example, a police officer acting within the scope of their employment as a police officer); 2) deprived the individual of their rights guaranteed by the U.S. Constitution or laws of the United States.

Now that we have laid a groundwork for the basic legal concepts underlying Fourth Amendment law, the following chapters will discuss the practical applications.

CHAPTER THREE

KNOW YOUR RIGHTS:
THE FOURTH AMENDMENT
Understanding The Warrant Requirement In Florida

I. INTRODUCTION AND OVERVIEW

The text of the Fourth Amendment requires that the government have a warrant based on probable cause when they want to invade our privacy or place us under arrest. Unfortunately, the words of the Fourth Amendment are not the end of the story. Over the years, the courts and the legislature have chipped away at the warrant requirement and created an incredible number of exceptions. So many, in fact, that today there are far more searches and seizures conducted without a warrant than with one. Despite this sad reality, warrants remain the general rule, and it is important to understand how they are obtained and executed.

II. WHAT IS THE WARRANT REQUIREMENT?

Let's start with the most basic question—what is a warrant? A warrant is a document issued by a government official, typically a magistrate judge, authorizing a police officer to arrest a person, search and/or seize property. A search warrant gives the government authority to conduct a search of a specified place and seize evidence of criminal acts or to install monitoring equipment in or on certain property. A magistrate can also issue a warrant that authorizes the "seizure" of a human being. This is called an arrest warrant, and it directs a law enforcement officer to arrest and bring "the body of the person" accused of criminal wrongdoing in front of the court.

PRACTICAL LEGAL TIP

What is a magistrate? Nearly every type of judge is a magistrate. The most common magistrate is a justice of the peace. Part of their duties include issuing warrants and advising those who have been arrested of their charges and initial legal rights. -David

A. How is a warrant issued?

First, police learn of activity leading them to believe a search or seizure of property will reveal evidence of a crime, or that a person has committed a criminal act. Police might gather this information through their own investigation and first-hand knowledge, or through information gathered by a confidential informant ("CI"). Next, the police officer drafts a sworn statement supporting the request to arrest or search. He will include all relevant facts he has gathered in his investigation or from his CI. He will often include photos, maps, or other visual evidence with his sworn statement. After the warrant is drafted, a neutral magistrate judge reviews the sworn statement and determines whether or not the officer has articulated probable cause for the arrest or search. See Chapter 2 for the definition of probable cause. If probable cause has been established, the magistrate judge signs the warrant, and police may then execute the warrant. This means the police now have full authority to search and/or seize property or persons described in the warrant.

Consider this example: Justin is arrested for possession of crack cocaine. Justin tells police where he bought the crack. Police write an affidavit describing details given by Justin about the crack house on Maple Street. The requested search warrant and attached affidavit are given to a magistrate who signs it, thus authorizing police to raid the crack house.

THE WARRANT PROCESS:

B. The "particularity requirement"

The text of the Fourth Amendment dictates that warrants must "particularly describe" the person or place at issue. How does this "particularity requirement" look in practical application? The warrant must specifically identify the person to be arrested, or describe the property to be searched for and seized. It must be done in such a manner that the average person could find the location or identify the persons and places named in the warrant. In an arrest warrant, particularity is generally satisfied by including the name and date of birth of the person to be arrested, the crime alleged, and the name of the victim, if any. A search warrant's requirements are a little more complicated. To cover all bases, a search warrant generally includes three separate descriptions of the location- the street address, visual characteristics of the land or building, and descriptors from the county property records. Police officers may also attach a photo of the location to the search warrant. The warrant must also describe the items the police want to seize and what they believe will be found in the location. Once probable cause is established, and the warrant is signed, it may be executed by a police officer.

C. How is a warrant executed?

1. General rule–police must "knock and announce"

It is generally required that the government "knock and announce" their presence before entering the premises to execute a warrant. However, in many states, there is an exception to this requirement, and this exception swallows the rule. If the police can state reasonable suspicion to believe that if they knocked or announced before entering it would be "dangerous, futile, or would frustrate the search's purpose," they may then disregard the knock and announce requirement. However, in Florida, by statute, the police must first knock before they can start breaking down doors and windows to gain admission pursuant to a warrant. *See* §933.09 Florida Statutes, which states, "The officer may break open any outer door, inner door or window of a house, or any part of a house or anything therein, to execute the warrant, if after due notice of the officer's authority and purpose he or she is refused admittance to said house or access to anything therein." Further, the Florida Supreme Court has held, "In absence of express statutory authorization, no-knock search warrants are without legal effect in Florida. *State v. Bamber*, 630 So.2d 1048 (1994). However, the police under certain circumstances do not need to wait very long at all, before entering after knocking and announcing. The Florida Supreme Court has also held that, "In determining the reasonableness of the amount of time an officer executing a search warrant waited after knocking and announcing his authority and purpose before forcing entry into a house, ... the question is whether, given the information known to law enforcement at the time of the warrant's execution, the officer can reasonably infer that he has been refused admittance by the occupants. *Mendez-Jorge v. State*, App. 5 Dist., 135 So.3d 464 (2014). Further, in the same case, the Supreme Court added, "In the face of exigent circumstances, such as the imminent destruction of evidence, the amount of time preceding forced entry into a house to execute a search warrant, after officers knock and announce their authority and purpose, is less imperative. *Mendez-Jorge v. State*, App. 5 Dist., 135 So.3d 464 (2014). What does all this mean? Generally in Florida, the police MUST "knock and announce" their purpose prior to entering when executing a search warrant, but the length of time they must wait prior to forcing entry can be minimal depending on the circumstances.

2. Is there a limit on destruction of your property?

It is a violation of the Fourth Amendment to cause unnecessary and excessive destruction of property when executing a search warrant. However, the U.S. Supreme Court clarified in *U.S. v. Ramirez*, 523 U.S. 65 (1998), that this violation does not mean that the evidence against you should be thrown out (see the previous chapter's discussion of exclusionary rule). Practically speaking, the police can justify highly destructive acts in the course of their search. If it is "necessary" in the execution of the search warrant, the police may go as far as ripping up your carpets or tearing open your furniture to find what they are looking for.

3. How long do the police have to execute a warrant?

Article Section 933.05 states that a search warrant shall be returned within ten days after issuance thereof.

4. What if you are in the wrong place at the wrong time?

You are at a friend's home when the police knock on the door with a search warrant for that address; what happens to you, the innocent bystander? If the police do not have probable cause to arrest or search other individuals present at the scene, they may be temporarily detained during the search for purposes of controlling the scene, officer safety, the preservation of evidence, or checks for outstanding arrest warrants. If there exists no probable cause that a detained person who is not named in the warrant is involved in criminal activity, they must be released. However, you may find yourself detained for several hours before the police decide to release you.

D. Do the police always need a warrant to perform a search and seizure?

No! The following chapter describes the many ways in which the warrant requirement has been eroded.

E. In Florida, what can be searched and/or seized?

Florida Statutes Section 933.02 lays out in detail under what circumstances property may be searched and/or seized. Section 933.02 reads—

Upon proper affidavits being made, a search warrant may be issued under the provisions of this chapter upon any of the following grounds:
(1) When the property shall have been stolen or embezzled in

violation of law;

(2) When any property shall have been used:

(a) As a means to commit any crime;

(b) In connection with gambling, gambling implements and appliances; or

(c) In violation of s. 847.011 or other laws in reference to obscene prints and literature;

(3) When any property constitutes evidence relevant to proving that a felony has been committed;

(4) When any property is being held or possessed:

(a) In violation of any of the laws prohibiting the manufacture, sale, and transportation of intoxicating liquors;

(b) In violation of the fish and game laws;

(c) In violation of the laws relative to food and drug; or

(d) In violation of the laws relative to citrus disease pursuant to s. 581.184; or

(5) When the laws in relation to cruelty to animals, as provided in chapter 828, have been or are violated in any particular building or place.

This section also applies to any papers or documents used as a means of or in aid of the commission of any offense against the laws of the state.

As you can see, almost anything is subject to a search and/or seizure with a warrant. What about when the police don't have a warrant? In the next chapter, we will discuss in detail the many, many exceptions to the warrant requirement.

> CHAPTER FOUR ◄

KNOW YOUR RIGHTS
THE FOURTH AMENDMENT
Practical Application:
Exceptions To The Warrant Requirement

I. INTRODUCTION AND OVERVIEW

Y ou are driving late at night when you look into your rearview mirror and see flashing blue and red lights. When the officer approaches your window, he tells you he is going to search your car because he saw you making "furtive movements." What are your rights? You are walking around your neighborhood when an officer approaches and tells you that you match the description of a burglary suspect. He frisks you for weapons. Can he do this without a warrant? When does the law allow police to avoid the warrant process to make an arrest or conduct a search of your private property?

Courts have eroded the strong protection of the warrant requirement over the years—there are so many present day exceptions to obtaining a warrant that the exceptions now swallow the rule. This chapter will discuss the many ways police can conduct warrantless arrests and warrantless searches of your body, vehicle, and home.

II. WHEN CAN THE POLICE SEARCH OR ARREST ME WITHOUT A WARRANT?

A. Stop and frisk

If a police officer has developed reasonable suspicion a person has committed a crime, he can detain and pat down that person to search for weapons. This "stop and frisk" is commonly referred to as a Terry stop. *Terry v. Ohio*, 392 U.S. 1, 29 (1968), confines this type of search to "...guns, knives, clubs, or other hidden instrumentalities for the assault of the police officer." Recall from Chapter 2 that reasonable suspicion is an extremely low standard. An officer has to have just a little more than a hunch that you might be involved in criminal activity. A Terry stop is limited to an over-the-clothes search for weapons, however, if an officer can determine through touch alone that a person is in possession of contraband (the "plain feel" doctrine), he can confiscate the contraband and charge the person with a criminal violation. How far does plain feel go? While the officer cannot squeeze, move, or manipulate the things in your pockets to see if the items feel like contraband, it is not uncommon for police officers to claim they could tell by plain feel that someone was in possession of a crack rock or a marijuana joint. If he feels contraband in your pockets, he can arrest you and the evidence he found on your body is admissible in court.

In 2017 the United States Fourth Circuit Court of Appeals issued an opinion in the case *U.S. v. Robinson*, which addressed a stop and frisk search situation that is relevant to all legal firearms owners. Basically the court reasoned that the presence of a firearm triggered a police officer's right to engage in a Terry search, even if the act of carrying a firearm is not illegal under state law. Under the reasoning of the Fourth Circuit's opinion, anyone exercising their Second Amendment rights effectively surrenders their Fourth Amendment rights against warrantless detentions and searches. At the time of the writing of this book, the U.S. Supreme Court has been asked to review this decision, therefore this issue may ultimately become settled.

B. On-site arrest

In Florida, the police have been given broad powers of arrest any time an officer has probable cause to believe someone is violating almost any law regardless of how minor, from serious felonies to minor municipal ordinances or violations of fishing and hunting regulations.

Because the police in Florida may arrest when they have probable cause that almost any crime has occurred or is occurring, there are literally hundreds of criminal offenses for which a person may be arrested. For example, if you are driving an automobile, you can be arrested for having an expired registration sticker or expired driver's license.

III. WHEN CAN THE POLICE SEARCH MY HOME WITHOUT A WARRANT?

Your home is about as private as any place can get. The government should always be required to get a warrant to search this ultra-private space, right? Wrong! There are several scenarios where the police can legally search your home or its surrounding areas. The following is a discussion of the most important exceptions.

A. Exigent circumstances

The police may enter and search a home in response to "exigent circumstances." Police officers typically claim exigency in order to protect life, protect property, prevent the destruction of evidence, or pursue a fleeing felon.

Once the crisis is contained, a further search of the home is not permitted. However, officers may seize any evidence or contraband that is in plain view inside the home. Further, what they see while in the home may be used to support probable cause for a search warrant.

EXAMPLE

The police are chasing Ricky the robbery suspect through a neighborhood. Unfortunately, Ricky decides to evade the cops by running into Howard's home! The police have every right to enter Howard's home without a warrant, and may search any place in his house that Ricky could possibly be hiding. To make matters worse, they see on Howard's kitchen counter what they believe are illegal gambling receipts. They can now seize those items to investigate, and can use them to develop probable cause for a search warrant or to arrest Howard.

B. Open fields

The police don't need a warrant to march around and search the open fields outside your home. What is an open field? It's any area "out of doors in fields, except in the area immediately surrounding the home." *Oliver v. United States*, 466 U.S. 170, 178 (1984). This area immediately surrounding your home is the "curtilage," and the police have to get a warrant to search this area. Why are the open fields different from the spaces immediately adjacent to your home? Courts have said that people do not have a reasonable expectation of privacy in the open fields outside because open fields aren't private enough to invoke the protections of the Fourth Amendment.

C. Abandoned property

Courts have consistently held that persons cannot object to the seizure and evidentiary admission of abandoned property. An officer only has to have a reasonable belief that a person has abandoned any reasonable expectation of privacy in the property. The most notable example of abandoned property is your garbage on the street awaiting collection.

D. Plain view

An officer may, without a warrant, seize contraband and evidence of criminal activity that is in plain view. The plain view doctrine, as courts have analyzed, has three requirements: 1) The officer must lawfully make an initial intrusion, or be in a lawful position to see the items; 2) the officer must make the discovery inadvertently, and may not use plain view as pretext; 3) it must be immediately apparent that the items are contraband or evidence of a crime. What does it mean to be in a "lawful position" to see the items? An officer walks up to your front door, and through your living room window, he sees your elaborate methamphetamine operation. He may enter and seize the items because they are in plain view. By contrast, if an officer suspects you have a meth lab somewhere in your home, and decides to jump your fence to look into your back window, anything he sees from that vantage does not fall under the "plain view" doctrine.

1. Can the police use sense enhancing devices?

It depends. Law enforcement's use of binoculars to peer into your home or your property is lawful and can constitute plain view. Similarly, aerial views of your property by airplane or helicopter are plain view and do not require a warrant. Infrared imaging and dog sniffs of your home, however, require warrants based on probable cause and do not constitute plain view (or smell).

2. Can the police claim "plain view" if you have "No Trespassing" signs?

Yes. A "No Trespassing" sign does not stop law enforcement officials from seizing items in plain view on your property. A "No Trespassing" sign might stop an officer from searching through your abandoned property or from physically setting foot on your property (unless one of the exceptions applies), but courts often allow officers to skirt this requirement by claiming they did not see any posted "No Trespassing" sign before entering the property.

IV. WHEN CAN THE POLICE SEARCH MY VEHICLE WITHOUT A WARRANT?

Many Americans would be shocked to learn that the Fourth Amendment provides very little protection for their personal vehicles. The Supreme Court justified this lessened expectation of privacy in the 1925 case of *Carrol v. United States*. In Carrol, they reasoned that a car's mobility makes it more difficult for the police to secure a search warrant, and because automobiles are already subject to increased government regulation, people should not expect the same security against warrantless searches that they have in their homes. As a result, there are very few circumstances in which the police have to seek a warrant to search a vehicle.

A. The probable cause search

This is the farthest reaching exception to searching without a warrant. In order to legally search a vehicle, a police officer only has to articulate probable cause that a crime has been, will be, or is being committed. (See detailed discussion of probable cause, Chapter 2). Once this occurs, an officer can search anywhere in the vehicle that could contain evidence of that crime without the requirement of obtaining a warrant.

It is a common misconception that police officer cannot search containers, bags, or other self-contained personal items present in a vehicle. Unfortunately, this is most often not the case. A police officer may search any part of the vehicle, including the glove box or trunk, which could contain evidence of the crime for which they developed probable cause.

For example, if an officer smells the odor of marijuana in a vehicle, he may search anywhere in the vehicle that could contain marijuana. Since marijuana could be stored in a very small space, there will be virtually no restrictions on where the officer may look. By contrast, if the officer has probable cause to believe you are a felon in possession of an AR-15, he will not be able to look in your glove box, center console, or small locked briefcase, as an AR-15 could not reasonably be stored in any of these locations.

What about the wheel well and body panel of the vehicle? An officer must have probable cause that contraband or evidence of a crime is specifically contained within these areas of your vehicle to justify a warrantless search. This makes some sense because searching these areas is more intrusive and damaging to your personal property than searching the passenger compartment.

How does the law treat other modes of transportation? Boats and planes are treated like motor vehicles, and warrantless searches are lawful based on probable cause. RVs and houseboats, however, are a different story—if the RV or houseboat is stationary and being used as a home at the time law enforcement wishes to conduct a search, they must seek a warrant. If the RV or houseboat is travelling, it is likely subject to a warrantless search.

B. Plain view in a motor vehicle

Just like an officer may seize contraband and evidence of a crime in plain view from your home and/or person (described in detail above), they may seize these items if they are in plain view in your vehicle. So if you leave your unholstered handgun laying out in plain view on your dashboard, an officer can seize it as evidence and arrest you for unlawfully carrying a firearm—no warrants required.

C. Search incident to arrest

Regardless of what the arrest was for, there is an exception to the warrant requirement that permits an officer to perform a warrantless search during or immediately after a lawful arrest. The exception is limited to the person arrested and the area immediately surrounding the person in which the person may gain possession of a weapon, in some way effect an escape, or destroy or hide evidence. If a person is arrested in the very near vicinity of his vehicle, this power to search will often extend to the passenger compartment of the vehicle. In 2009, the U.S. Supreme Court addressed this authority to search in the case of *Arizona v. Gant*, 556 U.S. 332. In Gant, the Court held that a search of the passenger compartment of the vehicle was lawful only if it was reasonable to believe the arrestee might access the vehicle at the time of search, or that the vehicle contains evidence of the crime for which the person has been arrested. Assume that an officer slaps the cuffs on you right outside your open car door for the aforementioned crime of unlawful carry. Now, the police can search your entire passenger compartment incident to your arrest! However, if you are arrested several yards away from your parked car, Gant does not allow the search of your car as being "incident" to the arrest.

D. Inventory search

The inventory search is the all-encompassing catch-all that will allow a thorough search of your vehicle anytime it comes into police custody. Anytime you are arrested with your vehicle; the police are authorized to remove the car and impound it for safe keeping. The contents of the car must be "inventoried" to protect the property of the person arrested as well as to protect the police from any false allegations of stealing or losing the property. For the search to provide admissible evidence, courts require that the police department must have procedures in place for performing inventories of automobiles. In practice, virtually every police agency has a valid inventory search policy. Many times, the police will use this opportunity to perform a thorough search of the car, its trunk, and all of its contents. The courts have determined that this "inventory" can be done without a warrant and any contraband or other evidence of criminal activity is lawfully obtained and constitutes admissible evidence.

E. Consent

In practice, this is the most common way police officers gain access to your home or vehicle to conduct a search. Most people are conditioned to respect the authority of a police officer, and so many people have a hard time saying no when an officer demands permission to search. An officer can ask permission to search for any reason, or no reason at all. There is no evidentiary standard required to ask a person for consent to conduct a search. The officer must simply obtain consent "voluntarily."

What is "voluntariness?" Florida courts have decided that "voluntariness" as it applies to consent to search means more than just the literal meaning of "a knowing choice." The state must prove that consent was voluntary by a preponderance of the evidence. [However], "[w]here there is an illegal detention or other illegal conduct on the part of the police, a consent will be found voluntary only if there is clear and convincing evidence that the consent was not a product of the illegal police action., and the court will look to the totality of the circumstances to make this determination. If an officer demands to search your vehicle, or else he is going to beat you to a bloody pulp, your consent is not voluntary under Florida law.

Do people have the right to refuse consent? Yes! However, an officer does not need to inform you of your right to refuse consent. In Florida consent may not be gained by a showing of authority. An officer may try to gain consent to search your vehicle by saying something to the effect of "I'm going to search your vehicle now, okay?" However, 'where the validity of a search rests on consent, the State has the burden of proving that the necessary consent was obtained and that it was freely and voluntarily given, a burden that is not satisfied by showing a mere submission to a claim of lawful authority.' " Reynolds, 592 So.2d at 1086 (quoting *Florida v. Royer*, 460 U.S. 491, 497, 103 S.Ct. 1319, 75 L.Ed.2d 229 (1983)) (alteration in original). There is at least a strong argument that when an officer asks for permission to search as in the statement above, your consent is not voluntary, but a submission to the officer's authority. How far does consent go? A person may limit the scope of their consent, and anything found outside that scope will not be admissible evidence. For example, if you grant an officer consent to look in your glove compartment, he may not use that same consent to conduct a search of your trunk. Further, you have the power to withdraw your consent or limit it, even after you have given consent.

V. OTHER SEARCH ISSUES
A. Inventory once in custody
No warrant is required to search an individual once they are in custody and booked into jail. Personal possessions are accounted for and logged into police custody. Depending on the officers and the offense you are suspected of committing, this search can be very invasive. Unfortunately, once you are in custody, there is no more permission needed for an officer to bring out the rubber gloves.

B. GPS tracking
The 2012 decision of *U.S. v. Jones*, 132 S.Ct. 945, determined that the installation and tracking of a GPS device on a vehicle is a Fourth Amendment search requiring a warrant. However, the U.S. Supreme Court has not yet issued any guidelines as to what conditions are required for the issuance of a warrant for GPS tracking.

C. Smart phones
In today's day and age, you might be hard-pressed to find someone who does not carry a smart phone on their person at all times. Most of these tiny, portable computers are overflowing with personal information such as texts, personal contacts, schedules, emails, and photos. What happens when police find a cell phone, say in an inventory search like the one above? How has Fourth Amendment

jurisprudence kept up with this technological development? In 2014, the U.S. Supreme Court handed down *Riley v. California*, 134 S.Ct. 2473, which directly addresses this issue. In Riley, the Court distinguished cell phones from other objects found on an individual by stating:

> Cell phones differ in both a quantitative and a qualitative sense from other objects that might be kept on an arrestee's person. The term "cell phone" is itself misleading shorthand; many of these devices are in fact minicomputers that also happen to have the capacity to be used as a telephone. They could just as easily be called cameras, video players, rolodexes, calendars, tape recorders, libraries, diaries, albums, televisions, maps, or newspapers. One of the most notable distinguishing features of modern cell phones is their immense storage capacity. Before cell phones, a search of a person was limited by physical realities and tended as a general matter to constitute only a narrow intrusion on privacy. 134 S.Ct. 2473, 2478-79 (2014).

Due to these distinguishing features, the Court ultimately concluded that police must obtain a warrant based on probable cause to search the contents of a cell phone.

D. Highly regulated businesses

Warrantless searches have been permitted by the courts if carried out by the state's administrative agents in any business or activity that is highly regulated by the government. For example, agents from the Bureau of Alcohol, Tobacco, Firearms & Explosives may conduct an audit of a gun store, or the Texas Alcoholic Beverage Commission may send their agents to inspect liquor stores or bars.

E. Airports/international borders

Warrantless searches are permitted at borders and airports under the legal theory that individuals have implicitly consented to be searched while traversing an international border or getting on an airplane. Further, warrantless searches are justified by public interest and the great risk to public safety in these areas.

F. Probationers/parolees

Persons on probation and parole have a lessened expectation of privacy due to their highly monitored status. As a result, they may be searched on reasonable suspicion alone. This standard even applies to the person's cell phone! Persons subject to government supervision lose nearly all of their Fourth Amendment rights.

G. Dog sniffs

As it applies to vehicles, a dog sniff is not considered a search under the Fourth Amendment. An officer may detain you for a reasonable amount of time to await a canine to conduct a sniff if he has a reasonable suspicion that drugs are contained in the vehicle. If the dog alerts on your vehicle, the officer then has probable cause to conduct a search of the vehicle for narcotics without a warrant. However, a dog sniff of the front porch of a home is a search under the Fourth Amendment, and cannot be done in the absence of a warrant. This is because the dog sniff takes place on the curtilage of the home which is a place where the occupant of the home has an expectation of privacy.

What is a "reasonable" amount of time? Courts examine this under the totality of the circumstances on a case by case basis. For example, in a large city with many canine officers, it is probably unreasonable to detain someone for over an hour to await the dog. In a small county with only one canine officer, this long wait may not be unreasonable if the dog is out on another crime scene. Ultimately, the lengths to which an officer is allowed to go to detain and search a particular person will be fought after the fact in the courtroom on this kind of "totality of the circumstances" analysis.

In April of 2015, the U.S. Supreme Court in *Rodriguez v. United States*, 135 S.Ct. 1609 (2015), considered the legality of dog sniff detentions at the conclusion of or during a traffic stop. The Court ruled that once the officer has concluded his investigation into the traffic stop, he may not detain a citizen to wait for a drug dog without independent reasonable suspicion that the person is in possession of illegal narcotics. Expect to see many lengthy traffic stops in the future as police officers attempt to stay on the right side of this decision.

H. Drones

The use of drones has become more and more prevalent. This includes aerial surveillance by both private individuals and law enforcement. Wherever a member of the public is allowed to fly their drones the police are allowed to fly theirs. However, as police expand the use of drones, the Fourth Amendment will certainly be implicated. It will be up to the courts to determine when these uses of police drones without a warrant will violate a person's expectation of privacy. Additionally, it will be important to see how a court addresses Fourth Amendment privacy concerns when a private citizen flies their drone over property and reports any suspicious activity to local law enforcement.

> CHAPTER FIVE ◄

LEGAL DEFINITIONS AND CLASSIFICATIONS OF FIREARMS:
WHAT IS LEGAL?

I. INTRODUCTION AND OVERVIEW

Before discussing the law of firearms and all its different facets, it is important first to understand what the law defines as a "firearm." Firearms laws are governed on both the federal and state levels; therefore, throughout this chapter we will explore the interactions between federal and state law, and the effect those interactions have on the purchase and possession of firearms.

A. What is a firearm?

FEDERAL DEFINITION

Under the federal law, a firearm is defined as "any weapon (including a starter gun) which will or is designed to or may readily be converted to expel a projectile by the action of an explosive." 18 U.S.C. §921(a)(3). The federal definition of a firearm also includes the frame or receiver of any such weapon, any firearm muffler or silencer, or any "destructive device." This is similar to the Florida definition, but not exactly the same.

FLORIDA DEFINITION

In the State of Florida, for purposes of applying state and not federal law, a firearm is defined by Florida Statutes in Section 790.001(6). Section 790.001(6) defines a firearm as "any weapon (including a starter gun) which will, is designed to, or may readily be converted to expel a projectile by the action of an explosive; the frame or receiver of any such weapon; any firearm muffler or firearm silencer; any destructive device; or any machine gun. The term 'firearm' does not include an antique firearm unless the antique firearm is used in the commission of a crime."

Why is it important to know the different ways "firearm" is defined under federal and state law? It is because if a person finds themselves charged with a crime by federal authorities, the federal definition of a firearm will apply. Likewise, if the charge is a violation of state law, then the Florida definition will apply. Thus, the primary difference in the definitions and their impact on a defendant charged with a crime involving a firearm lies with how a person is in trouble with the law. As we will see in the next section, the definitions of what is or is not a firearm, although similar in many respects, contain an array of differences that make violating the law unwittingly easy.

B. Definitions for handguns, rifles, and shotguns

In addition to defining what a firearm is, federal and Florida law further classify and define firearms into categories of handguns and long guns (rifles and shotguns). This section will provide an overview of how federal and state laws classify firearms as well as the physical requirements for a firearm to be legal.

1. What is a handgun?

Ultimately, whether looking at the federal or the Florida definition, the term handgun is defined in the same manner: it simply refers to any firearm that is designed to be fired by using only one hand. While it is true that most individuals will use two hands when firing a handgun for safety and accuracy purposes, the emphasis in the legal definition of a handgun rests purely in its design to be held or fired with a single hand.

FEDERAL DEFINITION

The United States Code of Federal Regulations defines a handgun as "(a) any firearm which has a short stock and is designed to be held and fired by the use of a single hand; and (b) any combination of parts from which a firearm described in paragraph (a) can be assembled." 27 CFR §478.11.

FLORIDA DEFINITION

Under Florida law, handguns are defined by the Constitution in Article I, Section 8. A handgun "means a firearm capable of being carried and used by one hand, such as a pistol or revolver." Surprisingly, outside of the law pertaining to handgun purchase waiting periods, the term handgun does not appear in the statutory definitions in Section 790, which deals with firearms in Florida.

2. What is a rifle?

Federal law defines a rifle as "a weapon designed or redesigned, made or remade, and intended to be fired from the shoulder, and designed or redesigned and made or remade to use the energy of the explosive in a fixed metallic cartridge to fire only a single projectile through a rifled bore for each single pull of the trigger." 27 CFR §478.11. In addition, a legal rifle must have a barrel length of 16 inches or greater, and includes any weapon made from a rifle which is at least 26 inches overall in length.

Florida law does not provide a definition for a rifle in our statutes, but it does classify illegal short-barreled rifles in the same manner as the federal definition. See Florida Statute §790.001(11)

Minimum lengths

A rifle must have a barrel of at least 16 inches or it will be subject to the National Firearms Act and classified as a short-barreled firearm under Florida law. The ATF procedure for measuring barrel length is accomplished by measuring from the closed bolt (or breech-face) to the furthermost end of the barrel or permanently attached muzzle device. Below is an example of a rifle that does not meet the minimum barrel length requirement after measurement:

The barrel is measured by inserting a dowel rod into the barrel until the rod stops against the bolt or breech-face. The rod is then marked at the furthermost end of the barrel or permanently attached muzzle device, withdrawn from the barrel, and then measured. Any measurement of less than 16 inches will classify the rifle as being short-barreled under Florida and federal law; subjecting the firearm to the NFA. For short-barreled rifles and other non-compliant firearms, see Chapter Fourteen, which discusses the NFA. Note: for overall length, rifles with collapsible/folding-stocks are measured from the "extreme ends," unless the stock is "easily detachable," in which case it is measured without the stock.

3. What is a shotgun?

The federal definition of a shotgun is "a weapon designed or redesigned, made or remade, and intended to be fired from the shoulder, and designed or redesigned and made or remade to use the energy of the explosive in a fixed shotgun shell to fire through a smooth bore either a number of ball shot or a single projectile for each single pull of the trigger." 27 CFR §478.11. Like rifles, legal shotguns have requirements for minimum barrel and overall lengths. Shotgun barrels must be at least 18 inches long and must also comply with the same 26 inch overall length requirement. Under Florida law, shotguns are classified in the same manner as they are under federal law. See Florida Statute §790.001(10).

Minimum lengths

In order for a shotgun to not be subject to the National Firearms Act or classified as a short-barreled firearm under Florida law, it must have a barrel of at least 18 inches in length. The ATF procedure for measuring the barrel length of a shotgun is the same as it is for a rifle. Below is an example of a shotgun that does not meet the minimum barrel length requirement after measurement:

Any measurement of less than 18 inches will classify the shotgun as a short-barreled weapon and illegal under Florida and federal law unless the requirements of the NFA are satisfied. For short-barreled shotguns and other non-compliant firearms, see Chapter Fourteen. Note: the collapsible/folding-stock rule that applies to rifles applies to shotguns as well.

C. Antique firearms and replica firearms

When is a firearm not legally a "firearm?" It is when the law defines it as not being one, such as with "antique" firearms.

1. Federal definition of "antique firearm"

1898 or prior

The federal definition of firearm under Title 18, Section 921 of the United States Code excludes "antique firearms." Even though an antique firearm still functions ballistically similar to a "modern" firearm, under federal law, antique firearms are regulated differently, if at all. An antique firearm under federal law includes any firearm with a matchlock, flintlock, or percussion cap, or similar type of ignition system manufactured in or before 1898 or any replica of a firearm just described so long as the replica "is not designed or redesigned for using rimfire or conventional centerfire fixed ammunition, or uses rimfire or centerfire ammunition that is no longer manufactured in the United States and is not readily available in ordinary channels of commerce." 18 U.S.C. §§921(16)(A) and (B). So, an "antique firearm" is not a "firearm" for purposes of federal regulation; it is an "antique firearm."

Muzzle loading

In addition, federal law does not consider "any muzzle loading rifle, muzzle loading shotgun, or muzzle loading pistol, which is designed to use black powder, or a black powder substitute, and which cannot use fixed ammunition" as a firearm. Be aware, however, that the term "antique firearm" does not include any weapon which incorporates a firearm frame or receiver, any firearm which is converted into a muzzle loading weapon, or any muzzle loading weapon which can be readily converted to fire fixed ammunition by replacing the barrel, bolt, breechlock, or any combination of these parts. 18 U.S.C. §921(a)(16)(C).

2. Florida definition of "antique firearm"
Pre-1899

Under Florida law, antique firearm means "any firearm manufactured in or before 1918 (including any matchlock, flintlock, percussion cap, or similar early type of ignition system) or replica thereof, whether actually manufactured before or after the year 1918, and also any firearm using fixed ammunition manufactured in or before 1918, for which ammunition is no longer manufactured in the United States and is not readily available in the ordinary channels of commercial trade." See Florida Statute §790.001(1)

D. What firearms are illegal?
Under Florida Statute §790.221, "(1) It is unlawful for any person

to own or to have in his or her care, custody, possession, or control any short-barreled rifle, short-barreled shotgun, or machine gun, which is, or may readily be made, operable; but this section shall not apply to antique firearms."

However, it is important to note that subsection (3) makes an exception for weapons owned in accordance with federal law. Subsection (3) reads: "(3) Firearms in violation hereof which are lawfully owned and possessed under provisions of federal law are excepted."

Under federal law, the same firearms that are prohibited weapons under state law, as well as others, are regulated by the National Firearms Act (NFA). These firearms include:
• short-barreled shotguns;
• short-barreled rifles;
• machine guns;
• firearm silencers or suppressors;
• weapons or devices capable of being concealed on the person from which a shot can be fired;
• pistols or revolvers having a smooth bore (as opposed to rifled bore) barrel designed to fire a fixed shotgun shell;
• pistols or revolvers with a vertical handgrip;
• destructive devices; and
• weapons classified as "Any Other Weapon," or AOWs.

See 26 U.S.C. §5845. For more information on these weapons, see Chapter Fourteen discussing the National Firearms Act.

On the surface, the federal and Florida prohibited firearms lists are similar, with the primary difference being that Florida law only prohibits the first three items on the federal list. However, although these firearms and/or weapons are prohibited by statute, it does not mean a person absolutely cannot possess one. Many of these weapons may be legally possessed with proper documentation under the National Firearms Act. For more information on these prohibited weapons and the NFA, see Chapter Fourteen.

E. How big of a gun can a person possess?

Federal law dictates that any firearm which has any barrel with a bore of more than one-half inch in diameter is a "destructive device" and is subject to the National Firearms Act. Possession of any such firearm without the proper paperwork associated with NFA firearms is illegal. Note, however, that some shotguns are regulated differently. For more information on destructive devices and the NFA, see Chapter Fourteen.

II. AMMUNITION AND THE LAW

No discussion concerning firearms laws would be complete without examining laws concerning the ammunition that goes into a firearm. Just like firearms, the law regulates the possession, sale, and even composition of "legal" ammunition. This section addresses the essential aspects of the law concerning ammunition and what gun owners need to know, both under federal and Florida law.

A. How does the law define ammunition?

Under federal law, the term ammunition is defined under 18 U.S.C. §921(a)(17)(A) as "ammunition or cartridge cases, primers, bullets, or propellant powder designed for use in any firearm." Thus, the federal definition of ammunition includes the finished product and all of the components in making a round of ammunition. However, the federal definition of ammunition does not include (1) any shotgun shot or pellet not designed for use as the single, complete projectile load for one shotgun hull or casing, nor (2) any unloaded, non-metallic shotgun hull or casing not having a primer. See 27 CFR §478.11. In other words, individual ammunition components are legally defined as ammunition themselves, even if they are simply parts, except that shotgun ammunition components, if not completely assembled, are not ammunition.

Under Florida law, the statutory definition for ammunition is an object consisting of all of the following:
a. A fixed metallic or nonmetallic hull or casing containing a primer.
b. One or more projectiles, one or more bullets, or shot.
c. Gunpowder.

Florida law also provides a definition for armor-piercing ammunition and other types of handgun and shotgun ammunition (which we will discuss later in this chapter). See Florida Statute §790.001(19).

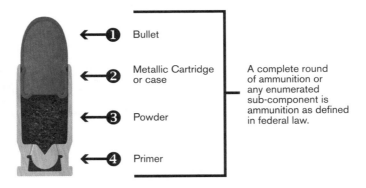

B. Is there a difference in ammunition that is used in different types of firearms?

Yes. Ammunition can be divided into two classifications: ammunition for handguns and ammunition for long guns. Long gun ammunition can be further divided into ammunition for rifles and ammunition for shotguns.

Handgun ammunition means ammunition that is meant to be fired from a handgun, and it comes in many different calibers. Rifle ammunition is meant to be fired from a rifle and is similar to handgun ammunition in that it comes in many different calibers. Shotgun ammunition, on the other hand, comes in self-contained cartridges loaded with some form of shot or a shotgun slug which is designed to be fired from a shotgun.

PRACTICAL LEGAL TIP

Even with firearms, having the right tool for the job is important. Practically speaking, you should choose the firearm and ammo that you feel most comfortable using. At the end of the day, why you started shooting is always more important than what you chose to shoot with. -David

C. What ammunition is illegal?

Armor-piercing handgun ammunition is the only ammunition which has explicit prohibitions under both federal and Florida law. The federal definition of armor-piercing ammunition found in 18 U.S.C. §921(a)(17)(B), is "[1] a projectile or projectile core which may be used in a handgun and which is constructed entirely (excluding the presence of traces of other substances) from one or a combination of tungsten alloys, steel, iron, brass, bronze, beryllium copper, or depleted uranium; or [2] a full jacketed projectile larger than .22 caliber designed and intended for use in a handgun and whose jacket has a weight of more than 25 percent of the total weight of the projectile."

Federal law

Under federal law, while there is no blanket prohibition on the mere possession of armor-piercing ammunition, it is prohibited under four conditions:

1. Prohibition one

It is illegal to make or import armor-piercing ammunition. Under 18 U.S.C. §922(a)(7) it is unlawful for any person to manufacture or import armor-piercing ammunition unless (1) the manufacture of such ammunition is for the use of the United States, any department or agency of the United States, any state, or any department, agency, or political subdivision of a state; (2) the manufacture of such ammunition is for the purpose of exportation; or (3) the manufacture or importation of such ammunition is for the purpose of testing or experimentation and has been authorized by the United States Attorney General.

2. Prohibition two

It is illegal for manufacturers and importers to sell or deliver armor-piercing ammunition. Federal law states that it is unlawful for any manufacturer or importer to sell or deliver armor-piercing ammunition unless such sale or delivery is (1) for the use of the United States, any department or agency of the United States, any state, or any department, agency, or political subdivision of a state; (2) for the purpose of exportation; or (3) for the purpose of testing or experimentation and has been authorized by the United States Attorney General. See 18 U.S.C. §922(a)(8).

3. Prohibition three

A Federal Firearms License (FFL) or other license-holder cannot sell or deliver armor-piercing ammunition without the proper documentation. Under 18 U.S.C. §922(b)(5), it is unlawful for any licensed importer, licensed manufacturer, licensed dealer, or licensed collector to sell or deliver armor-piercing ammunition to any person unless the licensee notes in his records, as required under 18 U.S.C. §923, the name, age, and place of residence of such person if the person is an individual, or the identity, and principal and local places of business of such person if the person is a corporation or other business entity.

4. Prohibition four

It is illegal to possess armor-piercing ammunition if a person is involved in a crime of violence or a drug-trafficking crime. Pursuant to 18 U.S.C. §924(c)(5), it is unlawful for "any person who, during and in relation to any crime of violence or drug trafficking crime (including a crime of violence or drug trafficking crime that provides for an enhanced punishment if committed by the use of a deadly or dangerous weapon or device) for which the person may be prosecuted in a court of the United States, use or carries armor piercing ammunition." Individuals who use or carry armor-piercing ammunition in the commission of a crime of violence or during a drug-trafficking crime are subject to heightened sentencing standards should they be found guilty.

As you can see, while possession of armor-piercing ammunition itself is not illegal, obtaining armor-piercing ammunition without violating one of the foregoing prohibitions is almost impossible.

Florida law

Florida Statute §790.31 defines armor-piercing ammunition as well as other types of ammunition which are illegal under Florida law. The following types of ammunition are illegal in Florida: armor-piercing, exploding ammunition, dragon's breath shotgun shells, bolo shells, or flechette shells.

These types of ammunition are defined in Florida Statute §790.31(1) as:

(a) "Armor-piercing bullet" means any bullet which has a steel inner core or core of equivalent hardness and a truncated cone and which is designed for use in a handgun as an armor-piercing or metal-piercing bullet.

(b) "Exploding bullet" means any bullet that can be fired from any firearm, if such bullet is designed or altered so as to detonate or forcibly break up through the use of an explosive or deflagrant contained wholly or partially within or attached to such bullet. The term does not include any bullet designed to expand or break up through the mechanical forces of impact alone or any signaling device or pest control device not designed to impact on any target.

Subsection (c) intentionally omitted

(d) "Dragon's breath shotgun shell" means any shotgun shell that contains exothermic pyrophoric misch metal as the projectile and that is designed for the sole purpose of throwing or spewing a flame or fireball to simulate a flamethrower.

(e) "Bolo shell" means any shell that can be fired in a firearm and that expels as projectiles two or more metal balls connected by solid metal wire.

(f) "Flechette shell" means any shell that can be fired in a firearm and that expels two or more pieces of fin-stabilized solid metal wire or two or more solid dart-type projectiles.

Florida Statute §790.31(2)(a) makes it a third-degree felony to manufacture, sell, offer for sale, or deliver any armor-piercing bullet, exploding bullet, dragon's breath shotgun shell, bolo shell, or flechette shell. Although it is not illegal to simply possess this type of ammunition, it is a third-degree felony to have any of these types of ammunition loaded in a handgun or firearm if the person has knowledge of its capabilities. See Florida Statute §790.31(2)(b). Finally, under Florida Statute §790.31(2)(c), it is a crime to possess the types of ammunition described above with the intent to use it in the commission of a crime. A person who violates this subsection commits a felony of the second degree.

Florida law does NOT make illegal the mere possession of any of these types of ammunition. Further, there is a notable exception located in the last part of Florida Statute §790.31. The exception is for law enforcement and law enforcement agencies. Florida Statute §790.31(3) allows for the possession, manufacture, and sale and delivery of the items described as prohibited if the possession, sale and manufacturing is done by or for law enforcement agencies.

EXCEPTIONS TO POSSESSING OTHERWISE ILLEGAL AMMUNITION; FLORIDA STATUTE §790.31(3)

(a) The possession of any item described in subsection (1) by any law enforcement officer, when possessed in connection with the performance of his or her duty as a law enforcement officer, or law enforcement agency.

(b) The manufacture of items described in subsection (1) exclusively for sale or delivery to law enforcement agencies.

(c) The sale or delivery of items described in subsection (1) to law enforcement agencies.

Notably, not all ammunition that can pierce armor is actually armor-piercing. Both the federal and Florida definitions contain specific requirements for a particular round of ammunition's composition to be considered armor-piercing. Federal law requires that the ammunition be comprised of certain alloys, while Florida law requires that the ammunition be designed of certain alloys, be for use in a handgun and designed for the purpose of penetrating armor or metal. For example, 5.7 millimeter ammunition for an FN57 handgun or a PS90 rifle, while capable of piercing armor based on its size and velocity, is not ammunition that is armor-piercing as defined under the law because such ammunition, sold commercially, is primarily for sporting purposes according to the ATF.

PS90

D. Does modifying traditional ammunition make it illegal?

No, outside of armor-piercing ammunition, and other types of ammunition mentioned above, there is no handgun or long gun ammunition that is prohibited under the federal or Florida law. In fact, there are many examples of hollow-point rounds which are modified in a way to become more lethal, such as the R.I.P. ammunition, Black Talons, etc., which star outward upon impact in order to do more internal damage and are still perfectly legal.

Factory and Expanded Hollow Point Rounds

E. Is it legal to use ammunition that works in both handguns and rifles?

Yes, except for armor-piercing ammunition that is used principally in handguns. This is because the federal and Florida definitions of armor-piercing ammunition contemplate handguns only. Armor-piercing ammunition for a rifle is perfectly legal, though it may complicate matters at trial in trying to demonstrate to the jury any differentiation. It is legal to use ammunition that is available in common calibers and that functions in both handguns and rifles, except for the specific type of armor-piercing ammunition mentioned above.

With a solid understanding of what is and is not a firearm and ammunition, as well as what firearms and ammunition a person may legally possess without the necessity of obtaining additional documentation, we are now ready to move to the next chapter discussing the purchase and possession of firearms.

CHAPTER SIX

PURCHASING, TRANSFERRING, AND POSSESSING FIREARMS
FIREARMS

I. LAWS OF PURCHASING AND POSSESSING: THE BASICS

The laws of purchasing, selling, gifting, or otherwise transferring a firearm are distinct and different from the laws of possessing a firearm. It may be legal for someone to possess a firearm, and it still be illegal for them to "purchase" the firearm. Further, each of these sets of laws for "purchasing" or "possessing" has a federal and a state component both of which must be satisfied in order to be on the right side of the law.

On the federal level, the Bureau of Alcohol, Tobacco, Firearms and Explosives ("ATF") is charged with regulating firearms, including sales, purchases, and transfers through Federal Firearms Licensees, however, a multitude of federal agencies can be involved in any given firearms law investigation or police function most currently falling under a branch of the U.S. Department of Homeland Security. Florida has no direct state-level counterpart to the ATF.

A. What is an FFL?

An "FFL" or Federal Firearms License is a license required by federal law for those persons or entities that are engaged in the business of buying and selling firearms. A federal firearms licensee is often called an "FFL" or "dealer." When an individual purchases, sells, or transfers a firearm through a dealer, the FFL and the individual must both comply with specific federal law requirements, paperwork, and procedures concerning the buying, selling, or transferring of those firearms. These requirements will be addressed throughout this chapter.

B. Who must obtain an FFL?

Federal law requires a Federal Firearms License if a person is engaged in business as a firearms dealer, manufacturer, or importer. For the purposes of our discussion in this chapter, a person is engaged in the business when the person "devotes time, attention, and labor to dealing in firearms as a regular course of trade or business with the principal objective of livelihood and profit through the repetitive purchase and resale of firearms, but such term shall not include a person who makes occasional sales, exchanges, or purchases of firearms for the enhancement of a personal collection or for a hobby, or who sells all or part of his personal collection of firearms." 18 U.S.C. §921(a)(21)(C).

C. What is a private sale?

A private sale is just what it sounds like: a sale, purchase, or transfer of a firearm by parties that are not licensed dealers. A private sale is perfectly legal for both handguns and long guns in Florida, as long as all other legal requirements are met. We will discuss the ins-and-outs of private sales in greater detail in this chapter under Section IV.

D. What is the legal age to purchase and possess a firearm?

Federal law controls all FFL firearms transactions and requires that a person be 21 years of age or older before they may purchase a handgun or 18 for the purchase of a long gun. However, under Florida law, a handgun or long gun may be purchased in a private sale by a person who is age 18. However, Florida Statute §790.17 makes it a crime for a person to "knowingly or willfully sell or transfer a firearm to a minor under 18 years of age." There are a few exceptions which are explained later in this chapter.

REQUIRED AGE TO PURCHASE FIREARMS	FEDERAL LAW: FROM DEALER	FLORIDA LAW: PRIVATE SALE
Handgun	21	18
Long gun	18	18

Under federal law, a person must be at least 18 years of age in order to possess a handgun or ammunition for a handgun. See 18 U.S.C. §922(x)(2). Unlike the law on purchasing a long gun, there is no federal age requirement for the possession of a rifle or shotgun. Florida Statute §790.22(3) provides that a minor under 18 years of age may not possess a firearm, other than an unloaded firearm at his or her home, unless certain other conditions are met.

E. Can I buy a firearm if I have a note from my parents?

If a person finds themselves charged with selling a firearm to a minor, Florida law provides an affirmative defense to prosecution of the seller that transfers ownership of the firearm to a minor with permission of the minor's parent or guardian and the parent or guardian maintains possession of the firearm. There is an exception found pursuant to certain circumstances enumerated in Florida Statute §790.22. Florida Statute §790.17(2)(a) & (b). This is the law whether the sale is for a handgun or a long gun. For the federal law regarding juveniles and handguns, see 18 U.S.C. §922(x). Note, however, that this state-law exception does not apply to FFL transactions, and an individual must be 21 years old to purchase a handgun from an FFL

F. Criminal liability for allowing a minor access to firearms

In Florida, under Florida Statute §790.174, a person who stores or leaves a loaded firearm on a property they control who has reason to know that the firearm might be accessed by a minor, must keep the firearm in a securely locked box or container or in a location which a reasonable person would believe to be secure or to secure it with a trigger lock. If the person is carrying the firearm on his or her body or has it close enough that he or she can retrieve and use it as easily and quickly as if he or she carried it on his or her body, then the above restriction does not apply.

Florida Statute §790.174 further provides that it is a misdemeanor of the second degree, punishable by up to 60 days in jail and/or up to a $500 fine, if a person fails to properly store a firearm and a minor gains access to it and possesses or exhibits it without the supervision required by law in a public place or in a rude, careless, angry or threatening manner.

However, it is an affirmative defense to prosecution when a child gains access to a firearm "as a result of an unlawful entry by any person." Florida Statute §790.174(2). This means that if a child illegally enters a person's premises and then takes possession of a firearm illegally, the gun owner has not committed a crime.

Florida Statute §790.22(4)(a) also makes it a third-degree felony for any parent or guardian of a minor, or other adult responsible for the welfare of the minor, to knowingly and willfully permit the minor to possess a firearm improperly under that section. Such a third-degree felony is punishable by up to five years in prison and up to a $5,000 fine.

G. When may children legally possess firearms?

Florida law allows for the legal possession of firearms by minors under specific exceptions included in the law. These exceptions or "affirmative defenses" include the following:

1. Unloaded firearm at his or her home

A minor child under 18 years of age may possess an unloaded firearm at his or her home. That exception is found in Florida Statute §790.22(3).

2. Exception for hunting activity

A minor child under 18 years of age may possess a firearm if the minor is engaged in a lawful hunting activity and is at least 16 years of age. If the child is under 16 years of age, then the child must be supervised by an adult. Florida Statute §790.22(3)(a).

3. Lawful sporting activities

A minor child may possess a firearm if the minor is engaged in a lawful marksmanship competition or practice or other lawful recreational shooting activity and is at least 16 years of age. If the child is under 16 years of age, then the child must be supervised by an adult who is acting with the consent of the minor's parent or guardian. Florida Statute §790.22(3)(b).

4. Self-defense

If a minor child's access to the firearm consisted of lawful defense by the child of themselves or other people, the child's possession of the gun is lawful. For obvious reasons, if a child uses a firearm in self-defense, or in defense of another person, there is a general public policy interest in not prosecuting the child who acted in self-defense.

EXAMPLE

One night, armed intruders break into Timmy's home and hold Timmy's parents at gunpoint while burglarizing the home. Timmy, who is 14, covertly sees what is transpiring from the top of the stairs and knowing that his father keeps a loaded handgun in his nightstand, retrieves the weapon. Timmy then shoots the burglar threatening his parents.

Two questions arise in this scenario: first, is Timmy legally justified in shooting the armed burglar? As we will see later in Chapters Four, Five, and Seven, yes, he is. Timmy is justified in defending a third person with deadly force under the circumstances. Second, is Timmy's father in trouble legally for leaving his firearm accessible to Timmy? No, he is not in trouble. Timmy's access to the firearm was the result of his necessity in defending his parents who were staring down the barrel of a burglar's gun!

H. Special duty of firearms dealers involving minors

Florida law requires that a dealer of firearms upon sale or retail transfer of any firearm, deliver a written warning to the purchaser, which must state the following warning written in block letters, not less than one fourth inch in height:

> **"IT IS UNLAWFUL, AND PUNISHABLE BY IMPRISONMENT AND FINE, FOR ANY ADULT TO STORE OR LEAVE A FIREARM IN ANY PLACE WITHIN THE REACH OR EASY ACCESS OF A MINOR UNDER 18 YEARS OF AGE OR TO KNOWINGLY SELL OR OTHERWISE TRANSFER OWNERSHIP OR POSSESSION OF A FIREARM TO A MINOR OR A PERSON OF UNSOUND MIND."**
> Florida Statute §790.175(1).

Further, Florida Statute §790.175(2) specifies that a similar warning must be conspicuously posted at each purchase counter of any retail or wholesale store, shop or sales outlet which sells firearms.

Federal law requires that FFLs who deliver handguns to non-licensees display at their licensed premises (including temporary business locations at gun shows) a sign that customers can readily see. These signs are provided by the ATF and contain the following language:

(1) The misuse of handguns is a leading contributor to juvenile violence and fatalities.

(2) Safely storing and securing firearms away from children will help prevent the unlawful possession of handguns by juveniles, stop accidents, and save lives.

(3) Federal law prohibits, except in certain limited circumstances, anyone under 18 years of age from knowingly possessing a handgun, or any person from transferring a handgun to a person under 18.

(4) A knowing violation of the prohibition against selling, delivering, or otherwise transferring a handgun to a person under the age of 18 is, under certain circumstances, punishable by up to 10 years in prison.

In addition to the displayed sign, federal law requires FFLs to provide non-licensee customers with a written notification containing the same four points as listed above as 18 U.S.C. §§922(x) and 924(a) (6). This written notification is available as a pamphlet published by the ATF entitled "Youth Handgun Safety Act Notice" and is sometimes referred to as ATF information 5300.2. Alternatively, this written notification may be delivered to customers on another type of written notification, such as a manufacturer's brochure accompanying the handgun or a sales receipt or invoice applied to the handgun package. Any written notification delivered to a customer other than the one provided by the ATF must include the language described here, and must be "legible, clear, and conspicuous, and the required language shall appear in type size no smaller than 10-point type." 27 CFR §478.103(c).

II. FEDERAL LAW DISQUALIFICATIONS FOR PURCHASING AND POSSESSING FIREARMS

Federal law lists categories of persons disqualified from legally purchasing and possessing a firearm. This list comprises disqualifications that come from several different pieces of federal legislation, including the Gun Control Act of 1968, the Brady Handgun Violence Protection Act, and the Violence Against Women Act. A disqualified person under these laws will not be able to legally buy a firearm from an FFL. Before an FFL may sell or otherwise transfer a firearm, the purchaser must fill out an ATF Form 4473. This form has questions concerning each of the criteria that disqualify a person from purchasing a firearm under federal law. These disqualifications include:

(1) If the person is not the actual purchaser of the firearm—also known as a "straw man purchaser;"

(2) If the person is under indictment or information in any court for a felony or any other crime for which the judge could imprison the person for more than one year;

(3) If the person has ever been convicted in any court for a felony or other crime for which the judge could imprison the person for more than one year;

(4) If the person is a fugitive from justice;

(5) If the person is an unlawful user of, or addicted to, marijuana, or any depressant, stimulant, narcotic drug, or controlled substance;

(6) if the person has ever been adjudicated as mentally defective or has been committed to a mental institution;

(7) If the person has been dishonorably discharged from the Armed Forces;

(8) If the person is subject to an active protective order restraining the person from harassing, stalking, or threatening the person's child, or an intimate partner or child of such partner;

(9) If the person has been convicted in any court for a misdemeanor crime of domestic violence;

(10) If the person has ever renounced their United States citizenship;

(11) If the person is an alien illegally in the United States; and

(12) If the person is admitted under a non-immigrant visa and does not qualify for an exception.

The purchaser must legally affirm that they are not subject to any of the criteria listed above before they may purchase a firearm. If a prospective purchaser answers any question on the form in a manner that indicates they are legally disqualified, it is illegal for the FFL to sell that person the firearm, and it is illegal for the purchaser to complete the transaction or possess the firearm.

A. Understanding who is disqualified

1. Can I buy a firearm for another person?

No. This would be a "straw man" purchase. In order to legally purchase a firearm from a dealer, you must be the "actual purchaser or transferee." If you are not the actual purchaser or transferee, it is illegal for you to complete the transfer or sale under federal law. Purchases for third persons are often called "straw man" purchases and are illegal. If you are not the actual purchaser, beware!

In fact, the ATF has a campaign called "Don't Lie for the Other Guy" that is targeted at (as they term it on their website) detection and deterrence of "straw man" purchases. The ATF website lists numerous examples of prosecutions for "straw man" purchases and a United States Supreme Court case examined and upheld federal law on this matter. *Abramski v. United States*, 134 S.Ct. 2259 (2014).

So who is the "actual" buyer or transferee so as not to be a "straw man?" The ATF states that you are the actual "transferee/buyer if you are purchasing the firearm for yourself or otherwise acquiring the firearm for yourself (e.g., redeeming the firearm from pawn/ retrieving it from consignment, firearm raffle winner)." The ATF goes on to state "you are also the actual transferee/buyer if you are legitimately purchasing the firearm as a gift for a third party."

EXAMPLE

Mr. Smith asks Mr. Jones to purchase a firearm for Mr. Smith. Mr. Smith gives Mr. Jones the money for the firearm. Mr. Jones then buys the firearm with Mr. Smith's money and gives Mr. Smith the firearm.

Mr. Jones is not the "actual buyer" (he is legally a "straw man") of the firearm and if Mr. Jones indicates that he is the "actual buyer" of the firearm on ATF Form 4473, he has committed a federal crime. However, under the Supreme Court ruling in Abramski, "gifts" of firearms are legal.

When completing ATF Form 4473: if a person checks "yes" to the box asking if the person is the "actual purchaser," then that person cannot have engaged in a separate transaction to sell or transfer the firearm privately. Please note: the Supreme Court's ruling held that a person cannot legally purchase a firearm on behalf of another even if the person receiving the firearm would not otherwise be prohibited from making the purchase themselves. So don't buy a firearm for another person no matter how good a friend, relative, or person they are—it is a crime!

FREQUENTLY ASKED QUESTION FROM ATF WEBSITE

Q: MAY I BUY A FIREARM FROM AN FFL AS A "GIFT" FOR ANOTHER PERSON?

A: Yes.

Editor's note: Instead of the previous example where Mr. Smith paid Mr. Jones to purchase a firearm for him, if Mr. Jones decides to buy a firearm with his own money and then give the firearm to Mr. Smith as a present, then Mr. Jones is the actual buyer/transferee of the firearm. Since Mr. Jones is the actual buyer, there exists no sham or "straw man," and the purchase is legal.

Q: MAY A PARENT OR GUARDIAN PURCHASE A FIREARM AS A GIFT FOR A JUVENILE?

A: Yes, however, possession of handguns by juveniles is generally unlawful under federal law. Juveniles may only receive and possess handguns with the written permission of a parent or guardian for limited purposes, e.g., employment, ranching, farming, target practice, or hunting.

See www.atf.gov.

2. A person cannot purchase a firearm if they have been convicted or are under "indictment or information" for a felony or certain misdemeanors

If a person has been convicted of a felony or other crime for which a judge may sentence, or could have sentenced the person, to more than one year imprisonment, that person may not legally purchase a firearm (unless the crime was a state misdemeanor punishable by imprisonment of two years or less). See 18 U.S.C §921(a)(20)(B). Likewise, if a person is under "indictment" or "information" for a felony, or any other crime for which a judge may sentence the person to more than one year imprisonment, that person is disqualified from purchasing a firearm. An "indictment" or "information" is a formal accusation of a crime punishable by imprisonment for a term exceeding one year. It is important to point out that the possible maximum sentence is the determining factor for disqualification, not the actual sentence received. For example, a person may have only been sentenced to 30 days imprisonment, but if the crime for which they were charged allowed a maximum penalty of five years, then that person is disqualified. See *Schrader v. Holder*, 831 F.Supp.2d 304 (D.D.C. 2011, aff'd, 704 F.3d 980 (D.C. Cir. 2013)).

3. What does it mean to be a "fugitive from justice" so as to be disqualified from purchasing a firearm?

A "fugitive from justice" is a person who, after having committed a crime, flees from the jurisdiction of the court where the crime was committed. A fugitive from justice may also be a person who goes into hiding to avoid facing charges for the crime of which he or she is accused. Such individuals are not eligible to purchase or possess firearms.

4. Unlawful users of or persons addicted to drugs are disqualified from purchasing firearms

Federal law is very broad in that it disqualifies persons from the purchase of firearms if they are either users of or addicted to marijuana or any depressant, stimulant, narcotic drug, or any controlled substance. Under federal law, an "addict" is defined as a person that "habitually uses any narcotic so as to endanger the public morals, health, safety, or welfare, or who is so far addicted to the use of narcotic drugs as to have lost the power of self-control with reference to his addiction." 21 U.S.C. §802(1). However, in using the terms "users of," no such frequency or dependence seems contemplated in the words, nor did Congress give further guidance. Illegal users and addicts are prohibited from purchasing firearms from any person under federal law, and are likewise prohibited from possessing firearms. See 18 U.S.C. §922(d) and (g).

a. Medical Marijuana

It is important to realize that although the State of Florida has recently passed medical marijuana legislation legalizing the use of marijuana for some people, the federal government still considers marijuana a controlled substance. Should you decide to use marijuana under a lawful prescription, you should realize that you will be giving up your right to carry, own, ship, transport, receive or in anyway possess a firearm under federal law. In fact, the ATF sent a letter to all Federal Firearm Licensees reminding them that 18 U.S. C. § 922(d)(3), makes it unlawful for any person to sell or otherwise dispose of any firearm or ammunition to any person knowing or having reasonable cause to believe that such person is an unlawful user of or addicted to a controlled substance. Having a valid lawful prescription of marijuana in Florida does NOT make you a lawful user of marijuana under federal law.

5. A person can't legally buy or possess firearms if they are "mentally defective"

What does "mentally defective" mean? A person is considered to have been adjudicated as "mentally defective" if there has been a "determination by a court, board, commission, or other lawful authority that a person, as a result of marked subnormal intelligence, or mental illness, incompetency, condition, or disease: is a danger to himself or others, or lacks the mental capacity to contract or manage his own affairs." The term "mentally defective" includes "a finding of insanity by a court in a criminal case, and those persons found incompetent to stand trial or found not guilty by reason of insanity or lack of mental responsibility." 27 CFR §478.11.

"Mentally defective" also includes a person who has been committed to a mental institution by a court, board, commission, or other lawful authority, or a commitment to a mental institution involuntarily. The term includes commitment for mental defectiveness or mental illness, and also includes commitment for other reasons, such as drug use. Importantly, it does not include a person in a mental institution for observation or a voluntary admission to a mental institution. Individuals who have been adjudicated as mentally defective are also prohibited from possessing firearms under federal law. See 18 U.S.C. §922(g)(4).

6. A person subject to a restraining order may not purchase or possess a firearm

Under 18 U.S.C. §922(g)(8), firearms may not be sold to or received by person subject to a court order that: (a) was issued after a hearing which the person received actual notice of and had an opportunity to participate in; (b) restrains the person from harassing, stalking, or threatening an intimate partner or child of such intimate partner or person, or engaging in other conduct that would place an intimate partner in reasonable fear of bodily injury to the partner or child; and (c) includes a finding that such person represents a credible threat to the physical safety of such intimate partner or child; or by its terms explicitly prohibits the use, attempted use, or threatened use of physical force against such intimate partner or child that a person would reasonably be expected to cause bodily injury. An "intimate partner" of a person is the spouse or former spouse of the person, the parent of a child of the person, or an individual who cohabitates with the person.

7. Domestic violence issues and disqualifications

A person who has ever been convicted of the crime of domestic violence may not purchase or possess firearms under federal law. These restrictions are found in what is known as the Violence Against Women Act in 1994 and amended in 1996. This is an often-misunderstood law, and, in fact, the ATF has numerous "Frequently Asked Questions" concerning this disqualification on its website: www.atf.gov. The ATF does a good job of explaining the scope of this subject in their FAQs. Due to the complexity of this issue, the ATF examples are included here:

A: A "misdemeanor crime of domestic violence" means an offense that:

1. is a misdemeanor under federal or state law;
2. has, as an element, the use or attempted use of physical force, or the threatened use of a deadly weapon; and
3. was committed by a current or former spouse, parent, or guardian of the victim, by a person with whom the victim shares a child in common, by a person who is cohabiting with or has cohabited with the victim as a spouse, parent, or guardian, or by a person similarly situated to a spouse, parent, or guardian of the victim.

HOWEVER, A PERSON IS NOT CONSIDERED TO HAVE BEEN CONVICTED OF A MISDEMEANOR CRIME OF DOMESTIC VIOLENCE UNLESS:

In addition, a conviction would not be disabling if it has been expunged or set aside, or is an offense for which the person has been pardoned or has had civil rights restored (if the law of the jurisdiction in which the proceedings were held provides for the loss of civil rights upon conviction for such an offense) unless the pardon, expunction, or restoration of civil rights expressly provides that the person may not ship, transport, possess, or receive firearms, and the person is not otherwise prohibited by the law of the jurisdiction in which the proceedings were held from receiving or possessing firearms. 18 U.S.C. §921(a)(33), 27 CFR §478.11.

Editor's note: A significant number of people make the mistake of overlooking or forgetting about a court issue or family law judicial proceeding. However, if you meet the above criteria, you are federally disqualified from possessing a firearm. The fact that it may have happened a long time ago, or that you did not understand the ramifications, is legally irrelevant.

Q: WHAT IS THE EFFECTIVE DATE OF THIS DISABILITY?

A: The law was effective September 30, 1996. However, the prohibition applies to persons convicted of such misdemeanors at any time, even if the conviction occurred prior to the law's effective date.

Editor's note: For those wondering why this is not an unconstitutional ex-post facto law, multiple federal appeals courts have ruled against that argument and the Supreme Court has consistently declined to review any of those cases, effectively accepting the ruling of the courts of appeals and upholding the law.

Q: X WAS CONVICTED OF MISDEMEANOR ASSAULT ON OCTOBER 10, 1996, FOR BEATING HIS WIFE. ASSAULT HAS AS AN ELEMENT THE USE OF PHYSICAL FORCE, BUT IS NOT SPECIFICALLY A DOMESTIC VIOLENCE OFFENSE. MAY X LAWFULLY POSSESS FIREARMS OR AMMUNITION?

A: No. X may not legally possess firearms or ammunition. 18 U.S.C. §922(g)(9), 27 CFR §478.32(a)(9).

Editor's note: In this situation because X's conviction for assault was against a person in the statute's protected class, the conviction would be, for purposes of firearms purchasing disqualification, a domestic violence conviction.

Q: X WAS CONVICTED OF A MISDEMEANOR CRIME OF DOMESTIC VIOLENCE ON SEPTEMBER 20, 1996, 10 DAYS BEFORE THE EFFECTIVE DATE OF THE STATUTE. HE POSSESSES A FIREARM ON OCTOBER 10, 2004. DOES X LAWFULLY POSSESS THE FIREARM?

A: No. If a person was convicted of a misdemeanor crime of domestic violence at any time, he or she may not lawfully possess firearms or ammunition on or after September 30, 1996. 18 U.S.C. §922(g)(9), 27 CFR §478.32(a)(9).

Q: IN DETERMINING WHETHER A CONVICTION IN A STATE COURT IS A "CONVICTION" OF A MISDEMEANOR CRIME OF DOMESTIC VIOLENCE, DOES FEDERAL OR STATE LAW APPLY?

A: State law applies. Therefore, if the state does not consider the person to be convicted, the person would not have the federal disability. 18 U.S.C. §921(a)(33), 27 CFR §478.11.

Q: IS A PERSON WHO RECEIVED "PROBATION BEFORE JUDGMENT" OR SOME OTHER TYPE OF DEFERRED ADJUDICATION SUBJECT TO THE DISABILITY?

A: What is a conviction is determined by the law of the jurisdiction in which the proceedings were held. If the state law where the proceedings were held does not consider probation before judgment or deferred adjudication to be a conviction, the person would not be subject to the disability. 18 U.S.C. §921(a)(33), 27 CFR §478.11.

A: The definition of misdemeanor crime of domestic violence in the GCA (the Gun Control Act of 1968) includes any offense classified as a "misdemeanor" under federal or state law. In states that do not classify offenses as misdemeanors, the definition includes any state or local offense punishable by imprisonment for a term of 1 year or less or punishable by a fine. For example, if state A has an offense classified as a "domestic violence misdemeanor" that is punishable by up to 5 years imprisonment, it would be a misdemeanor crime of domestic violence. If state B does not characterize offenses as misdemeanors, but has a domestic violence offense that is punishable by no more than 1 year imprisonment, this offense would be a misdemeanor crime of domestic violence. 18 U.S.C. §921(a)(33), 27 CFR 478.11.

Q: ARE LOCAL CRIMINAL ORDINANCES "MISDEMEANORS UNDER STATE LAW" FOR PURPOSES OF SECTIONS 922(d)(9) AND (g)(9)?

A: Yes, assuming a violation of the ordinance meets the definition of "misdemeanor crime of domestic violence" in all other respects.

Q: IN ORDER FOR AN OFFENSE TO QUALIFY AS A "MISDEMEANOR CRIME OF DOMESTIC VIOLENCE," DOES IT HAVE TO HAVE AS AN ELEMENT THE RELATIONSHIP PART OF THE DEFINITION (E.G., COMMITTED BY A SPOUSE, PARENT, OR GUARDIAN)?

A: No. The "as an element" language in the definition of "misdemeanor crime of domestic violence" only applies to the use of force provision of the statute and not the relationship provision. However, to be disabling, the offense must have been committed by one of the defined parties. 18 U.S.C. §921(a)(33), 27 CFR §478.11.

Editor's note: This basically means that regardless of the language in the underlying statute, if the illegal force was used against a member of the protected class under the statute, federal law will deem this as satisfying the requirements and disqualify the individual from purchasing and possessing firearms.

Q: WHAT SHOULD AN INDIVIDUAL DO IF HE OR SHE HAS BEEN CONVICTED OF A MISDEMEANOR CRIME OF DOMESTIC VIOLENCE?

A: Individuals subject to this disability should immediately dispose of their firearms and ammunition. ATF recommends that such persons transfer their firearms and ammunition to a third party who may lawfully receive and possess them, such as their attorney, a local police agency, or a federal firearms dealer. The continued possession of firearms and ammunition by persons under this disability is a violation of law and may subject the possessor to criminal penalties. In addition, such firearms and ammunition are subject to seizure and forfeiture. 18 U.S.C. §922(g)(9) and §924(d)(1), 27 CFR §478.152.

A: Yes. The Gun Control Act was amended so that employees of government agencies convicted of misdemeanor crimes of domestic violence would not be exempt from disabilities with respect to their receipt or possession of firearms or ammunition. Thus, law enforcement officers and other government officials who have been convicted of a disqualifying misdemeanor may not lawfully possess or receive firearms or ammunition for any purpose, including performance of their official duties. The disability applies to firearms and ammunition issued by government agencies, purchased by government employees for use in performing their official duties, and personal firearms and ammunition possessed by such employees. 18 U.S.C. §922(g)(9) and §925(a)(1), 27 CFR §478.32(a)(9) and §478.141.

Q: IS AN INDIVIDUAL WHO HAS BEEN PARDONED, OR WHOSE CONVICTION WAS EXPUNGED OR SET ASIDE, OR WHOSE CIVIL RIGHTS HAVE BEEN RESTORED, CONSIDERED CONVICTED OF A MISDEMEANOR CRIME OF DOMESTIC VIOLENCE?

A: No, as long as the pardon, expungement, or restoration does not expressly provide that the person may not ship, transport, possess, or receive firearms.

If you or a loved one are going through court proceedings involving family issues and a restraining or protective order is entered in your case, it can suspend your ability to purchase or possess firearms. Language in the court order prohibiting any acts of family violence whether or not family violence actually occurred, make it so the person against whom the order is entered is legally barred from the purchase or possession of any firearm. Believe it or not, the Family Courts have the ability to suspend your Second Amendment rights. -David

8. Illegal aliens or aliens admitted under a non-immigrant visa

Persons who are illegally in the United States may not legally purchase, possess, or transport firearms. Generally, non-immigrant aliens are also prohibited from legally purchasing, possessing, or transporting firearms.

Exceptions for nonimmigrant aliens

However, a nonimmigrant alien who has been admitted under a non-immigrant visa is not prohibited from purchasing, receiving, or possessing a firearm if the person falls within one of the following exceptions:

1. If the person was admitted to the United States for lawful hunting or sporting purposes or is in possession of a hunting license or permit lawfully issued in the United States;
2. If the person is an official representative of a foreign government

who is accredited to the United States Government or the Government's mission to an international organization having its headquarters in the United States;

3. If the person is an official representative of a foreign government who is en route to or from another country to which that alien is accredited;

4. If the person is an official of a foreign government or a distinguished foreign visitor who has been so designated by the Department of State;

5. If the person is a foreign law enforcement officer of a friendly foreign government entering the United States on official law enforcement business;

6. If the person has received a waiver from the prohibition from the Attorney General of the United States.

See 18 U.S.C. §922(y).

III. FLORIDA LAW DISQUALIFICATIONS:
WHO CANNOT BUY A FIREARM UNDER FLORIDA LAW?

As mentioned earlier, Florida has restrictions on the sale, transfer, and possession of firearms that are separate and distinct from the federal restrictions. If a person runs afoul of the law, they could potentially face prosecution in both state and federal court.

A. Florida law disqualifications for "purchasing" a firearm

The disqualifications for purchasing firearms from a licensed importer, licensed manufacturer or licensed dealer of firearms under Florida law are partly enumerated in Florida Statute §790.065. The following constitute some of the reasons why the purchase of a firearm by a person may be denied:

(1) The person has been convicted of a felony;

(2) The person has been convicted of a misdemeanor crime of domestic violence;

(3) The person has had adjudication of guilt withheld or imposition of sentence suspended on any felony or misdemeanor crime of domestic violence unless three years have elapsed since probation or any other conditions set by the court have been fulfilled or expunction has occurred;

(4) The person has been adjudicated mentally defective or has been committed to a mental institution by a court;

(5) The person has been indicted or has had an information filed against him or her for an offense that is a felony under either state or federal law, or, as mandated by federal law, has had an injunction for protection against domestic violence entered against person, has had an injunction for protection against repeat violence entered against the person, or has been arrested for any of the following crimes:

a. arson;

b. aggravated assault;

c. aggravated battery;

d. illegal use of explosives;

e. child abuse or aggravated child abuse;

f. abuse of an elderly person or disabled adult, or aggravated abuse of an elderly person or disabled adult;

g. aircraft piracy;

h. kidnapping;

i. homicide;

j. manslaughter;

k. sexual battery;

l. robbery;

m. carjacking;

n. lewd, lascivious, or indecent assault or act upon or in presence of a child under the age of 16 years;

o. sexual activity with a child, who is 12 years of age or older but less than 18 years of age, by or at solicitation of person in familial or custodial authority;

p. burglary of a dwelling;

q. stalking and aggravated stalking;

r. act of domestic violence;

s. home invasion robbery;

t. act of terrorism;

u. manufacturing any substances in violation of the controlled substance laws;

v. attempting or conspiring to commit any of the above-referenced crimes;

w. criminal anarchy;

x. extortion;

y. explosives violations;

z. controlled substances violations;

    aa. resisting an officer with violence;

    bb. weapons and firearms violations;

    cc. treason;

    dd. assisting self-murder;

    ee. sabotage;

(6) The person has an active warrant (felony or misdemeanor);

(7) The person is addicted to any controlled substance;

(8) The person's status is that of an illegal alien;

(9) The person was dishonorably discharged from the US Armed Forces;

(10) The person has renounced their United States citizenship.

B. Florida law disqualifications for "possessing" firearms

Similar to the disqualifications for purchasing firearms under Florida law, Chapter 790 of the Florida Statutes also includes prohibitions on the possession of firearms. The following are some of the prohibitions on the possession of firearms included within Chapter 790:

(1) Persons who have been adjudged mentally incompetent, who are addicted to the use of narcotics or any similar drug, or who are habitual or chronic alcoholics, or persons using weapons or firearms in violation of Florida Statutes §§790.07-790.115, 790.145-790.19, 790.22-790.24;

(2) Persons in or about a place of nuisance as defined in Florida Statute §823.05, unless such person is there for law enforcement or some other lawful purpose;

(3) Persons who have been convicted of a felony in the courts of Florida;

(4) Persons who have been found by the courts of Florida to have committed a delinquent act that would be a felony if committed by an adult and such person is under 24 years of age;

(5) Persons convicted of or found to have committed a crime against the United States which is designated as a felony;

(6) Persons found to have committed a delinquent act in another state, territory, or country that would be a felony if committed by an adult and which was punishable by imprisonment for a term exceeding one year and such person is under 24 years of age;

(7) Persons found guilty of an offense that is a felony in another state, territory or country and which was punishable by imprisonment for a term exceeding one year;

(8) Persons who have been issued a final injunction that is currently in force and effect, restraining that person from committing acts of domestic violence or committing acts of stalking or cyberstalking;

(9) Persons who are under the influence of alcoholic beverages, any chemical substance set forth in Florida Statute §877.111, or

any substance control under Florida Statute Chapter 893, when affected to the extent that his or her normal faculties are impaired.

Note: Even though a person may not be disqualified from possession of a firearm under state law, that person may nevertheless still be disqualified to possess a firearm under federal law.

EXAMPLE

Scott was convicted of a misdemeanor of domestic violence in 1992. He has a Smith & Wesson .357 Magnum in his nightstand for self-defense.

Under Florida law, Scott may be in legal possession of his firearm. However, Scott is in unlawful possession of a firearm under federal laws 18 U.S.C. §922(g)(9) and 27 CFR §478.32(a)(9), regardless of how legal he might be under state law.

IV. UNDERSTANDING "PRIVATE SALES" LAWS

A. What are the legal restrictions on "private sales" of firearms?

Private individuals may legally buy, sell, gift, or otherwise transfer firearms to another private individual in Florida. However, when doing so, careful attention needs to be paid to not violate the laws regulating these transactions. So what are the legal restrictions? First, the ATF website has an informative pamphlet entitled "Best Practices: Transfers of Firearms by Private Sellers" located on its website. This pamphlet is a must-read before entering into a "private sales" transaction involving a firearm.

1. Residency requirements

Under federal law, an unlicensed (non-dealer) may only "transfer" a firearm to another unlicensed person in the same state. This means that if a person is a resident of Florida, federal law prohibits the person from directly (not through a dealer) selling or transferring the firearm to a resident of another state. Federal law makes these transactions illegal from both the buyer/transferee and seller/transferor perspective. It is illegal for a private individual to transport into or receive within his own state a firearm which was purchased in another state from a private seller. See 18 U.S.C. §922(a)(3). Likewise, it is illegal for a private seller to sell or deliver a firearm to an individual whom the private seller knows or has reason to believe is not a resident of the seller's state. See 18 U.S.C. §922(a)(5).

EXAMPLE

Bob is visiting his best friend from high school, Jim. Ten years ago after high school was over, Bob moved to Nebraska from Florida. One night, Bob and Jim decide to go to the shooting range during Bob's trip back to Florida, and Bob borrows one of Jim's handguns. After shooting at the range, impressed with both the feel and action of Jim's handgun, Bob asks Jim if he could buy it from him. Since they've been friends for so many years, Jim says yes, and even offers him a good price for the transaction. Before leaving to go home to Nebraska, Bob pays Jim and packs his new handgun.

Has Jim committed a crime in selling the handgun to Bob? Has Bob committed a crime in purchasing the handgun from Jim? The answer to both questions is yes! Under federal law, Bob is not allowed to privately purchase a handgun in another state and transport it back to his home state. Likewise, Jim is not allowed to sell a firearm legally to a person he knows lives in another state. In this example, both Bob and Jim know that Bob is not a Florida resident—the place where Jim has sold his firearm. Bob has committed the crime of willful receipt of a firearm from an out-of-state unlicensed person while Jim has committed the federal crime of willful sale of a firearm to an out-of-state resident. See 18 U.S.C. §924(a)(1)(D). The penalties for these crimes include jail time of up to 5 years and/or a fine of $250,000!

What if the situation is less obvious? Let's take a look at an example where "reasonable cause to believe" comes into play.

Frank, a Florida resident, recently posted his Glock 19 for sale on an internet message board in Florida. Frank receives an email from a person named Ted who would like to buy the handgun. Frank and Ted agree, via email, on a purchase price and arrange to meet at a place in Florida one week later to facilitate the transfer. When Ted pulls up in his 1978 Ford LTD Wagon, Frank notices the car's Tennessee license plates. Nevertheless, Frank shrugs and sells Ted the gun anyway without going through any of the formalities of a bill-of-sale, or asking for identification. Two weeks later, Frank finds himself at an FBI field office in Houston answering questions about a shooting that took place with his (former) Glock 19.

Is Frank in trouble? It is highly likely. Although Frank is not the center of the shooting investigation, Frank is probably the center of an investigation for illegally selling the firearm to an out-of-state resident under federal law.

2. Private sales: don't knowingly sell to the "wrong" people
A private individual may sell a firearm to a private buyer in the same state so long as the seller does not know or have reasonable cause to believe that the person purchasing the firearm is prohibited

from possessing or receiving a firearm under federal or state law. See 18 U.S.C. §922(d).

EXAMPLE

> Gordon and Josh are friends and Josh tells Gordon that he has just attempted to buy a gun from a local FFL and that he was denied because he was disqualified for some reason under federal law (something about a conviction or restraining order or drug use or psychiatric problems—Josh was too mad to remember!). Gordon says, "No problem, I'll just sell you one of mine," and he does.

Gordon has just committed a federal crime, because he knew (or at least had reasonable cause to believe) that Josh was prohibited from purchasing a firearm under the law.

B. How does the law determine a person's residence when buying or selling a firearm?

1. Individuals with one residence

For the purpose of firearms purchases, the person's state of residence is the state in which the person is present and where the individual has an intention of making a home. 27 CFR §478.11.

2. What if a person maintains a home in two states?

If a person maintains a home in two (or more) states and resides in those states for periods of the year, he or she may, during the period of time the person actually resides in a particular state, purchase a firearm in that state. However, simply owning property in another state does not qualify a person as a resident of that state so as to purchase a firearm in that state. To meet the residency requirements, a person must actually maintain a home in a state which includes an intention to make a particular state a residence.

See 27 CFR §478.11. This issue may ultimately be a fact question with evidence of residency including a driver's license, insurance records, recurring expenses in the state, as well as other things related to making a state a person's residence.

3. Members of the Armed Forces

A member of the Armed Forces on active duty is a resident of the state in which his or her permanent duty station is located. If a member of the Armed Forces maintains a home in one state and the member's permanent duty station is in a nearby state to which he or she commutes each day, then the member has two states of residence and may purchase a firearm in either state. See 18 U.S.C. §921(b). See also ATF FAQs on residency at www.atf.gov.

4. Nonimmigrant aliens

Persons who are legally present in the United States are residents of the state in which they reside and where they intend to make a home. Such persons, provided they meet all other requirements and are not otherwise prohibited from purchasing a firearm, are lawfully permitted to purchase a firearm.

C. Suggestion on how to document a private firearms sale

Protect yourself! This is practical advice that should not be ignored. If you engage in the private sale of a firearm, here are some practical tips:

- Ask for identification whether you are the buyer/transferee or seller/transferor to establish residency;
- Get and/or give a "bill of sale" for the transfer and keep a copy— identify the firearm including make, model, and serial number, as well as the date and place of transfer;
- Put the residency information on the "bill of sale" including

names, addresses, and phone numbers;

- Do not sell or transfer a firearm or ammunition if you think the person may not be permitted or is prohibited from receiving the firearm.

Why do this? Not only will it help establish residency, but if you unfortunately happen to buy or sell a firearm that was previously used in a crime, or if you sell or transfer a gun that is later used in a crime, you want to be able to establish when you did and did not own or possess the firearm.

Further, as a matter of good course, if you are a seller or transferor in a private sale, you might ask whether there is any reason the buyer/transferee cannot own a firearm. Why? So that if there is an issue later, you can at a minimum say that you had no reason to know the buyer could not legally possess firearms. However, do not overlook behavior that may indicate the buyer is not telling you the truth, because law enforcement will not overlook facts that show you did know, or should have had reasonable cause to believe that the buyer/transferee could not own a firearm at the time of the transfer if a legal issue arises later.

V. BUYING, SELLING, AND TRANSFERRING THROUGH AN FFL
A. Basic procedures

Persons purchasing firearms through dealers must comply with all legal requirements imposed by federal law. These include both paperwork, and appropriate background checks or screenings to ensure that the purchaser is not prohibited from the purchase or possession of a firearm under federal law.

When purchasing through a dealer, the first thing a prospective buyer will do is select a firearm. Once a selection has been made, the prospective purchaser is required to show proper identification and complete ATF Form 4473. This form requires the applicant, under penalty of law, to provide accurate identifying information, as well as answer certain questions in order to establish whether a person may legally purchase a firearm. The information provided on Form 4473 is then provided to the National Instant Criminal Background Check System (NICS) for processing and approval in order to proceed with the transfer (however, no NICS background may be required if the transferee is legally exempt for reasons such as possessing a state-issued firearms license like a Florida CWFL). A FFL dealer can submit the check to NICS either by telephone or through the online website and only after the FFL completes all of these steps successfully is a purchaser/transferee allowed to take possession of the firearm.

B. What is Form 4473?

ATF Form 4473 is known as a Firearms Transaction Record, which must be completed when a person purchases a firearm from an FFL. See 27 CFR §478.124. Form 4473 requires the applicant to provide their name, address, birth date, state of residence, and other information including government issued photo identification. The form also contains information blanks to be filled-in including the NICS background check transaction number, the make, model, and serial number of the firearm to be purchased, and a series of questions that a person must answer. See 27 CFR §478.124(c). This series of questions and the corresponding answers help determine a purchaser's eligibility under federal law to purchase a firearm. Once the form is completed, the prospective purchaser will sign the form and attest that the information provided thereon is truthful and accurate under penalty of federal law. This means that if you lie or make false statements on this form, the Feds can and will prosecute you for a crime!

Likewise, the dealer must also sign the Form 4473 and retain it for at least 20 years. The ATF is permitted to inspect, as well as receive a copy of Form 4473 from the dealer both during audits and during the course of a criminal investigation. The 4473 records must be surrendered to the Bureau of Alcohol, Tobacco, Firearms and Explosives in the event the FFL dealer retires or ceases business.

C. How are background checks administered when purchasing a firearm?

1. NICS: National Instant Criminal Background Check System

Background checks by dealers when transferring firearms are completed through the National Instant Criminal Background Check System or NICS, if required, prior to the transfer of a firearm from an FFL dealer to a non-dealer. When the prospective purchaser/transferee's information is given to NICS, the system will check the applicant against at least three different databases containing various types of records. Applicants are checked against the records maintained by the Interstate Identification Index (III) which contains criminal history records, the National Crime Information Center (NCIC) which contains records including warrants and protective orders, as well as the NICS Index which contains records of individuals who are prohibited from purchasing or possessing firearms under either federal or state law. In addition, if the applicant is not a United States Citizen, the application is processed for an Immigration Alien Query (IAQ) through the Department of Homeland Security's Immigration and Customs Enforcement Division.

2. Responses from NICS

NICS responses to background checks come in three basic forms: proceed, delay, or deny. The "proceed" response allows for the transfer to be completed. The "delay" response means that the transfer may not legally proceed. If the dealer receives a response of "delay," NICS has three business days to research the applicant further. If the dealer has not received a notice that the transfer is denied after the three business days, then the transfer may proceed. "Deny" means the transfer does not take place; a transferee's options after a "deny" are discussed below.

3. What transactions require background checks?

A background check is required before each and every sale or other transfer of a firearm from an FFL to a non-licensee unless an exception is provided under the law. For every transaction that requires a background check, the purchaser/transferee must also complete ATF Form 4473. This includes:
- The sale or trade of a firearm;
- The return of a consigned firearm;
- The redemption of a pawned firearm;
- The loan or rental of a firearm for use off of an FFL's licensed premises;

PRACTICAL LEGAL TIP

Thinking about buying a gun on behalf of your buddy? Not a good idea! One of the purposes of ATF Form 4473 is to conduct a background check on individuals who want to purchase firearms in order to make sure they are legally allowed to do so. Acting as a "straw man" by purchasing it for your buddy circumvents this process and is a crime. -David

4. What transactions do not require a background check?

A background check is not required under the following circumstances:

- The sale or transfer of a firearm where the transferee presents a valid state permit/license that allows the transferee to carry a firearm (for example, a CWFL) from the state where the FFL is located and the state permit/license is recognized by the ATF as a qualifying alternative to the background check requirement;
- The transfer of a firearm from one FFL to another FFL;
- The return of a repaired firearm to the person from whom it was received;
- The sale of a firearm to a law enforcement agency or a law enforcement officer for official duties if the transaction meets the specific requirements of 27 CFR §478.134, including providing a signed certification from a person in authority on agency letterhead stating that the officer will use the firearm in official duties and where a records check reveals the officer does not have any misdemeanor convictions for domestic violence;
- The transfer of a replacement firearm of the same kind and type to the person from whom a firearm was received;
- The transfer of a firearm that is subject to the National Firearms Act if the transfer was pre-approved by the ATF.

Note: A Florida Concealed Weapons License currently does not qualify as an alternative to the NICS background check requirement. A complete permit chart for all states is available on the ATF's website at www.atf.gov (see Permanent Brady Permit Chart).

5. If a person buys multiple handguns, a dealer must report that person to the ATF

Under federal law, FFLs are required to report to the ATF any sale or transfer of two or more pistols, revolvers, or any combination of pistols and revolvers totaling two or more to an unlicensed (non-FFL) individual that takes place at one time or during any five consecutive business days. This report is made to the ATF on Form 3310.4 and is completed in triplicate with the original copy sent to the ATF, one sent to the designated state police or local law enforcement agency in the jurisdiction where the sale took place, and one retained by the dealer and held for no less than five years.

6. FFLs must report persons who purchase more than one rifle in southwest border states

In Florida, Arizona, New Mexico, and California, dealers are required to report the sale or other transfer of more than one semiautomatic rifle capable of accepting a detachable magazine and with a caliber greater than .22 (including .223 caliber/5.56 millimeter) to an unlicensed person at one time or during any five consecutive business days. See 18 U.S.C. §923(g)(3)(A). This report is made via ATF Form 3310.12 and must be reported no later than the close of business on the day the multiple sale or other disposition took place. This requirement includes (but is not limited to) purchases of popular semiautomatic rifles such as AR-15s, AK-47s, Ruger Mini-14s, and Tavor bullpup rifles.

VI. WHAT IF I'M DENIED THE RIGHT TO PURCHASE A FIREARM?
A. If I am denied the right to purchase, how do I appeal?

Persons who believe they have been erroneously denied or delayed a firearm transfer based on a match to a record returned by the NICS may request an appeal of their "deny" or "delay" decision. All appeal inquiries must be submitted to the NICS Section's Appeal Service Team (AST) in writing, either online on the FBI's website at www.fbi.gov or via mail. An appellant must provide their complete name, complete mailing address, and NICS Transaction Number. For persons appealing a delayed transaction, a fingerprint card is required and must be submitted with the appeal, although the fingerprint card is merely recommended on appeals for denied applications. This may seem counter-intuitive, but it is required per the FBI's website.

B. What if I keep getting erroneously delayed or denied when I am attempting to buy a firearm?

Apply for a PIN (personal identification number) that is designed to solve this issue. Some individuals may have a name which is common enough (or happens to be flagged for other reasons) that it causes undue delays or denials in the background check verification process through NICS. For that reason, NICS maintains the Voluntary Appeal File database (VAF) which allows any applicant to apply by submitting an appeal request and then obtain a UPIN or Unique Personal Identification Number. A person who has been cleared through the VAF and receives a UPIN will then be able to use their UPIN when completing Form 4473 in order to help avoid further erroneous denials or extended delays. A person can obtain a UPIN by following the procedures outlined on the FBI's website at www.fbi.gov.

VII. ADDITIONAL CONSIDERATIONS IN FIREARMS PURCHASING AND POSSESSION LAWS

A. How can I legally purchase a firearm from someone in another state?

Any individual who wishes to purchase a firearm from a person that lives in another state than the purchaser must complete the transaction through an FFL. Sellers or transferors are legally authorized to facilitate a private transaction or transfer by shipping the firearm to the purchaser's FFL in the recipient/buyer's state, where the FFL will complete the transfer process. It is a federal crime to sell or transfer a firearm between persons who are residents of different states, or where a transfer takes place in a state other than the transferee/transferor's singular state of residence.

B. Can I purchase firearms on the Internet?

Yes. However, all legal requirements for a transfer must be followed. If the buyer and seller are both residents of Florida, then the two may lawfully conduct a private sale so long as all other legal issues are satisfied (see our earlier discussion on disqualifications to purchasing and possessing firearms in this chapter). However, if buyer and seller are not residents of the same state, the transaction can only be legally facilitated through the intervention of an FFL.

C. Shipping firearms

1. Can I ship my firearm through the postal service?

Long guns: yes. Handguns: no. However, under federal law, a non-licensed individual may not transfer (and this would include shipping to someone) a firearm to a non-licensed resident (non-FFL) of another state. However, a non-licensed individual may mail a long gun to a resident of his or her own state, and they may also mail a long gun to an FFL of another state. To that end, the USPS recommends that long guns be mailed via registered mail and that the packaging used to mail the long gun be ambiguous so as to not identify the contents. Handguns are not allowed to be mailed through USPS. See 18 U.S.C. §§1715, 922(a)(3), 922(a)(5), and 922(a)(2)(A). Rather, handguns must be shipped using a common or contract carrier (e.g., UPS or FedEx).

2. Shipping handguns and other firearms through a common or contract carrier

Under federal law, a non-licensed individual may ship a firearm (including a handgun) by a common or contract carrier (e.g., UPS or FedEx) to a resident of his or her own state, or to a licensed individual (FFL) in another state. However, it is illegal to ship any firearm to a non-FFL in another state. It is a requirement that the carrier be notified that the shipment contains a firearm, however, carriers are prohibited from requiring any identifying marks on the package which may be used to identify the contents as containing a firearm. See 18 U.S.C. §§922(a)(2)(A), 922(a)(3), 922(a)(5), 922(e), 27 CFR 478.31 and 478.30.

D. Can I ship my firearm to myself for use in another state?

Yes. In accordance with the law as described in the preceding section, a person may ship a firearm to himself or herself in care of another person in another state where he or she intends to hunt or engage in other lawful activity. The package should be addressed to the owner and persons other than the owner should not open the package and take possession of the firearm.

E. If I am moving out of Florida, may I have movers move my firearms?

Yes, a person who lawfully possesses firearms may transport or ship the firearms interstate when changing the person's state of residence so long as the person complies with the requirements for shipping and transporting firearms as outlined earlier. See 18 U.S.C. §922(e) and 27 CFR §478.31. However, certain NFA items such as destructive devices, machine guns, short-barreled shotguns or rifles, and so forth require approval from the ATF before they can be moved interstate. See 18 U.S.C. §922(a)(4) and 27 CFR

§478.28. It is important that the person seeking to move the firearms also check state and local laws where the firearms will be relocated to ensure that the movement of the firearms into the new state does not violate any state law or local ordinance.

F. May I loan my firearm to another person?

There is no prohibition on loaning a firearm to another person, so long as the person receiving the firearm may lawfully possess one.

G. What happens to my firearms when I die?

Depending on the manner in which a person leaves his or her estate behind, firearms may be bequeathed in a customary manner like other personal property. However, firearms held in an estate are still subject to the laws of transfer and possession. Thus careful consideration needs to be given in estate planning with consideration for firearms law of both the jurisdiction in which the estate is located as well as consideration of who is to receive the firearms.

VIII. AMMUNITION: THE LAW OF PURCHASING AND POSSESSION

A. Who is legally prohibited from purchasing ammunition under federal law?

Under federal law, there are six primary situations where a person is prohibited from buying, selling, or possessing ammunition (beyond armor-piercing ammunition which was discussed in Chapter Two).

1. Under 18 U.S.C. §922(b)(1), it is unlawful for a person to sell long gun ammunition to a person under the age of 18;
2. Under 18 U.S.C. §922(b)(1), it is unlawful for a person to sell handgun ammunition to a person under the age of 21;
3. Under 18 U.S.C. §922(x)(2)(B), it is unlawful for a juvenile to possess handgun ammunition;

4. Under 18 U.S.C. §922(d), it is unlawful to sell ammunition to a person who is prohibited from purchasing firearms;

5. Under 18 U.S.C. §922(g), it is unlawful for a person who is disqualified from purchasing or possessing firearms to possess firearm ammunition if such ammunition has moved in interstate commerce (which is nearly all ammunition); and

6. Under 18 U.S.C. §922(h), it is unlawful for a person who is employed by a person who is disqualified from purchasing or possessing ammunition to possess or transport ammunition for the disqualified individual.

For the statutes that involve juveniles, there are a couple of notable exceptions to the law: first, the law against selling handgun ammunition to a juvenile and possession of handgun ammunition by a juvenile does not apply to a temporary transfer of ammunition to a juvenile or to the possession or use of ammunition by a juvenile if the handgun and ammunition are possessed and used by the juvenile in the course of employment, in the course of ranching or farming-related activities at the residence of the juvenile (or on property used for ranching or farming at which the juvenile, with the permission of the property owner or lessee, is performing activities related to the operation of the farm or ranch), target practice, hunting, or a course of instruction in the safe and lawful use of a handgun. The law also does not apply to the temporary transfer to or use of ammunition by a juvenile if the juvenile has been provided with prior written consent by his or her parent or guardian who is not prohibited by federal, state, or local law from possessing firearms. See 18 U.S.C. §922(x)(3).

Additionally, juveniles who (1) are members of the Armed Forces of the United States or the National Guard who possesses or is armed with a handgun in the line of duty, (2) receive ammunition by inheritance, or (3) possess ammunition in the course of self-defense or defense of others are permitted to possess ammunition.

B. When is a person prohibited from purchasing or possessing ammunition under Florida law?

The Florida Statutes provide three occasions where the sale of ammunition is prohibited: (1) to felons and persons found delinquent of felonies when those persons found delinquent are under 24 years of age (Florida Statute §790.23); (2) to persons who have been issued final injunctions that are currently in force and effect, restraining those persons from committing acts of domestic violence or from committing acts of stalking or cyberstalking (Florida Statute §790.233); and (3) certain types of ammunition, such as armor-piercing bullets, exploding bullets, dragon's breath shotgun shells, bolo shells and flechette shells (Florida Statute §790.23).

C. Can a person be disqualified from purchasing ammunition if they are disqualified from purchasing firearms?

Yes, under federal law. Under 18 U.S.C. §922(g) it is unlawful for a person who is disqualified from purchasing or possessing firearms to purchase ammunition if the ammunition has moved in interstate commerce. Since nearly all ammunition or ammunition components move through interstate commerce in one form or another, this disqualification includes essentially all ammunition.

D. Can a person purchase ammunition that is labeled "law enforcement use only"?

Yes. Although some handgun ammunition is sold with a label "law enforcement use," such a label has no legal meaning and is only reflective of a company policy or, viewed less positively, as a marketing strategy.

> CHAPTER SEVEN ◄

WHEN CAN I LEGALLY USE MY GUN: PART I
UNDERSTANDING THE LAW OF JUSTIFICATION
Some Basic Legal Concepts

I. IGNORANCE OF THE LAW IS NO EXCUSE!
When is it legal to use a weapon?

L et's take a look at some basic legal concepts of when and under what circumstances a person may be legally justified in using force or deadly force against persons or animals. Understanding the law can be the difference between a conviction and freedom. Not knowing the law can and will get many good people in legal trouble. The defense of "It was an honest mistake!" holds zero bearing in a court of law.

II. TO LEGALLY USE FORCE OR DEADLY FORCE, YOU MUST BE "JUSTIFIED." WHAT IS LEGAL JUSTIFICATION?

A. Basic definition of justification: an acceptable excuse

A legal justification allows for what would otherwise be an unlawful act to be a lawful, excusable act. Even though a crime has been committed, justice dictates that a person should not be punished for the act.

For instance, a robber unlawfully breaks into a home while the homeowner is making dinner in the kitchen. The homeowner hears his front door busted down. The homeowner grabs his 9 mm handgun, shoots and kills the robber. Technically, the homeowner did an illegal act – he killed another human being. However, since the circumstances surrounding the shooting involved a person unlawfully entering another's home while occupied by the homeowner, it is highly likely the shooting is excused under the law because justice and society dictates such a conclusion.

B. Basic requirement: you must admit your action

How can a person receive a justification defense? In order to be able to assert a justification defense, a person can't say "I didn't do it, but if I did I was justified." When claiming a justification defense, a person admits to the commission of a crime. *Martinez v. State*, 981 So.2d 449 (Fla. 2008). A justification claim is both a confession of committing a crime and an avoidance of being punished for the crime. *Hopson v. State*, 127 Fla. 243, 168 So. 810, 811 (Fla. 1936).

Evidence must be presented at trial pertaining to a person's justification defense in order for a jury to be instructed that they may consider whether a person was justified in their use of force or deadly force. "Any evidence" presented to support a justification means that a court must instruct the jury to consider the defendant's justification claim. See *Goode v. State*, 856 So.2d 1101, 1104 (Fla. 1st DCA 2003). Once a defendant presents "any evidence" in support of a justification claim, the state's attorney (the prosecutor) is required to prove beyond a reasonable doubt that the defendant's actions were not justified under the law.

C. What does "any evidence" mean?

A jury instruction must include a justification defense if "any evidence" of self-defense is presented during trial. The "any evidence" standard is a very low one. Even if the evidence is weak or contradictory to other evidence, a jury instruction must include the justification defense as long as the defense requests such an instruction. *Martinez v. State*, 981 So.2d 449 (Fla. 2008). This evidence may be in the form of the defendant's testimony, witness testimony, or physical evidence.

III. WEAPONS LAWS YOU NEED TO KNOW!

Where do you find these justification defenses in the law? Florida's justification statutes are found in Florida Statutes Title XLVI Chapter 776. This chapter, entitled "Justifiable Use of Force," lays out when a person will be legally justified in using force or deadly force. Further and perhaps even more importantly, Chapter 776 explains when a person will lose their justification defense.

A. Categories of force for justification under Chapter 776

Basically, a justification defense hinges on the type of force used in a given set of facts, i.e. the type of force used will determine whether a person is legally justified. There are three categories of force in Florida: force, deadly force, and the threat of force or deadly force.

1. What if a person uses greater force than the law allows?

If a person uses a greater amount of force than the law allows, they will not be legally justified in their action and may be ultimately convicted of a crime. It is important to know the degree of force that is legally justified in order to stay on the right side of the law.

Category 1: Force

Interestingly enough, there is no specific definition of "force" in Florida's "Justifiable Use of Force" chapter. A prerequisite of using deadly force is the requirement that the use of mere force would be justified.

Florida Standard Criminal Jury Instruction 3.6(g) defines non-deadly force as "force not likely to cause death or great bodily harm." If we boil this definition down, force may be described as unwanted physical contact that will not cause a person to die or sustain great bodily harm. What about displaying a firearm in order to deter an attack? A firearm is a deadly weapon capable of causing death or great bodily harm. Does pointing a gun at someone amount to the use of deadly force as opposed to mere force? No, pointing a gun without firing it is considered force, not deadly force. *Rivero v. State*, 871 So.2d 953, 954 (Fla. 3d DCA 2004). What about waving a gun around? The act of waving the gun is also considered force, not deadly force. Id.

Category 2: Deadly Force

Now that we know what mere force means, let's discuss the concept of "deadly force." Florida Standard Criminal Jury Instruction 3.6(f) defines deadly force as force likely to cause death or great bodily harm. Deadly force does not have to cause death!

The term "deadly force" seems to have a pretty straight forward definition. But, the term is a little trickier than what first meets the eye. Death is not a requirement of deadly force. Inflicting great bodily harm on another is considered the use of deadly force under the law. So how much harm is required to enter into the realm of great bodily harm? A Florida court described it as more than "slight, trivial, minor or moderate harm [and][a]s such, does not include mere bruises..." *Heck v. State*, 774 So.2d 844, 845 (Fla. App. 2000). Facial fractures, a fractured leg, and scars have all been determined to constitute great bodily harm by Florida courts. Id. It appears that broken bones, loss of an organ function, and disfigurement would all be considered great bodily harm.

2. Does a deadly weapon have to be involved in order for force to be classified as deadly force?

No. The use of a weapon does not always constitute the use of deadly force. As mentioned earlier, Florida courts have ruled that pointing a gun is classified as force. However, discharging a firearm in the vicinity of other people is considered deadly force. *Rivero v. State*, 871 So.2d 953, 954 (Fla. 3d DCA 2004), See *Howard v. State*, 698 So.2d 923 (Fla. 4th DCA 1997). Keep in mind, that everyday items can cause death or great bodily harm like hammers, baseball bats, or flower pots. A jury will look at how the item was used rather than its intended manufactured purpose.

3. Does the law recognize a person's fist as a deadly weapon?

Maybe. We all know that a person's hands are capable of killing or causing great bodily harm. A deadly weapon is an instrument which will likely cause death or great bodily harm when used in the ordinary and usual manner contemplated by its design and construction, or an object which is used or threatened to be used in such a way that it would be likely to cause death or great bodily harm. *Butler v. State*, 602 So.2d 1303 (Fla. 1st DCA 1992).

So, who decides whether an object is a deadly weapon? A jury will be tasked with making this decision. The Supreme Court of Florida held that the determination of whether an unloaded BB gun was a deadly weapon is a jury question. *Dale v. State*, 22 FLW 670 (Fla. 1997). Even though most of us would agree that an unloaded BB gun is not likely to cause death or great bodily harm, a jury will look through the eyes of the victim (or complaining witness) as to what they perceived the object to be. See also, *Mitchell v. State*, 1997 Fla.App.Lexis 7870 (2nd DCA 1997) and *J.M.P. v. State*, 35 Fla.L.Weekly D2072 (Fla. 4th DCA 2010).

B. Threats of Force

Florida law allows for the justified use of force in particular situations, in turn; it makes sense that Florida law allows for the justified threat of force in similar situations. Threats of force are justified as long as they meet the requirements laid out in Chapter 776. A threat can be described as a communicated intent that a person will inflict harm against another. *United States v. White*, 258 F.3d 374, 383 (5th Cir. 2001).

USE OR THREATENED USE OF FORCE IN DEFENSE OF PERSON; FLORIDA STATUTE §776.012(1)

A person is justified in using or threatening to use deadly force, except deadly force, against another when and to the extent that the person reasonably believes that such conduct is necessary to defend himself or herself or another against the other's imminent use of unlawful force. A person who uses or threatens to use force in accordance with this subsection does not have a duty to retreat before using or threatening to use such force.

The plain reading of this statute indicates when a person is faced with force they may threaten to use force against the perpetrator. They cannot threaten deadly force and be justified under §776.012(1). As discussed previously, case law suggests that the display of a firearm is considered force not deadly force. So, yelling that you will pull your gun on another is a threat of force because the mere display is considered force.

USE OR THREATENED USE OF FORCE IN DEFENSE OF PERSON; FLORIDA STATUTE §776.012(2)

A person is justified in using or threatening to use deadly force if he or she reasonably believes that using or threatening to use such force is necessary to prevent imminent death or great bodily harm to himself or herself or another or to prevent the imminent commission of a forcible felony. A person who uses or threatens to use deadly force in accordance with this subsection does not have a duty to retreat and has the right to stand his or her ground if the person using or threatening to use the deadly force is not engaged in a criminal activity and is in a place where he or she has a right to be.

It would appear that a threat of deadly force is only justified if a person is faced with unlawful deadly force. A person would not be justified in threatening deadly force in a mere use of force scenario. Threatening deadly force may be seen as more force than allowed and not legally justified under the law if the set of facts only amount to force. Thus, yelling at a perpetrator that you will pull your gun and shoot him is considered a threat of deadly force and a person must be in a deadly force scenario in order to be justified in the threat.

IV. WARNING SHOTS: "BUT, I NEVER MEANT TO HURT ANYONE!"

Are warning shots a use of deadly force? As mentioned earlier, discharging a firearm in another person's vicinity is considered deadly force. *Rivero v. State*, 871 So.2d 953, 954 (Fla. 3d DCA 2004). The media touted that Florida's House Bill 89 condones the use of warning shots. This simply isn't true. The bill, which has now become law, allows for a person to threaten the use of force or deadly force as long as they meet the requirements under Chapter 776(1) or (2), respectively. In other words, a person may threaten deadly force by shooting a warning shot if they would be justified under the law in using deadly force. A person is justified in using deadly force if they reasonably believe that deadly force is necessary to defend against another's imminent use of unlawful deadly force or to prevent the imminent commission of a forcible felony. If something less than deadly force should have been used, a person may be charged and convicted of a crime. (See the section above for a discussion of justifiable threats of force/deadly force under Chapter 776(1) and (2)).

V. WHAT DOES IT MEAN TO REASONABLY BELIEVE THAT FORCE IS NECESSARY TO DEFEND FROM ANOTHER'S IMMINENT USE OF UNLAWFUL FORCE?

In order to be justified in using/threatening force or deadly force in Florida, a person must have a reasonable belief that the use of force/ deadly force is necessary to defend against another's imminent use of unlawful force.

A. How does the law determine "reasonable?"

In determining whether a person is justified in their use of force, a jury will evaluate whether a person's action was "reasonable." How does a reasonable person act? At the end of the day, the jury will determine whether an action is deemed reasonable.

Basically, a person must reasonably believe that force is necessary to defend themselves. Other people (a jury) must agree that they would have done the same thing if presented with similar circumstances. If a person is found to have acted unreasonably in using such force, their actions will not be justified under the law. Under the reasonable person standard, a jury will look at the facts through the eyes of the defendant and determine whether the use of force was something a "reasonable person" would have done.

B. What does "imminent use of unlawful force" mean under the law?

When does someone have a reasonable belief that they must use force in order to protect themselves from an "imminent use of unlawful force" by another? In Florida, the decision will be ultimately decided by a jury. Let's focus on the word "imminent." Florida courts have said that imminent means an act that is about to happen immediately. *Gaffney v. State*, 742 So.2d 358 (Fla. 2d DCA 1999). It is not something that will happen in the next hour, next week, or even next month. It is an action that will be made within the next few seconds. A jury is tasked in deciding whether your use of force was used to prevent another's imminent use of unlawful force. You must be protecting yourself from an act that is seconds away from happening.

A conditional threat such as, "If I see you on this side of town again, I'll bury you!" is not imminent because it has to do with an act that must be taken in the future. Since "I'll bury you!" is something that will happen in the future (not immediately) and it is conditional upon coming back to that particular part of town, it is not imminent.

Therefore, it is unlikely that a person will be justified in using force against this particular threat since it lacks imminence.

Certain circumstances receive the presumption that you had a reasonable fear of imminent peril of death or great bodily harm. This presumption of reasonableness is a powerful legal tool. It prevents a prosecutor from second-guessing that a person did not have a reasonable fear of imminent death or great bodily harm. A jury will be told if a given set of circumstances exist, (for instance a person is unlawfully breaking into your occupied home), the law will presume the person in the home held a reasonable fear of imminent death or great bodily harm, and that a person's use of force or deadly force against the home invader would be justified. We will dive in to what scenarios receive the presumption of reasonableness in the next chapter.

C. No presumption of reasonableness: prosecutors are allowed to second-guess

As discussed above, there are situations where a person will receive the presumption of reasonableness. However, there are many scenarios where a person will not be afforded the presumption that they held a reasonable fear of death or great bodily harm. What happens in those cases? A prosecutor will be able to second-guess a person's use of force or deadly force. They will be able to attempt to poke holes in a person's assertion that they were in reasonable fear of imminent force or deadly force. The timing and the degree of force used will definitely be attacked! The prosecutor may also argue that a person should have retreated, should have used lesser force, or that there was no imminent threat. In some areas of the law, there are NO legal presumptions! In these scenarios, the ultimate decision is up to a jury on whether you held a reasonable belief that force or deadly force was necessary.

VI. THE BURDEN OF PROOF IN CRIMINAL CASES.

In criminal cases, the State's attorneys (or prosecutors) have the burden of proof. It is the State's job to present evidence of a crime to attempt to prove that a defendant did in fact commit that crime. The burden of proof that the State must meet is "beyond a reasonable doubt." It is the highest burden of proof in the American justice system. At trial, the state must prove the defendant's guilt beyond a reasonable doubt. This means that the prosecution must eliminate all reasonable doubt whatsoever from the jury's mind that the defendant's action was justified.

VII. AM I SUBJECT TO A STATUTORY MINIMUM SENTENCE IF I USE A WEAPON TO DEFEND MYSELF?

Maybe. Under Florida Statute §775.087, if a person is in possession of a weapon during the commission of one of the following crimes, there is a statutory minimum sentence required under the statute: murder, sexual battery, robbery, burglary, arson, aggravated battery, kidnapping, escape, aircraft piracy, aggravated child abuse, aggravated abuse of an elderly or disabled person, carjacking, home-invasion robbery, aggravated stalking, drug trafficking, unlawful throwing/placing/discharge of a destructive device, or possession of firearm by a convicted felon.

VIII. WHAT IS THE PROBLEM WITH STATUTORY MINIMUM SENTENCES?

Statutorily required minimum sentences take out the human element and basically stop a judge or jury from making a decision based on the facts presented at trial. Statutory minimums put every scenario in a cookie-cutter box, and frankly, that's not how the law should work. It leaves a judge or jury with their hands tied, preventing them from making a decision based on logic and common sense. In 2014, the Florida Legislature addressed the issue finding that people have been criminally prosecuted and sentenced to mandatory minimum terms of imprisonment for threatening to use force/deadly force under circumstances that would have been justifiable under Chapter 776.

Mandatory Firearm Sentences

i. 10 years – firearm/destructive device possessed in any listed felony;

ii. 15 years – possessed semi-automatic firearm with high capacity detachable box magazine capable of holding 20 centerfire cartridges; or machine gun, during any of the listed felonies or their attempt;

iii. 20 years – discharged a firearm or destructive device during any of listed felonies or their attempt;

iv. 25 to life – same as previous, and as a result death or great bodily harm inflicted on any person.

The crime of aggravated assault was recently removed from the enumerated list above. What does that mean? A person charged with aggravated assault (a very common offense weapons owners are charged with), will not be subject to the statutory minimum sentence requirement, but still faces up to 5 years in prison.

Now we are ready to move onto when a person is legally justified in using deadly force to protect themselves and others!

> CHAPTER EIGHT ◄

WHEN CAN I LEGALLY USE MY GUN: PART II
SELF-DEFENSE AND DEFENSE OF OTHERS
Understanding When Force And Deadly Force Can Be Legally Used Against Another Person

I. INTRODUCTION AND OVERVIEW

The question of "when can a person legally use deaThe question of "when can a person legally use deadly force against another person" is of critical importance if you are a legal Florida firearms owner. Although a firearm is nothing more than a tool, it is a tool that by its very nature has the ability to deliver deadly force. Thus, all responsible firearms owners should understand when they are justified in using force and deadly force under the law. Failure to understand the law gets lots of good people in serious trouble!

The primary laws dealing with self-defense and defense of other people are contained in Chapter 776 of Title XLVI of the Florida Statutes, specifically Florida Statutes §776.012: Use Of Force In Defense Of Person and §776.013: Home Protection; Use Of Threatened Use Of Deadly Force.

The law of justified self-defense is split between justification for the use of force and justification for the use of deadly force in Section 776.012. Section 776.013 contains legal presumptions of reasonableness that are available under certain circumstances and are extremely powerful when deciding if a use of force or deadly force was legally justified, also known as the "Castle Doctrine." Likewise, the language of both sections contains versions of the "Stand Your Ground" laws. Finally, Section 776.012 combines force and deadly force in providing justification for defense of third persons.

In the previous chapter, several legal concepts, such as reasonableness, imminent use, and the categorization of force and deadly force were discussed. Those concepts have practical applications in this chapter. In this chapter, we will expand upon those topics to include when a person may be justified in using force or deadly force in self-defense, as well as those circumstances when the law specifically prohibits the use of force or deadly force.

II. DEFENDING PEOPLE WITH FORCE OR DEADLY FORCE
A. The Self-Defense Justification: Florida Statute §776.012
The primary self-defense statute in Florida is in Section 776.012. This section lays out the legal requirements for the justified use of force and deadly force for self-defense. This section establishes that a person is legally justified in using force when he or she has a reasonable belief that their "conduct is necessary to defend himself

or herself against the other's imminent use of unlawful force." Florida Statute §776.012(1).

Similarly, Florida Statute §776.012(2) establishes a general standard for the justified use of deadly force. A person may use deadly force when they reasonably believe such force is necessary to prevent imminent death or great bodily harm to themselves, or to prevent the imminent commission of a forcible felony. As discussed in the previous chapter, what a person believes is "imminent" and whether their belief that force or deadly force was necessary is reasonable is the difference between justification (not guilty) and conviction (guilty).

Who decides whether an actor's belief is or is not reasonable that force or deadly force is immediately necessary? Who decides if the degree of force used by someone was reasonable under a particular set of circumstances? The answer to both of these questions is the jury.

Therefore, if a person finds himself or herself facing a criminal charge and is claiming self-defense under the general self-defense provisions contained in Section 776.012, the jury will decide if that person's belief was or was not reasonable that deadly force was necessary to prevent imminent death, great bodily harm, or the commission of a forcible felony. This leaves a lot of room for juries to interpret what actions are reasonable or not. It also leaves the door open for legal second-guessing by prosecutors as to when and how much force was used, including arguments that neither death nor great bodily harm was imminent, making the force used unreasonable. If the prosecutor convinces a jury that a person used force or deadly force that was not "reasonably believed" to be necessary to prevent the imminent threat, that person will be guilty of using unlawful force or deadly force.

B. What are forcible felonies?

A person may use deadly force to prevent the imminent commission of a forcible felony; this begs the question, "What is a forcible felony?" Florida Statute §776.08 lists a series of crimes that constitute forcible felonies, which include:

> Treason; murder; manslaughter; sexual battery; carjacking; home-invasion robbery; robbery; burglary; arson; kidnapping; aggravated assault; aggravated battery; aggravated stalking; aircraft piracy; unlawful throwing, placing, or discharging of a destructive device or bomb; and any other felony which involves the use or threat of physical force or violence against any individual.

While some of these crimes are intuitive and easy to mentally grasp, such as unlawfully throwing a bomb, other crimes require some explanation to fully grasp.

1. Treason

Treason is defined in Florida Statute §876.32 as "levying war" against the state, or adhering to the enemies of the state or giving them aid and comfort. For better or for worse, there are no cases involving self-defense against individuals committing treason, so this is more an intellectual exercise than a day-to-day concern.

2. Murder

Murder in Florida is detailed in §782.04 of the Florida Statutes. Murder is when a person is unlawfully killed. Florida recognizes murder in the 1st degree, which is punishable as a capital crime by death or life in prison; murder in the 2nd degree, punishable as a 1st degree felony by a jail sentence up to life in prison; and murder in the 3rd degree, which is punishable as a 2nd degree felony with a prison sentence not to exceed 15 years.

The facts surrounding the murder determine what degree it is. There are three circumstances under Florida law that are recognized as 1st degree murder: 1) premeditated (preplanned) killing of a human being; 2) the killing of a human being while the killer is engaged in one of the felonies listed in the statute, including but not limited to sexual battery, robbery, burglary, kidnapping, escape and many others1 and 3) the killing of a human being which is the result of the unlawful distribution of certain controlled substances, when the substance causes the death of the user.

2nd degree murder is defined in two ways in Florida. The first is the killing of a human being, which is caused by an imminently dangerous act to another, which shows a depraved mind not concerned with human life, but without any preplanned design to cause the death of another.

The second way a person commits 2nd degree murder is when a human being is killed during the commission of any felony listed in footnote 1 by someone other than the perpetrator of the offense.

3rd degree murder is committed when a person is committing any other felony offense not listed in footnote[1] and a human being is killed during the commission of that offense without any preplanned design to cause the death of another.

[1]These felony crimes include: offenses prohibited by s. 893.135(1), arson, sexual battery, robbery, burglary, kidnapping, escape, aggravated child abuse, aggravated abuse of an elderly person or disabled adult, aircraft piracy, unlawful throwing, placing, or discharging of a destructive device or bomb, carjacking, home-invasion robbery, aggravated stalking, murder of another human being, resisting an officer with violence to his or her person, aggravated fleeing or eluding with serious bodily injury or death, any felony that is an act of terrorism or is in furtherance of an act of terrorism.

Shaun is jealous of Gordon because he has a beautiful girlfriend. He thinks that with Gordon out of the way, he will have a chance of being noticed by her. One day, he follows Gordon to work, and as Gordon exits his car aims his gun at Gordon. A co-worker of Gordon, named Bob, sees Shaun with his gun aimed at Gordon and fires at him to prevent the murder. Bob's bullet hits Mary, an innocent bystander, killing her. Shaun fires his gun and kills Gordon. Shaun is arrested later that day.

Under Florida Law, Shaun will likely be charged with 1st degree murder for the killing of Gordon and 2nd degree murder for the death of Mary which occurred when Bob hit her accidentally.

3. Manslaughter

Manslaughter is defined by Florida Statute §782.07 as the killing of a human being by the act, procurement, or culpable negligence of another, without lawful justification according to the provisions of Chapter 776 and in cases in which such killing shall not be excusable homicide or murder, according to the provisions of this chapter, a felony of the second degree. Explained more simply, manslaughter is the killing of a human being, without lawful justification, and which does not fall into any of the murder categories.

4. Sexual Battery

Florida Statute §794.011 defines sexual battery as oral, anal, or vaginal penetration by, or union with, the sexual organ of another or the anal or vaginal penetration of another by any other object; however, sexual battery does not include an act done for a bona fide medical purpose.

5. Carjacking

Found in Florida Statute §812.133, carjacking means: the taking of a motor vehicle which may be the subject of larceny from the person or custody of another, with intent to either permanently or temporarily deprive the person or the owner of the motor vehicle, when in the course of the taking there is the use of force, violence, assault, or putting in fear. More simply, forcibly taking someone's car either permanently or temporarily.

6. Robbery

The taking of money or other property which may be the subject of larceny from the person or custody of another, with intent to either permanently or temporarily deprive the person or the owner of the money or other property, when in the course of the taking there is the use of force, violence, assault, or putting in fear. More simply stated, taking someone's stuff either temporarily or permanently using violence, force or threat.

"In the course of" means any act which occurs in an attempt to commit robbery or in flight (escaping) from the attempt or commission of a robbery. Additionally, acts are deemed "in the course of the taking" if it occurs either prior to, at the same time as, or immediately after the taking of the property in one continuous series of acts or events. See Florida Statute §812.13.

7. Home-invasion Robbery

Whenever a robbery occurs when the offender enters a dwelling with the intent to commit a robbery, and does commit a robbery of the occupants inside, it is considered a home-invasion robbery in the State of Florida, pursuant to Florida Statute §812.135.

8. Burglary

Burglary, per Florida Statute §810.02, is:

Entering a dwelling, a structure, or a conveyance with the intent to commit an offense therein, unless the premises are at the time open to the public or the defendant is licensed or invited to enter; or Notwithstanding a licensed or invited entry, remaining in a dwelling, structure, or conveyance:

a. Surreptitiously, with the intent to commit an offense therein;
b. After permission to remain therein has been withdrawn, with the intent to commit an offense therein; or
c. To commit or attempt to commit a forcible felony, as defined in Florida Statute §776.08.

9. Arson

Found in Florida Statute §806.01, arson occurs when any person willfully and unlawfully, or while in the commission of any felony, by fire or explosion, damages or causes to be damaged:

Any dwelling, occupied or not, or its contents

Any structure, or its contents, where persons are normally present (such as jails, prisons, detention centers, hospitals, nursing homes, other health care facilities, department stores, office buildings, business establishments, churches, or educational institutions, or other similar structures) during normal hours of occupancy

Any other structure that he or she knew or had reasonable grounds to believe was occupied by a human being.

10. Kidnapping

Kidnapping means forcibly; secretly; or by threat; confining, abducting, or imprisoning another person against her or his will and without lawful authority, with intent to hold them for ransom or reward, use them as a shield or hostage, commit or facilitate commission of any felony, inflict bodily harm upon them, to terrorize the victim or another person, or to interfere with the performance of any governmental or political function. This definition is found in Florida Statute §787.01.

11. Aggravated Assault

An aggravated assault is an assault with a deadly weapon without the intent to kill, or with the intent to commit a felony. This definition is found in Florida Statute §784.021. The definition of assault, however, is found in Section 784.011, and is defined as an intentional, unlawful threat by word or act to do violence to the person of another, coupled with an apparent ability to do so, and doing some act which creates a well-founded fear in such other person that such violence is imminent. Keep in mind that only the aggravated assault is a forcible felony in Florida, not the lesser misdemeanor assault!

12. Aggravated Battery

Found in Florida Statute §784.045, an aggravated battery is a battery where the offender intentionally or knowingly causes great bodily harm, permanent disability, or permanent disfigurement, or uses a deadly weapon, or if the victim was pregnant and the offender knew or should have known she was pregnant. What then is a battery (as opposed to an aggravated battery)? According to Florida Statute §784.03, whenever a person actually and intentionally touches or strikes another person against that person's will, or intentionally causes bodily injury to another person a battery has occurred. Keep in mind that only aggravated battery is something against which you can defend with deadly force, not mere battery!

13. Aggravated Stalking

Florida law defines aggravated stalking as willfully, maliciously, and repeatedly following, harassing, or cyberstalking another person, and making a credible threat with the intent to place that person in reasonable fear of death or bodily injury of the person, or the person's child, sibling, spouse, parent, or dependent. Florida Statute §784.048.

14. Aircraft Piracy

While images of eye-patched peg-legged swashbucklers, flying the Jolly Roger, attacking a plane may be what springs to mind, that is not the definition assigned by Florida Statute §860.16. Aircraft piracy occurs whenever a person, without lawful authority, seizes or exercises control by force or violence and with wrongful intent, any aircraft containing a non-consenting person or persons within the State of Florida.

PRACTICAL LEGAL TIP

Juries tend to ignore the rule of "innocent until proven guilty." Even though every person has a Constitutional right to remain silent, Jurors will often want to hear both sides of the story. If they do not, it can cloud a juror's mind so as to make the notion of innocent until proven guilty less meaningful. -James

C. The "Castle Doctrine" and "Stand Your Ground" laws
1. Castle Doctrine

The term "Castle Doctrine" does not appear in Florida law, however, the legal concept comes from the philosophy that every person is a King or Queen of his or her "castle." As such, no king or queen is required to retreat before using force or deadly force against an intruder in his or her castle. In Florida, these "Castle Doctrine" type laws are implemented in Section 776.013 of Title XLVI, and include a powerful "presumption of reasonableness." Florida "Castle Doctrine" laws extend to a person's dwelling, residence, or occupied vehicle.

Florida Statute §776.013 was modified during the 2017 legislative session and changes were made to the Stand Your Ground section of the law. These changes will be covered later in this chapter.

If you are a victim of unlawful force or deadly force when you are in a dwelling, your residence, or an occupied vehicle, the law will provide you protection beyond the general rules of self-defense. In these "Castle Doctrine" circumstances, the law will presume "reasonable" your belief that force or deadly force was necessary to defend against unlawful force likely to cause imminent death or great bodily harm. Under these statutes, a person's belief that it was necessary to use force or deadly force against an imminent threat will be presumed reasonable. This legal presumption, if available to an accused, is a potentially powerful legal argument and requires the prosecutor to overcome the presumption with evidence showing that the defendant's fear of death or great bodily harm was unreasonable.

So how does a person qualify for "Castle Doctrine" protection? Florida law requires that two conditions be present:
1. The person against whom deadly force was used was in the process of unlawfully and forcefully entering, or had unlawfully

and forcibly entered a dwelling, residence, or occupied vehicle, or they had removed or were attempting to remove another against that person's will from the dwelling, residence, or occupied vehicle, and

2. The person who uses defensive force knew or had reason to believe that an unlawful and forcible entry or unlawful and forcible act was occurring or had occurred.

As can be seen, section (1) covers conditions when someone is entering or attempting to enter your "castle," or is removing or attempting to remove you from your "castle;" section (2) further requires that you knew this was happening, or had reason to know it happened. If you meet these two requirements, you qualify for "Castle Doctrine" protection, which is a powerful legal tool for any person who is accused of a crime and claiming justification. The presumption will be further enhanced by having no duty to retreat (see No Duty to Retreat later in this chapter). These presumptions are available only for dwellings, residences, or occupied vehicles.

2. What are dwellings and residences under the "Castle Doctrine?"
Florida law, in defining "Castle Doctrine" rights, does not use the term home, house, or property; it uses the terms dwelling or residence. A dwelling is a building or conveyance of any kind, including any attached porch, whether the building or conveyance is temporary or permanent, mobile or immobile, which has a roof over it, including a tent, and is designed to be occupied by people lodging therein at night. A residence is a dwelling in which a person resides either temporarily or permanently or is visiting as an invited guest. As you can see the presumptions of reasonableness found in the "Castle Doctrine" are limited, specific, and do not cover an entire piece of real property – just a dwelling or residence.

3. What is an occupied vehicle under the "Castle Doctrine?"

Florida's "Castle Doctrine" legal presumptions and protections are applicable to occupied vehicles. If a person is attempting to unlawfully and forcefully enter your vehicle while you are in it, or unlawfully remove you from your vehicle, you will fall under the "Castle Doctrine." What does Florida law define as a vehicle? "A conveyance of any kind, whether or not motorized, which is designed to transport people or property." Florida Statute §776.013. This is a very broad definition and appears to include just about anything that is designed to carry people or property from one place to another, including cars, boats, airplanes, golf carts, and so forth.

4. How can I lose the presumption of reasonableness under the "Castle Doctrine?"

There are a few ways that a person can lose "Castle Doctrine" protection and the presumption of reasonableness regarding their actions. The first is if the person against whom the force was used had the right to be in, or was a lawful resident of, the dwelling, residence, or vehicle, and there was not an injunction for protection from domestic violence or a written pretrial supervision order of no contact against that person. For example, spouses that both have a right to live in the marital home and have no injunctions against them, titleholders to vehicles, owners of property, or lease holders.

Another way "Castle Doctrine" protection can be lost is if a child's guardian is attempting to remove their child, grandchild, or a person otherwise in their lawful custody or guardianship. So, if a child's lawful guardian is attempting to remove them from a dwelling or residence, you will not be presumed to be reasonable should you defend the child under the auspices of the "Castle Doctrine."

If you are engaged in an unlawful activity or are using the dwelling, residence, or occupied vehicle to further an unlawful activity, you lose the presumption of reasonableness provided by the "Castle Doctrine." Even though you are in your vehicle, if a police officer attempts to remove you after your attempted bank robbery get-away, you will not receive "Castle Doctrine" protection!

You cannot use the "Castle Doctrine" if the person against whom the defensive force is used is a law enforcement officer, who enters or attempts to enter a dwelling, residence, or vehicle in the performance of his or her official duties and the officer identified himself or herself in accordance with any applicable law, or you knew or reasonably should have known that the person entering or attempting to enter was a law enforcement officer. What is a Law Enforcement Officer? Florida Statute §943.10(14) defines an Officer as, "any person employed or appointed as a full-time, part time, or auxiliary law enforcement officer, correctional officer, or correctional probation officer."

A second presumption is found in Florida's Castle Doctrine; one which presumes the bad guy is entering the castle to do bad things. Section 776.013(4) states that, "A person who unlawfully and by force enters or attempts to enter a person's dwelling, residence, or occupied vehicle is presumed to be doing so with the intent to commit an unlawful act involving force or violence."

Florida's Castle Doctrine is one of the strongest defensive weapons a gun owner has. Many states offer some protections to firearms owners in their own homes, however, as you can see above, Florida's Castle Doctrine does much more and perhaps provides the greatest protections in the country.

D. Standing Your Ground: "Stand Your Ground" laws in Florida

"Stand Your Ground" is a common term for laws that provide a person no legal duty to retreat before using force or deadly force against a person that is a threat. Florida law states that a person not engaged in unlawful activity, who is attacked in a place where they have a right to be, has no duty to retreat and has the right to stand his or her ground and meet force with force, including deadly force, if he or she reasonably believes it is necessary to do so to prevent death or great bodily harm to himself or herself or another or to prevent the commission of a forcible felony (Florida Statute §776.012(1) & (2)).

The requirements of the statute are threefold:
1. You cannot be engaged in unlawful activity;
2. You have to be attacked in a place where you have a right to be; and
3. You reasonably believe that the non-deadly force you use is necessary to defend yourself from the other's imminent use of force OR
3. You have to reasonably believe deadly force is necessary either to:
 a. to prevent imminent death or great bodily harm to yourself or another, or
 b. to prevent the commission of a forcible felony.

If all three of these conditions (both of the first two and either of the last two depending on whether you use force or deadly force) are satisfied, then the Florida "Stand Your Ground" law applies, and you have no duty to retreat, and may meet force with force, including deadly force. If you do not meet all of these requirements, you will not qualify for this protection. The prosecutor will be free to argue that because you could have but did not retreat, your belief that it was necessary to use force or deadly force was not reasonable.

Other states have "no duty to retreat" laws similar to Florida's, that do not require fleeing before the legal use of deadly force. However, several states impose a duty on a person to retreat if reasonably available before using deadly force. Some even require retreat in a person's own home. So, when traveling, make sure you know the law of the state you are visiting. -David

EXAMPLE

One day, looking for a shortcut through the neighborhood, Tom hops a fence (a trespass) and is walking across open property to reach the street on the other side of the property. Tom is confronted by the property owner and tries to explain that he meant no harm and was just taking a shortcut. However, the property owner becomes irate and cocks his gun, aims it at Tom, and says "I'm going to kill you!"

Under this example, Tom is a trespasser, and since trespassing is considered being "engaged in criminal activity" under the statute, Tom is disqualified from the "Stand Your Ground" protection. Additionally, as a trespasser he has no legal right to be at his "location," a second reason Tom will not be entitled to the protections of the stand your ground law. Thus, a prosecutor could argue that before the use of force or deadly force by Tom was immediately necessary, Tom should have retreated. It does not mean Tom may not be ultimately legally justified in defending himself; it just makes it more difficult to convince a jury of his justification.

Another "Stand Your Ground" styled law exists, to protect law enforcement officers and people that have been summoned or directed to assist them, in arresting an individual. It states simply that neither the law enforcement officer, nor the person that was summoned or directed to assist, are required to retreat or desist in their efforts to make a lawful arrest because of resistance or threatened resistance to the arrest. (Florida Statute §776.05)

1. Standing your ground in a Castle Doctrine location

As mentioned previously, Florida Statutes §776.013 was modified in July 2017. Former subsection 3 of the statute previously read, "(3) A person who is attacked in his or her dwelling, residence, or vehicle has no duty to retreat and has the right to stand his or her ground and use or threaten to use force, including deadly force, if he or she uses or threatens to use force in accordance with s. 776.012(1) or (2) or 776.31(1) or (2)." The new statute moved this section to the beginning of §776.013 and reworded it as follows:

(1) A person who is in a dwelling or residence in which the person has a right to be has no duty to retreat and has the right to stand his or her ground and use or threaten to use:

(a) Nondeadly force against another when and to the extent that the person reasonably believes that such conduct is necessary to defend himself or herself or another against the other's imminent use of unlawful force; or

(b) Deadly force if he or she reasonably believes that using or threatening to use such force is necessary to prevent imminent death or great bodily harm to himself or herself or another or to prevent the imminent commission of a forcible felony.

What is the difference? First, you will notice that the requirement of being attacked has been removed from the statutory language before having the right to stand your ground and defend yourself. Second, "vehicle" has been removed from this subsection. Finally, the phrase, "if he or she uses or threatens to use force in accordance with §776.012(1) or (2) or §776.031(1) or (2) has been replaced with the actual language of §776.012(1) and (2), eliminating §776.031 entirely.

What are the practical effects of the changes? Not much. In the law there is a requirement that statutes are read in pari materia with other statutes. This means that each law is read individually, but also as a whole with the other laws. For example, if you read only the new §776.013 by itself, you might think the legislature has eliminated your right to stand your ground if you are attacked in your vehicle. After all, they eliminated "vehicle" from the list of places in the new statute. However, reading the new §776.013 as part of a whole body of law, you realize that §776.012, still protects your right to stand your ground while you are in a vehicle. Remember from the discussion above that §776.012 allows you to use force, including deadly force as long as the following apply:

1. You cannot be engaged in unlawful activity;
2. You have to be attacked in a place where you have a right to be; and
3. you reasonably believe that the non-deadly force you use is necessary to defend yourself from the other's imminent use of force OR
4. You reasonably believe deadly force is necessary either to:

a. to prevent imminent death or great bodily harm to yourself or another, or

b. to prevent the commission of a forcible felony.

Further, you still get the presumptions present in the castle doctrine when you are in an occupied vehicle. Although the Legislature removed "vehicle" from part of the statute, they left "occupied vehicle" along with dwelling and residence as a location under which the castle doctrine presumptions apply.

Finally, the legislature removed the word "attacked" from the statute. However, remember that although the language no longer requires a person to be attacked prior to using defensive force, you still must use defensive force to prevent the use of force or deadly force against you.

E. When is the use of force or deadly force not legally justified under Florida Statute §776.012?

1. Force is never legally justified for verbal provocation alone

If you think back to your childhood, you probably remember the saying: "sticks and stones will break my bones, but words will never hurt me!" Believe it or not, the law agrees wholeheartedly with this concept. Under Florida case law, a person is not justified in using force when words are the only provocation to a situation. *Gibbs v. State*, 789 So. 2d 443 (Fla. 4th DCA 2001).

EXAMPLE

Samantha is walking to her car in the grocery store parking lot when a woman starts screaming at her: "you're a terrible driver, and you park like an idiot!" Samantha runs over to the woman and punches the woman in the face.

In this instance, Samantha is not legally justified in her use of force because the only thing happening was the other woman screaming at her—a mere verbal provocation.

2. Force not legally justified to resist arrest or search

A person will not be justified in using force to resist an arrest by a law enforcement officer, or to resist a law enforcement officer who is engaged in the execution of a legal duty, if the law enforcement officer was acting in good faith and he or she is known, or reasonably appears, to be a law enforcement officer. (FS §776.051).

EXAMPLE

Justin has been pulled over for speeding and is removed from his vehicle by a uniformed police officer. While sitting on the curb, the officer begins to search Justin's vehicle without his consent and without probable cause. Feeling violated, Justin gets up and pulls the officer out of his car and throws the officer to the ground.

Even though the officer's behavior is unusual for a mere speeding violation, and even though it appears Justin is being subjected to an illegal search and seizure, his legally justifiable recourse is to pursue the matter through the court system— not to use force against the officer!

3. Force not justified when aiding illegal arrest

Strangely enough, a person that has been summoned or directed to assist a law enforcement officer is not justified in using force if the arrest or execution of a legal duty is unlawful and known by the person to be unlawful. See Florida Statute §776.051. Of note is the fact that the unlawful nature of the arrest must be known in order for this justification exception to control. So, if you know someone is being unlawfully arrested, don't help with the unlawful arrest!

4. A person who is attempting to commit, is committing, or is escaping after committing a forcible felony is not entitled to justification

Florida law provides that self-defense is not available as a defense if you are attempting to commit, committing, or escaping after the commission of a forcible felony. The definition of what constitutes a forcible felony has been examined in great detail previously in this chapter.

5. A person who provokes an attack is not entitled to legal justification

Self-defense is not available if you initially provoke the use of force against yourself. Unfortunately, Florida law does not give us a concrete answer as to precisely what the word "provoke" means. However, if you have provoked the use of force against yourself, there are two exceptions where you are allowed to defend yourself:

i. If you reasonably believe that you are in imminent danger of death or great bodily harm and that you have exhausted every reasonable means to escape such danger other than the use of force which is likely to cause death or great bodily harm to the assailant; or

ii. In good faith, you withdraw from physical contact with the assailant and indicate clearly to the assailant your desire to withdraw and terminate the use of force, but the assailant continues or resumes the use of force.

Exception 1: A group of teens is hanging out at a party. Without provocation one of the teenagers picks a fight with another. Big mistake. The second teenager is much stronger than the first and eventually gets the attacker on the ground. After climbing on top of the original attacker, the larger teen begins slamming the attackers head into the concrete.

In this scenario, the original attacker reasonably fearing death or great bodily harm, with no means of escape as the larger teenager is on top of him, will regain the right to use deadly force to save his own life, even though he "started it".

Exception 2: Dave is at a bar when he notices another man checking-out his girlfriend. Dave tells the other man, "take a hike or you'll regret it" and slightly shoves the admirer. The other man responds by punching Dave in the face. Dave, who didn't really want a confrontation, holds both his hands up in surrender and says, "I don't want any more trouble!" However, the other man pulls out a knife and lunges at Dave.

In this scenario, Dave is legally justified to fight back: he attempted to abandon the incident and made his intention known to the other person. When the other man continued to attack, Dave is now legally justified to defend himself, even though he made the initial provocation.

F. When can I threaten to use force or deadly force?

In 2014, Florida changed the law to explicitly state that either the threat or use of force would be justified as discussed above.

Therefore, if you would be justified to use force or [force], you may also threaten force or deadly force, respec[tively]. However, note that the threat of deadly force is justified only under the circumstances when deadly force could be used; you cannot threaten deadly force when you are only justified to use force! See Florida Statutes §§776.012, 776.013.

III. DEFENSE OF A THIRD PERSON

When does Florida law allow for the justifiable use of deadly force to protect someone else?

In past sections, we addressed the law of legal justification for the use of force or deadly force for self-defense. We now turn to when the law allows the justified use of force or deadly force to protect another person or persons. In general, if you place yourself in the "shoes" of the third person, and if the law would allow the third person to use force or deadly force to protect themselves, then you are legally justified to use the same level of force to protect a third person. In fact, the law specifies "or another" when talking about defending yourself from death or great bodily harm, or from a forcible felony in Florida Statute §776.012(2). Just as with defending yourself, you can also qualify for the additional "Stand Your Ground" protection discussed earlier.

EXAMPLE

Steve walks into a convenience store and see the cashier being forced to empty the register at gun point. He pulls out his gun and kills the robber.

In this example, since the clerk had a right to use deadly force in his own defense, a third party (Steve, in this example) would have a right to use deadly force to protect him. Since the clerk was being threatened with deadly force, Steve had a right to defend him with deadly force.

IV. "IMMUNITY" FROM CRIMINAL PROSECUTION

Can I be criminally prosecuted, even if I use force legally in self-defense?

Possibly, possibly not. Florida Law has a unique provision that provides "immunity" from criminal prosecution, assuming a person qualifies for it. This means that the individual may avoid entanglement with the Florida Criminal Justice System, which is always a good day! Specifically, Florida's Immunity Statue prohibits "criminal prosecution" including arresting, detaining in custody, and charging or prosecuting the defendant. Essentially, the statute "grants defendants a substantive right to assert immunity from prosecution and to avoid being subjected to a trial." *Dennis v. State*, 51 So.3d 456, 462 (Fla. 2010).

So how does one qualify for this immunity? First, your use of force or deadly force must be justified. Second, you cannot have used the force against a law enforcement officer who was acting in the performance of his or her official duties and who identified himself or herself in accordance with any applicable law or you knew or reasonably should have known that the person was a law enforcement officer.

Does this mean you can tell responding officers to the scene of your self-defense to hit the bricks when they first show up? Probably not. Florida law provides that a law enforcement agency may use standard procedures for investigating the use of force, but the agency may not arrest the person for using force unless it determines that there is probable cause that the force that was used was unlawful. This is really no different from what the law always required. Police officers have always had to have probable cause that a crime was committed before making an arrest.

PRACTICAL LEGAL TIP

The right to remain silent is a fundamental Constitutional right which is why it is so disturbing that in 2010, the U.S. Supreme Court held that you have to say the magic words of "I invoke my right to remain silent and to counsel" in order to trigger it. Seemingly, by the Court's standard, if you don't say the magic words, police could interrogate you until the end of time. -James

In 2017, the legislature amended the immunity law contained in Florida Statute 776.032 adding subsection 4, which reads, "(4)   In a criminal prosecution, once a prima facie claim of self-defense immunity from criminal prosecution has been raised by the defendant at a pretrial immunity hearing, the burden of proof by clear and convincing evidence is on the party seeking to overcome the immunity from criminal prosecution provided in subsection (1)."

Prior to this amendment , a defendant who was arrested (in other words, the police do not agree the use of force was justified) was required to file a motion in court to invoke this statutory immunity. This has not changed under the amended statute. Further, under the old and the new versions of the statute, the court would hold a pre-trial evidentiary hearing, to determine if one qualified for this immunity. This is where the similarities end. You will note that in the prior version of the statute, courts were not provided any guidance as to who had the burden of proof, or what that burden was. In a series of appellate cases, the courts determined what the procedure would be and what the burden of proof would be in an immunity hearing. The case law developed to the point that a defendant was required to prove that he had acted lawfully in his use of force by a "preponderance of the evidence." See *State v. Yaqubie*, 51 So.3d 474, 476 (Fla. 3d DCA 2010). In other words, the defendant was the one who had to prove that they qualified for immunity; it was not "presumed" to apply, and it was not the State's burden to show that the accused did not qualify. While the State could have presented evidence to chip away at their case, it was ultimately up to the accused and their attorney to prove they qualified for this defense.

Under the new immunity law, the burden of proof and the level of proof required to meet that burden have both been changed. The legislature shifted the burden from the Defendant to the State. Under the new law, if the Defendant shows the minimal elements for a claim of self-defense, the burden then becomes the prosecution's to prove by "clear and convincing evidence" that the defendant is not entitled to immunity. If the prosecution cannot meet its burden, the court must grant immunity. According to Florida's Standard Jury Instructions, "clear and convincing" evidence is "evidence that is precise, explicit, lacking in confusion, and of such weight that it produces a firm belief or conviction, without hesitation, about the matter in issue." Fl. St. Cr. Jury Inst. 2.03.

If the court, after hearing both sides, decides that immunity does not apply, does this mean you are automatically found to be guilty? No; it simply means you do not qualify for immunity from prosecution.

In 2011, a tourist from Indiana who was a passenger in a car that was almost side-swiped by a truck was arrested and asserted an immunity defense. Here is what happened:

The driver of the truck stopped in front of the tourist's vehicle, got out of the truck and approached the car unarmed. The Defendant's father, then held up a gun and the truck's driver went back to his vehicle.

The Defendant then got out of the vehicle and approached the truck aiming the gun at the truck driver. Eventually, the Defendant, went back to the car he was traveling in with his family, but continued pointing the gun at the truck's driver. Police arrived after receiving 911 calls, and believing that the use or threatened use of force by the Defendant was more than necessary, and therefore illegal, the Defendant was arrested and charged with aggravated assault with a firearm.

After an immunity hearing, a circuit judge ruled that the Defendant was not entitled to immunity from prosecution. The judge ruled that the "threat was no longer imminent, and in fact, the possible volatile situation had been diffused. The defendant's subjective fear was no longer reasonable" as the truck's driver had retreated to his own vehicle and was no longer in a position to harm the Defendant or his family.

In 2012, the Tampa Bay Times researched the percent of successful immunity challenges under Florida Law and found that nearly 70% of the time the challenges were successful.

Recently, the new version of the immunity law has made national news. Miami-Dade County Circuit Judge Milton Hirsch recently ruled that the new version of the immunity law contains unconstitutional changes. Specifically, the Judge pointed to the separation of powers required in Florida's constitution.

ARTICLE V, SECTION 2.
ADMINISTRATION; PRACTICE AND PROCEDURE.–

(a) The supreme court shall adopt rules for the practice and procedure in all courts including the time for seeking appellate review, the administrative supervision of all courts, the transfer to the court having jurisdiction of any proceeding when the jurisdiction of another court has been improvidently invoked, and a requirement that no cause shall be dismissed because an improper remedy has been sought. The supreme court shall adopt rules to allow the court and the district courts of appeal to submit questions relating to military law to the federal Court of Appeals for the Armed Forces for an advisory opinion. Rules of court may be repealed by general law enacted by two-thirds vote of the membership of each house of the legislature. (emphasis added)

Art. V, §2(a), Fla. Const;

Judge Hirsch ruled that per the Florida Constitution the legislature could only change the procedure used to determine immunity with a 2/3 "super-majority", which they failed to accomplish. Therefore, the legislatively enacted changes to the procedure used in immunity hearings were unconstitutional. He did not rule that immunity itself was unconstitutional as was reported in the media across this country.

It is important to know that Judge Hirsch's ruling was not made in an appellate case but in a case of original jurisdiction. To you and me, this means that it has no binding legal effect anywhere but Judge Hirsch's courtroom. A prosecutor could use Judge Hirsch's opinion to try to persuade another Judge to declare the new law unconstitutional, but the Judge is free to ignore Judge Hirsch's ruling should he or she choose. In fact, other Judges in Miami-Dade County have come to different conclusions than Judge Hirsch and are giving full-effect to the new immunity law. It is highly likely that this matter will ultimately be resolved in an appellate decision by the Florida Supreme Court, until then, should you find yourself facing a judge after a self-defense incident, it is important to know which version of the law is being used in their courtroom. In other words, is the Judge following the law as written by the elected legislature or does the Judge agree with Judge Hirsch that the law is unconstitutional and is therefore following the older version of the law?

CHAPTER NINE

WHEN CAN I LEGALLY USE MY GUN: PART III
DEADLY FORCE
Understanding When Deadly Force Can Be Used Against Animals

I. WHAT IS AN "ANIMAL" UNDER FLORIDA LAW?

Before beginning a discussion of when deadly force may be used against animals, it is important to understand what constitutes an "animal" under Florida law. The Florida law prohibiting cruelty to animals provides a general definition to this term in Section 828.02 of the Florida Statutes, specifying that "every dumb living creature" is an animal. Does this definition strike you as too broad? You wouldn't be the first to think so. In *Wilkerson v. Florida*, 401 So. 2d 1110 (Fla. 1981), the defendant argued, amongst other things, that this definition was invalid because it is unconstitutionally vague. The Supreme Court of Florida disagreed, and upheld the validity of this broad definition even though this definition includes every non-human creature. To date there are no published animal cruelty decisions that mention any non-mammalian animal. Does this mean that you can use your neighbor's squawking parrot for target practice? No. Under the black letter of the law, virtually all living creatures still fall under the statutory definition.

II. NO GENERAL "DEFENSE AGAINST ANIMALS" STATUTE

Florida gives no general statutory authorization to use deadly force in self-defense against an animal that is attacking a human. Floridians must instead rely on common law and the specific wording of the animal cruelty statute to defend against potential charges if a dog is attacking a human. In other words, there is no statutory provision in Florida that explicitly allows a person to kill a dog in order to stop an attack. People are forced to rely on the requirement in the animal cruelty statutes that a killing be "necessary" in order to defend against the charge of animal cruelty.

III. CAN I LEGALLY USE DEADLY FORCE AGAINST ANIMALS?

Now that we have presented the basics of this topic, the rest of the chapter will delve deeper into the animal cruelty requirement that the killing of an animal be "necessary," and discuss the laws that exist relating to the use of deadly force against an animal assailant.

A. Self-defense & "necessary" killings

As discussed above, the animal cruelty statute specifically criminalizes the "unnecessary" killing of animals. The statute reads:

> A person who unnecessarily overloads, overdrives, torments, deprives of necessary sustenance or shelter, or unnecessarily mutilates, or kills any animal, or cause the same to be done, or carries in or upon any vehicle, or otherwise, any animal in a cruel or inhumane manner, commits animal cruelty, a misdemeanor of the first degree...
> *Florida Statute §828.12 (emphasis added).*

Therefore, a person presumably does not violate Florida law if the killing or wounding of an animal was "necessary."

B. What is a "necessary" killing?

Unfortunately, there is not yet any case law that directly addresses or defines what is a "necessary" killing. The only time it has been addressed in a written opinion is within *Wilkerson v. Florida*, where, along with the definition of "animal," the court concluded that the term "unnecessary" was not unconstitutionally vague.

Where does this leave us in defining necessary killing? Though not well-fleshed out by case law, a necessary killing appears to be two-fold: 1) it must be necessary to protect against an imminent danger to a human being; 2) it causes no more pain or suffering than is absolutely necessary to accomplish that goal.

EXAMPLE

Bartlett v. Florida, 929 So. 2d 1125 (Fla. 4th Dist. 2006): Defendant shot and chased away an opossum from his garage. It appears that this on its own would not have garnered an animal cruelty charge. However, the Defendant pursued the animal away from his home, and riddled the creature's body with BB pellets. The overkill seems to be what violated the statute, because it resulted in more pain and an "unnecessary" level of cruelty.

Furthermore, Florida Statute §828.24, requires that any killing of an animal be done in a "approved humane method," where the animal is "rapidly and effectively rendered insensitive to pain," and includes killing an animal with a firearm. Florida Statute §828.23(6)(a).

To decide if the killing was "necessary" we look to the affirmative defense of "necessity." Necessity is a defense to a crime, including animal cruelty, and other laws regulating firearm use. In order for a person to be found justified in using force or deadly force against an animal attacking, he or she must meet the following requirements:

1. The actor reasonably believed a danger or an emergency existed which was not intentionally caused by himself or herself;
2. The danger or emergency threatened significant harm to himself, herself, or a third person;
3. The threatened harm must have been real, imminent, and impending;
4. The actor had no reasonable means to avoid the danger or emergency except by committing the crime;
5. The crime charged must have been committed out of necessity to avoid the danger or emergency;
6. The harm that the actor avoided must outweigh the harm caused by committing the crime.

There are some important definitions in these six requirements that one must be aware of in deciding if he or she should use force or deadly force in self-defense against an attacking animal. These definitions can be found in Florida Standard Jury Instruction 3.6(k). "Imminent and impending" means that the danger or emergency is about to take place and cannot be avoided by using other means. A threat of future harm is not sufficient to prove the defense of "necessity." If your neighbor tells you that he is going to release his dog on you tomorrow if you don't mow your yard, you cannot shoot his dog in anticipation of an attack the next day. Furthermore, a person cannot use the defense of necessity if he or she used force or deadly force against the animal, after the danger from the threatened harm had passed. In other words, a person who survives the animal attack cannot go seek revenge against the animal that attacked him or her.

C. Dogs attacking livestock or domestic animals

In order to use deadly force against an animal attacking a human, it must be "necessary." What about when dogs attack a person's livestock or domestic animals? According to Florida Statute §767.03, in a criminal prosecution or action for damages, a person has a defense if "satisfactory proof" is put forward that the dog had been or was killing any domestic animal or livestock. What is "satisfactory proof?" "Satisfactory proof" is not defined in Florida Statutes or by case law. Ultimately, it is up to the trier of fact (the jury) to determine what this means, and decide whether you have met this common-sense burden of proof.

1. How are "domestic animal" and "livestock" defined under Florida law?

Section 585.01 of the Florida Statutes, defines "domestic animal" as any equine or bovine animal, goat, sheep, swine, domestic cat, dog, poultry, ostrich, emu, rhea, or other domesticated beast or bird. The same statute defines "livestock" as grazing animals, such as cattle, horses, sheep, swine, goats, other hoofed animals, ostriches, emus, and rheas which are raised for private use or commercial purposes.

2. Does this apply to any animal that attacks my animals?

Probably not. The statutory allowance is for dogs only, and does not appear to apply to other wild animals that are killing or attacking livestock or domestic animals.

D. Fur-bearing animals

When does the law authorize deadly force against small mammals? There is no general, independent statutory authorization to dispatch these animals. The only mention of this issue is within Florida Statute §379.354, which allows the "taking" of fur-bearing animals by those with a valid hunting license participating in recreational hunting activities. What are fur-bearing animals? Under Florida Statute §379.101(19), "fur-bearing animals" include muskrat, mink, raccoon, otter, civet cat, skunk, red and gray fox, and opossum.

1. What does it mean to "take" these animals?

Florida Statute 379.101(38) tells us "take" as it pertains to animals means taking, attempting to take, pursuing, hunting, molesting, capturing, or killing any wildlife or freshwater or saltwater fish, or their nests or eggs, by any means, whether or not such actions result in obtaining possession of such wildlife or freshwater or saltwater fish or their nests or eggs.

2. Is the statutory authorization only for persons with a valid hunting license during recreational hunting activities?

Under the plain language of the statute, yes. However, it does appear from the Bartlett case, as noted earlier, that humanely dispatching small fur-bearing mammals interfering or ravaging one's property will not run up against the animal cruelty statute. The Court seems to take issue not with the fact that Mr. Bartlett killed an opossum outside the purview of recreational hunting activities, but rather that he did so unnecessarily and inhumanely, causing unnecessary pain and suffering to the animal. So even though the statute is narrowly tailored in its allowance for dispatching these animals, it may not be applied so strictly.

E. Can I use a BB gun or other weapons to defend against animals?

Florida law vacillates on whether BB guns are classified as deadly weapons. However, discharging your BB gun at an animal will still land you an animal cruelty charge unless it was "necessary." *C.W.*

v. State, 528 So. 2d 66 (Fla. 3d DCA 1988). (Also, see Bartlett case earlier.) This also applies if you unnecessarily use other weapons such as tasers, clubs, pepper spray, etc. In contrast, one neighboring State, Alabama, does not criminalize discharging BB guns at animals on one's property. Ala. Code §13A-11-246(4).

F. Dogs that kill sheep

If, by chance, you spot a dog that is "known to have killed sheep" roaming unattended, Florida Statute §767.02 specifically authorizes the killing of that dog. What is the standard to label a dog a "sheep-killer?" Your guess is as good as ours!

G. Federal law defenses

Federal law, in a comprehensive fashion, has actually had the foresight to specifically provide that a person may kill in self-defense an animal protected by federal law, such as the regulations concerning the Mexican gray wolf in 50 CFR §17.84(k)(3)(xii), or the grizzly bear in 50 CFR §17.40(b)(1)(i)(B). Therefore, if you are carrying a firearm in a National Park (see Chapter Nine) and you find yourself face to face with a grizzly bear, you will have a legal defense for protecting yourself.

CHAPTER TEN

WHEN CAN I LEGALLY USE MY GUN: PART IV
PROTECTING PROPERTY
Understanding When Deadly Force Can Be Used To Protect Property

I. OVERVIEW AND LOCATION OF THE LAW TO PROTECT PROPERTY

Florida law allows a person to protect, with force, their property from another's unlawful interference or trespass on their property or the property of another. Further, Florida law, under certain circumstances, will also allow a person to use legally justified deadly force to protect property. The sections in the Florida Statutes dealing with legally justified force or deadly force to defend property are as follows:

776.031(1): Protection of One's Own Property

776.031(2): Deadly Force to Protect Property

776.031(1),(2): Protection of a Third Person's Property

Protection of property will be analyzed under the same "reasonable person" standard discussed in Chapters Four and Five and will have the same requirements for a person reasonably believing that the force or deadly force used was "necessary."

II. WHEN IS SOMEONE LEGALLY JUSTIFIED TO USE "FORCE" BUT NOT "DEADLY FORCE" TO PROTECT THEIR OWN PROPERTY?

A. Prevent or terminate interference with property

The law answers this question based upon the statutory law of the justified use of force to protect property contained in Section 776.031(1) of Florida Statutes. Under Section 776.031(1) a person is justified in using force to prevent or terminate another person's unlawful trespass or interference with their property, *e.g.*, stealing property, vandalizing property, etc.

1. If you catch someone in the act

In plain terms, if someone is unlawfully taking your personal property, you are justified in using force to stop them.

JUSTIFIED USE OF FORCE TO PROTECT YOUR PROPERTY; FLORIDA STATUTE §776.031(1)

A person is justified in using or threatening to use force, except deadly force, against another when and to the extent that the person reasonably believes that such conduct is necessary to prevent or terminate the other's trespass on, or other tortious or criminal interference with, either real property other than a dwelling or personal property, lawfully in his or her possession or in the possession of another who is a member of his or her immediate family or household or of a person whose property he or she has a legal duty to protect. A person who uses or threatens to use force in accordance with this subsection does not have a duty to retreat before using or threatening to use such force.

---

2. After property is taken

In the event a person's property has already been stolen, a person is not generally justified to use force to recover it after it was stolen. A person is certainly not allowed to use force to go and recover the property days, weeks, or months later. There is no justification if the victim of a theft beats up the thief in the process of recovery of their property at a later date. However, if you catch a person in the act of taking your property, you can use force to stop them from leaving the scene with it.

B. No legal presumption of reasonableness when defending property

Florida law provides no legal presumptions of reasonableness for uses of force to protect property, whether it is preventing or terminating a trespass or interference with property. Thus, the jury will be the ultimate arbiter of the reasonableness of conduct.

The analysis so far leads us to the question: if force may legally be used to prevent or terminate trespass or interference with property, what constitutes a trespass or interference with property?

C. What is trespassing?

The commonly understood meaning of trespass is "an unlawful interference with one's person, property, or rights." This definition has been expanded to refer typically to "any unauthorized intrusion or invasion of private premises or land of another." Black's Law Dictionary, 6th ed. This commonly understood definition of trespass is different and more expansive than the offense of criminal trespass found in Section 810 of the Florida Statues. Florida Statutes provide a separate definition for trespass depending upon what type of property the trespass is occurring. However, all the definitions have in common that a trespass occurs when without being authorized, licensed, or invited, a person willfully enters or remains on another's property.

> **TRESPASS IN A STRUCTURE OR CONVEYANCE; FLORIDA STATUTE §810.08(1)**
>
> Whoever, without being authorized, licensed, or invited, willfully enters or remains in any structure or conveyance, or, having been authorized, licensed, or invited, is warned by the owner or lessee of the premises, or by a person authorized by the owner or lessee, to depart and refuses to do so, commits the offense of trespass in a structure or conveyance.

> **TRESPASS ON PROPERTY OTHER THAN STRUCTURE OR CONVEYANCE; FLORIDA STATUTE §810.09(1)(a)**
>
> A person who, without being authorized, licensed, or invited, willfully enters upon or remains in any property other than a structure or conveyance: 1. As to which notice against entering or remaining is given, either by actual communication to the offender or by posting, fencing, or cultivation as described in s. 810.011; or 2. If the property is the unenclosed curtilage of a dwelling and the offender enters or remains with the intent to commit an offense thereon, other than the offense of trespass, commits the offense of trespass on property other than a structure or conveyance.

In other words, unlike the common definition of trespass where a person becomes a trespasser whether they realized it or not (unwittingly walking across the King's hunting grounds, for instance), under Florida Law prior to committing a criminal offense a person must have knowledge that they are in a place they do not belong or are not welcome. In addition, the crime of criminal trespass is strictly limited to when a person is found in or on a piece of property without permission—the offense does not cover situations involving personal property.

D. Trespass, for legal justification, is not just "Criminal Trespass"

How, then, is "trespasser" defined in Section 776.031(1) for purposes of defending property? Because the plain language of Section 776.031(1) refers only to terminating "the other's trespass" and does not reference a "criminal trespass," we must make clear under Florida law a trespass to property only occurs if the person has notice not to be on the property either by actual communication, posting, fencing, etc. In other words, a person is not likely to be legally justified in using force against a person found trespassing on their land—unless that person has committed the crime of criminal trespass and has notice that they do not belong there. However, in the event an unwitting trespasser has no intention of remaining on or damaging the property, the use of force is not likely to be found to be reasonably necessary. In many cases, a jury will be the ultimate arbiter of whether or not a person had a reasonable belief that it was necessary to use force to terminate another person's trespass on the land. Remember, on property that is not a building or vehicle, if someone voluntarily leaves and they have not been previously warned that they are trespassing, they are not usually trespassers under Florida law.

EXAMPLE

Jim looks out his back window and sees the neighbor's kids in his backyard walking toward their home. He goes outside and tells them that he just planted a new garden where they are walking and tells them to leave and stay away. They apologize and leave.

In this situation, if Jim were to call the police to report a crime, he would likely be told that no crime was committed as the kids were not in a building and left as soon as they were asked.

E. What is unlawful interference with property?

You have a legal right to prevent or terminate "tortious or criminal interference with property," but what does this mean? It can be a theft, destruction, vandalism, or anything else that diminishes a person's right to their property. Whether particular conduct rises to "tortious or criminal interference with property" is an issue that a jury decides.

F. Is there a statutory minimum value of property before force may be legally used to protect it?

No. There exists no statutory minimum value for property before force may be used to protect it. Section 776.031 does not specify that property a person seeks to protect must be of a certain, minimum dollar value in order for a person to protect it. Having said that, what Florida Law says, is that a person must reasonably believe that the force used is necessary to prevent or terminate the other's trespass on, or other tortious or criminal interference with property before a person would be justified in using force.

Realistically, even though a person may be in the process of taking your property, some property may be of so little value that the use of force or deadly force to protect or recover it would not be deemed reasonable by a jury.

One day at work, Fred walks into Ricky's office and takes a potato chip from a bag of chips on Ricky's desk. As he brings the chip toward his mouth, Ricky, upset at having his favorite chips pilfered, jumps up and shoves Fred to the ground, beating on Fred to recover his chip.

Was Ricky's use of force against Fred legally justified? Maybe, but maybe not. It may be a very hard sell to a jury that a person was beat up over a potato chip. However, some members of a jury may value a potato chip much differently. What if a thief is stealing irreplaceable family photos? There's no monetary value to be placed there—only personal sentiment. Again, the law is silent on the subject of any minimum monetary value of property to be defended.

The point to be made here is that some items simply may not have enough value (financial, sentimental, or otherwise) to provide a person with a reasonable belief that the use of force is necessary to prevent the tortious or criminal interference. In this example, not only do the chips have little monetary value, but it is also not common in our culture to beat someone over eating one of your chips. It would be hard to imagine a jury finding a person to be justified in using any force other than possibly grabbing the single chip back from Fred, let alone beating him for such a petty larceny!

There are plenty of clever signs and bumper stickers out there advocating the use of a firearm. "Keep honking, I'm reloading," and even "Trespassers Will Be Shot" are seen often on the bumpers of cars in Florida and the fence posts of Florida homeowners. But these signs, despite the chuckle they may elicit from a passerby, are not a good idea. Even if meant only to prompt a laugh, if you are forced to use your firearm to defend yourself and end up in court, you can bet that the prosecutor will bring these signs up to the jury for consideration. Remember, a prosecutor will use every avenue to paint you in the worst light possible. Keep the laughs to yourself and take the signs down! -David

III. WHEN IS SOMEONE LEGALLY JUSTIFIED IN USING "DEADLY FORCE" TO PROTECT OR RECOVER THEIR OWN PROPERTY?

When a person may legally use deadly force (force likely to cause death or great bodily harm) to defend his or her property is addressed in Section 776.031 of the Florida Statutes.

JUSTIFIED USE OF DEADLY FORCE TO PROTECT YOUR PROPERTY; FLORIDA STATUTES §776.031(2)

A person is justified in using or threatening to use deadly force only if he or she reasonably believes that such conduct is necessary to prevent the imminent commission of a forcible felony. A person who uses or threatens to use deadly force in accordance with this subsection does not have a duty to retreat and has the right to stand his or her ground if the person using or threatening to use the deadly force is not engaged in a criminal activity and is in a place where he or she has a right to be.

Legal justification under Section 776.031(2)

Legal justification for deadly force to protect property under Section 776.031 is not accompanied with any legal presumptions of reasonableness; the jury will be the ultimate arbiter in deciding whether a person acted reasonably in a given incident.

First, the jury will be responsible for determining whether the person (now a defendant) involved in the use of deadly force was justified in using said force. Judging the defendant by the circumstances that surrounded them at the time the force was used, a jury will determine whether a reasonably cautious and prudent person under the same circumstances would have believed that the danger could be avoided only through the use of that force.

Second, the jury must decide whether a defendant had a reasonable belief that deadly force was necessary to prevent the imminent commission of a forcible felony.

FORCIBLE FELONIES; FLORIDA STATUTE §776.08

"Forcible felony" means treason; murder; manslaughter; sexual battery; carjacking; home-invasion robbery; robbery; burglary; arson; kidnapping; aggravated assault; aggravated battery; aggravated stalking; aircraft piracy; unlawful throwing, placing, or discharging of a destructive device or bomb; and any other felony which involves the use or threat of physical force or violence against any individual.

EXAMPLE

After a long day at work, Gordon finally pulls into his driveway just in time to see two masked men running out of his front door with his favorite television and his grandfather's expensive watch on one of the men's wrists. Gordon gets out of his car and demands that the men stop where they are, but they ignore him and run away. Gordon pulls his Glock 17 and fires at the fleeing men, killing one and injuring the other, both men shot in the back.

Was Gordon justified under Section 776.031 to use deadly force? To answer this question, start the analysis above. First, Gordon has to show a jury that he had a reasonable belief that deadly force was necessary to prevent the imminent commission of a forcible felony. Here, the felony being committed was a burglary. Checking our list of forcible felonies, we find that burglary is included on that list. Next, was Gordon's belief that deadly force was necessary to stop the imminent commission of a forcible felony? This is where

Gordon runs into problems. Based on the facts given, the felony was already complete and the bad guys were leaving the scene and ran away when Gordon told them to stop. Gordon was probably not in any danger from the fleeing bad guys as they were running with their backs to him. Further, while the bad guys were running away, nothing was imminent. Therefore, a jury may find that the force used was unreasonable or excessive and Gordon may be convicted of manslaughter and aggravated assault with a firearm.

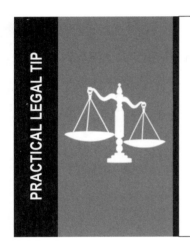

PRACTICAL LEGAL TIP

Notice that Florida Statutes never give the right to use deadly force to prevent escape, however, this right may still be available in a very limited number of situations as a defense under the common law. Of course, if they are firing a weapon while running, deadly force would be justified as an act of self-defense. -David

IV. CAN I PROTECT ANOTHER PERSON'S PROPERTY?

Florida Statute §776.031(1) allows the use of non-deadly force to protect the property of another if that person is a member of your family or household or another person whose property you have a lawful duty to protect. Nowhere in the statute does it give you permission to protect an unrelated neighbor's property. However, Section 776.031(2) gives you the right to use all force reasonably necessary up to and including deadly force to prevent the commission of a forcible felony. Importantly, the law does not say to prevent a forcible felony against yourself or your property.

Therefore, if a forcible felony is being committed against the property of another, under this statute you can use force, including deadly force to prevent the imminent commission of that forcible felony. Let's look at another example.

EXAMPLE

After a long day at work, Gordon pulls into his own driveway and witnesses two men looking at a bicycle in front of his neighbor's house. Gordon immediately recognizes it as his neighbor's antique, collectible, extremely rare, 1890 bicycle which he knows is valued at over $100,000 dollars.

Is Gordon legally justified in using force under this scenario? Not likely. Even though a felony theft is being committed (it is not a forcible felony), Gordon is not related to his neighbor, they are not members of the same household and our facts do not indicate any legal duty that would require Gordon to protect his neighbor's property.

EXAMPLE

After a long day at work, Gordon pulls into his own driveway and witnesses two men physically and forcibly attempting to remove his neighbor from the seat of his bicycle and steal it. Gordon immediately recognizes his neighbor and the bicycle. Gordon knows that the bicycle is worth $150 dollars because he gave it to his neighbor for his birthday, just a week ago.

Is Gordon legally justified in using force under this scenario? Very likely, including deadly force. Florida Statute §776.031(2) allows the use of all force up to and including deadly force to prevent the imminent commission of a forcible felony. The taking of the bicycle in this case is a robbery, which Florida law defines as "the taking of money or other property ... from the person or custody of another, with intent to either permanently or temporarily deprive the person or the owner of the money or other property, [and] when in the course of the taking there is the use of force, violence, assault, or putting in fear."

Although we caution about saying too much to 911, in fairness to law enforcement, I believe that when you call 911 if there is still a threat or the possibility of other armed assailants in the area, that you should share this information with 911 so the police know they are arriving into a hostile or potentially deadly situation. Further, if suspects have fled the scene, informing 911 of a basic description and a direction they fled can help law enforcement catch the bad guys. -David

V. HOW ARE THE CRIMES ASSOCIATED WITH DEFENDING PROPERTY DEFINED UNDER FLORIDA LAW?

In the previous sections, we discussed circumstances where if certain crimes are being or have been committed, a person may have a legal justification in using force or deadly force to defend their property. How does Florida law define those crimes?

1. Arson

When a person willfully and unlawfully or during the commission of a felony causes a structure to be damaged by fire, or explosion commits arson. The type of structure and whether or not it is occupied determines what level an offense is committed. *See* Florida Statute §806.

2. Burglary

Entering a dwelling, a structure, or a conveyance with the intent to commit an offense therein. If entry is lawful, but one stays in the dwelling structure or conveyance secretly after permission to remain is withdrawn with the intent to commit an offense. *See* Florida Statute §810.02.

3. Robbery

The taking of money or other property ... from the person or custody of another, with intent to either permanently or temporarily deprive the person or the owner of the money or other property, when in the course of the taking there is the use of force, violence, assault, or putting in fear. *See* Florida Statute §812.13.

4. Robbery by snatching

"Robbery by sudden snatching" means the taking of money or other property from the victim's person, with intent to permanently or temporarily deprive the victim or the owner of the money or other property, when, in the course of the taking, the victim was or became aware of the taking. *See* Florida Statute §812.131.

5. Carjacking

The taking of a motor vehicle which may be the subject of larceny from the person or custody of another, with intent to either permanently or temporarily deprive the person or the owner of the motor vehicle, when in the course of the taking there is the use of force, violence, assault, or putting in fear. *See* Florida Statute §812.133.

6. Home-invasion robbery

Any robbery that occurs when the offender enters a dwelling with the intent to commit a robbery, and does commit a robbery of the occupants therein. *See* Florida Statute §812.135.

7. Theft

Knowingly obtaining or using, or endeavoring to obtain or to use, the property of another with intent to, either temporarily or permanently:

(a) Deprive the other person of a right to the property or a benefit from the property.

(b) Appropriate the property to his or her own use or to the use of any person not entitled to the use of the property. *See* Florida Statute §812.014.

8. Criminal Mischief

When a person, willfully and maliciously injures or damages by any means any real or personal property belonging to another, including, but not limited to, the placement of graffiti thereon or other acts of vandalism thereto. *See* Florida Statute §806.13(a).

VI. HOW CAN I ASSIST LAW ENFORCEMENT?

A. Acting under a police officer's direction

Almost without fail, as attorneys we are regularly asked about whether you can make a citizen's arrest, and how you can best assist law enforcement in dicey situations. Since every legal situation is unique, here we'll just provide a brief summary of the general law, as well as references to some of the statutes governing the law of citizen's arrests and how to assist authorities.

First, Florida Statute §843.04 states that you must assist a prison officer or correctional officer to make a search or arrest of a convict who has escaped if they tell you to. Failure to assist is a misdemeanor punishable by up to one year in jail. Further, Florida Statute §843.06 imposes the same duty to assist at the direction of any law enforcement officer to aid in the execution of their duties in a criminal case or the preservation of the peace. Failure to assist is a 2nd degree misdemeanor punishable by up to 60 days in jail.

Additionally, when an officer summons a citizen to assist them, the citizen may use any force necessary that the officer could lawfully use. Florida Statute §776.05 states that the officer, or any person whom they have summoned to assist, does not need to retreat or stop efforts to make a lawful arrest because of resistance or threat, and is justified in using any force necessary to defend himself or herself from bodily harm while making an arrest in retaking felons who have escaped or in arresting felons fleeing from justice. However, with regard to a fleeing felon, deadly force can only be used if three conditions are met: 1) the officer or person directed by them used deadly force necessary to prevent the arrest from failing due to the felon fleeing, 2) some warning has been given if possible, and 3) the officer or person reasonably believes that the fleeing felon poses a threat of death or serious physical harm to the officer or others, or reasonably believes that the fleeing felon has committed a crime involving the infliction or threat of infliction of serious physical harm to another.

This would appear to eliminate the very idea of a "citizen's arrest" in the traditional sense and looks much more like a field-commission to deputy!

Section 776.05 operates as the statute under which law enforcement is able to use force against a suspect. In order to enable officers to use all available resources at their disposal (such as an ordinary citizen), the statute is expanded to include individuals acting at an officer's direction.

B. Not acting under a police officer's direction

Nowhere in Florida statutory law is there any authorization for a citizen to make an arrest. However, our courts have recognized a citizen's right to make an arrest under common law principles. In order to make an arrest under Florida law, a citizen must either witness a felony being committed or have probable cause that the person they are arresting is guilty of having committed a felony. Further, a citizen's arrest is also authorized for a misdemeanor crime if it constitutes a breach of the peace.

PRACTICAL LEGAL TIP

When declining to speak with the police, be polite. Further, even if you are not going to answer questions, follow law enforcements commands. If they ask you to stay away from the area where the incident occurred, arguing with them or disobeying could land you in jail. -David

C. Detaining potential thieves: "retailer's privilege"

Florida Statute §812.015(3)(a) grants a retailer or their employee authority to detain a person in order to investigate potential theft:

> **AUTHORIZATION TO DETAIN POTENTIAL THIEF; FLORIDA STATUTE §812.015(3)(a)**
>
> A law enforcement officer, a merchant, a farmer, or a transit agency's employee or agent, who has probable cause to believe that a retail theft, farm theft, a transit fare evasion, or trespass, or unlawful use or attempted use of any antishoplifting or inventory control device countermeasure, has been committed by a person and, in the case of retail or farm theft, that the property can be recovered by taking the offender into custody may, for the purpose of attempting to effect such recovery or for prosecution, take the offender into custody and detain the offender in a reasonable manner for a reasonable length of time. In the case of a farmer, taking into custody shall be effectuated only on property owned or leased by the farmer. In the event the merchant, merchant's employee, farmer, or a transit agency's employee or agent takes the person into custody, a law enforcement officer shall be called to the scene immediately after the person has been taken into custody.

The most common application of this particular statute is in the retail-store setting. Thus, it is often called "retailer's" or "shopkeeper's privilege" or right. Common scenarios include when a loss prevention officer for the store detains a customer while they investigate whether an item was stolen from their business.

VII. WHAT CRIMES CAN I BE CHARGED WITH WHEN MY USE OF DEADLY FORCE IS NOT JUSTIFIED?

We've reached the end of our discussion on when you may be justified to use a weapon in defense of your person or property. Now it's time to give a brief summary of what kind of legal trouble you could find yourself in if you don't meet the elements of justification as we've described throughout this book.

The following tables lists some of the crimes involving the use of deadly force or a firearm and where relevant provisions may be found in Florida law:

CRIMES INVOLVING DEADLY FORCE OR A FIREARM:

1. Murder: *see* Florida Statute §782.04
2. Excusable Homicide: *see* Florida Statute §782.03
3. Manslaughter: *see* Florida Statute §782.07
4. Vehicular Homicide: *see* Florida Statute §782.071
5. Vessel Homicide: *see* Florida Statute §782.072
6. Unnecessary Killing: *see* Florida Statute §782.11
7. Aggravated Assault: *see* Florida Statute §784.021
8. Aggravated Battery: *see* Florida Statute §784.045
9. False Imprisonment: *see* Florida Statute §787.02

CRIMES INVOLVING DEADLY FORCE OR A FIREARM:

1. DISPLAY OF FIREARMS:

a. Improper Exhibition of a Dangerous Weapon or Firearm states that it is a misdemeanor to exhibit a firearm (or any dirk, sword, sword cane, electric weapon or device, or other weapon) in a rude, careless, angry, or threatening manner, not in necessary self-defense. *See* Florida Statute §790.10;

b. Open Carrying of Weapons states that a person licensed to carry a concealed firearm as provided in s. 790.06(1), and who is lawfully carrying a firearm in a concealed manner, commits a misdemeanor by intentionally displaying the firearm in an angry or threatening manner, not in necessary self-defense. *See* Florida Statute §790.053(1);

c. Aggravated Assault is a felony of the third degree that occurs when a person intentionally and unlawfully threatens, by word or act, with a deadly weapon without intent to kill, to do violence to another, coupled with an apparent ability to do so and does some act which creates a well-founded fear in the other person that such violence is imminent. *See* Florida Statute §784.021(1)(a)

2. DISCHARGE OF FIREARMS:

a. It is a misdemeanor to knowingly discharge a firearm in any public place or on or over the right-of-way of any paved public road, highway or street, or over any occupied premises; or who recklessly or negligently discharges a firearm outdoors on any property used primarily as a dwelling or zoned exclusively for residential use; not in necessary self-defense nor while performing official duties which require the discharge of a firearm. *See* Florida Statute §790.15(1).

b. It is a felony of the second and third degrees respectively, to knowingly and willfully discharge any firearm from a vehicle within 1,000 feet of any person; and for any driver or owner of any vehicle, whether occupying said vehicle or not, to knowingly direct any other person to discharge any firearm from the vehicle. *See* Florida Statute §790.15(2) & §790.15(3).

c. It is a prohibited felony to discharge any weapon or firearm at a school-sponsored event or on the property of any school, school bus, or school bus stop; not in lawful defense of self or another. *See* Florida Statute §790.115(2)(d).

WHAT DO I DO IMMEDIATELY AFTER I USE MY FIREARM?

1. Make sure that the threat is contained or neutralized.
2. Call 911 and tell them you (or another person) has been the victim of a crime. Give the operator your location and description. Avoid giving any unnecessary information, and avoid telling them you shot someone. It may be wise to suggest an ambulance is needed. Further, if armed assailants ran from the scene or may still be present, let 911 know that gunman are in the area and if possible provide a basic description. Then hang up with 911.
3. Call the Florida specific U.S. Law Shield Emergency Hotline on the back of your membership card and follow the instructions your program attorney gives you.
4. Return your firearm to safekeeping if you are no longer in danger.
5. Wait for police and do not touch any evidence.
6. If directed by your attorney, provide police only simple details of the crime against you otherwise keep your mouth shut.
7. Be careful of police questions and always be ready to invoke your right to silence and your right to counsel at any time. Let the police know that you will not answer any questions until advised to do so by your attorney.

If you use your firearm for defensive purposes, the first number you should call is 911. But keep your call brief: you only need to tell the operator that you have been the victim of a crime, where you are located, and some identifying information. After that, hang up! You are not required to remain on the line. Continuing to talk to the 911 operator could cause you problems later. Remember, all 911 calls are recorded and operators are trained to gather as much information as possible. No matter how justified you are in your use of a firearm, something you say on a 911 call may become a real headache later at trial. -David

> CHAPTER ELEVEN ◄

LAW OF CONCEALED CARRY: PART I
CONCEALED WEAPONS OR FIREARMS
The License Qualifications, Requirements, Appeals, And Regulations

In 1987, the Florida Legislature passed a law allowing for the issuance of licenses to carry concealed weapons or firearms (CWFLs). In Florida, qualified individuals may obtain a CWFL, which allows the carrying of a concealed weapon on their person for any lawful purpose. To obtain a CWFL, a person must meet certain requirements and submit an application to the Florida Department of Agriculture and Consumer Services. A CWFL allows for the lawful carry of a handgun, electronic weapon or device, tear gas gun, knife, or billie; but specifically, does not include a machine gun. This chapter deals exclusively with the licensed carrying of a handgun in Florida.

I. THE EVOLUTION OF THE FLORIDA CONCEALED CARRY LAW

Florida is a "shall issue" state which means, as long as the prescribed requirements are met, a concealed weapons license shall be issued by the Department of Agriculture. Florida allows for licenses to be issued both to residents and non-residents. There are currently more than 1.3 million Concealed Weapons or Firearm License holders in the State of Florida.

Florida Statutes Chapter 790, Section 06, entitled "License to Carry Concealed Weapon or Firearm," contains the law on how concealed weapons licenses are administered in this state. Throughout this chapter, we will discuss the requirements, the application process, as well as the rights given to CWFL holders for carrying a firearm in the State of Florida. A CWFL does not allow a person to open carry a handgun in public generally. However, open carry of firearms and other weapons is permitted in public under Florida Statutes Chapter 790, Section 25 under certain circumstances including but not limited to members of the armed forces, law enforcement and other approved officials, guards, or carriers, a person engaged in fishing, camping, or lawful hunting, a person firing weapons for testing or target practice under safe conditions and in a safe place not prohibited by law, a person traveling by private conveyance when the weapon is securely encased, a person possessing arms at his or her home or place of business, etc.

II. QUALIFICATIONS FOR AND STEPS TO GET A CWFL
A. Persons who are legally qualified to obtain a CWFL

In this section, we will discuss the requirements to apply for a Florida CWFL, as well as potential disqualifications. In addition to the requirements listed below, applicants must also be deemed competent with a firearm and provide proof of the same.

Florida Statute §790.06, states that to be generally eligible for a CWFL in Florida, a person must:

1. Be a resident of the United States and a citizen of the United States or a permanent resident alien of the United States;

2. Be 21 years of age or older;

3. Not suffer from a physical infirmity which prevents the safe handling of a weapon or firearm;

4. Not be ineligible to possess a firearm pursuant to Fla. Stat. §790.23 by virtue of having been convicted of a felony;

5. Not have been committed for the abuse of a controlled substance or been found guilty of a crime under the provisions of Florida Statute Chapter 893: Drug Abuse Prevention and Control or similar laws of any other state relating to controlled substances within a three-year period immediately preceding the date on which the application is submitted;

6. Not chronically and habitually use alcoholic beverages or other substances to the extent that his or her normal faculties are impaired;

7. Desire a legal means to carry a concealed weapon or firearm for lawful self-defense;

8. Demonstrate competence with a firearm by any of the approved courses;

9. Not have been adjudicated an incapacitated person under Florida Statute §744.331, or similar laws of any other state, unless five

years have elapsed since the applicant's restoration to capacity by court order;

10. Not have been committed to a mental institution under Florida Statute Chapter 394: Mental Health, or similar laws of any other state, unless the applicant produces a certificate from a licensed psychiatrist that he or she has not suffered from disability for at least five years prior to the date of submission of the application;

11. Not have had an adjudication of guilt withheld or imposition of sentence suspended on any felony or misdemeanor crime of domestic violence unless 3 years have elapsed since probation or any other conditions set by the court have been fulfilled, or the record has been sealed or expunged;

12. Not have been issued an injunction that is currently in force and effect and that restrains the applicant from committing acts of violence or acts of repeat violence; and

13. Not be prohibited from purchasing or possessing a firearm by any other provision of Florida or federal law.

B. What does it mean to be a "chronic and habitual user of alcohol or substances to the extent normal faculties are impaired" so as to be disqualified from receiving a CWFL?

A person is legally disqualified from receiving a CWFL if that person is a chronic and habitual user of alcohol or other substances to the extent that person's normal faculties are impaired.

Florida Statute §790.06 states that it shall be presumed that an applicant chronically and habitually uses alcoholic beverages or other substances to the extent that his or her normal faculties are impaired if:

1. The applicant has been committed under Florida Statute Chapter

397: Public Health Substance Abuse (or under the provisions of former chapter 396);

2. Or has been convicted under Florida Statute §790.151 which penalizes the use of a firearm while under the influence of alcoholic beverages, chemical substances, or controlled substances;

3. Or has been deemed a habitual offender under subsection 3 of Florida Statute §856.011: Disorderly Intoxication;

4. Or has had two or more convictions under Florida Statute §316.193: Driving Under the Influence or similar laws of any other state, within the three-year period immediately preceding the date on which the application is submitted.

Individuals who possess any of the characteristics listed in this section will not legally qualify for a CWFL under Florida law.

C. What does it mean to be "incapacitated person" so as to be disqualified from receiving a CWFL?

Florida Statute §744.102 defines an incapacitated person as a person who has been judicially determined to lack the capacity to manage at least some of their property or to meet some of their own essential health and safety requirements. The court order determining incapacity pursuant to Florida Statute §744.331 relies on a clear and convincing evidence standard and requires the court to make findings of fact and to determine the particular right or rights to which the person is incapacitated. Specifically, the court shall make the following findings: 1. The exact nature and scope of the person's incapacities; 2. The exact areas in a which the person lacks capacity to make informed decisions about care and treatment services or to meet the essential requirements for her or his physical or mental health or safety; 3. The specific legal disabilities to which the person is subject; and 4. The specific rights that the person is incapable of exercising. Individuals who have been found to be incapacitated by a court of competent jurisdiction within five years of applying for a CWFL will not legally qualify for one under Florida law.

D. How does a person prove they are competent with a firearm?

Florida law requires a photocopy of the certificate of completion from any of the approved courses or classes. Do not send in originals. Also acceptable as qualifying evidence of competence with a firearm is an affidavit from the instructor, school, club, organization, or group that conducted or taught said course or class, attesting to the completion of the course or class by the applicant; or a copy of any document which shows completion of the course or class or evidences participation in firearms competition.

The following list includes the approved ways a person can demonstrate competence with a firearm as required by Florida Statute §790.06(8):

1. Completion of any hunter education or hunter safety course approved by the Fish and Wildlife Conservation Commission or a similar agency of another state;
2. Completion of any National Rifle Association firearms safety or training course;
3. Completion of any firearms safety or training course or class available to the general public offered by a law enforcement, junior college, college, or private or public institution or organization or firearms training school, utilizing instructors certified by the National Rifle Association, Criminal Justice Standards and Training Commission, or the Department of Agriculture and Consumer Services;
4. Completion of any law enforcement firearms safety or training

course or class offered for security guards, investigators, special deputies, or any division or subdivision of law enforcement or security enforcement;

5. Presents evidence of equivalent experience with a firearm through participation in organized shooting competition or military service;
6. Is licensed or has been licensed to carry a firearm in this state or a county or municipality of this state, unless such license has been revoked for cause; or
7. Completion of any firearms training or safety course or class conducted by a state-certified or National Rifle Association certified firearms instructor.

E. If you don't disclose, you can expect your application to be delayed or denied!

The qualifying factor that probably delays the majority of applications revolves around when a person fails to make a full disclosure of material facts. To qualify for a Florida CWFL, a person must not make any material misrepresentation or fail to disclose any material fact in his or her CWFL application. Most often, this is due to a person failing to disclose a criminal conviction of one nature or another.

Many applicants forget about things that may have happened many years ago, but which require disclosure in the application. The best practice is: when in doubt, disclose! Otherwise, a person may face unwanted delays or even a denial of their application.

Note: Be very careful in the wording of your disclosures. We have seen many applicants encounter difficulties in not using precise descriptions of their legal history, medical condition, etc. Be careful with your words!

F. What if I received a "withhold of adjudication?" Can I get a CWFL?

As discussed elsewhere, being convicted of certain crimes can result in an application for a CWFL being denied or a CWFL being revoked if one had been issued. The question arises, when is a person "convicted" such that their ability to obtain or retain a CWFL is negatively affected?

What is a "withhold of adjudication?"

Under Florida Statute §948.01(1), "[i]f it appears to the court upon a hearing of the matter that the defendant is not likely again to engage in a criminal course of conduct and that the ends of justice and the welfare of society do not require that the defendant presently suffer the penalty imposed by law, the court, in its discretion, may either adjudge the defendant to be guilty or stay and withhold the adjudication of guilt." If a court adjudicates a person "guilty" of a criminal offense, then that person has been "convicted" of the crime. Conversely, if a court withholds adjudication of guilt, then for most purposes that person has not been convicted of the crime. That being said, there are times when Florida law considers a withhold of adjudication to be a conviction for purposes of causing certain negative legal consequences.

The issue of whether or not a withhold of adjudication constitutes a "conviction" for purposes of firearms restrictions imposed upon "convicted felons" was addressed in *State v. Menuto*, 912 So.2d 603, 607 (Fla. 2nd DCA 2005). In Menuto, Florida's Second District Court of Appeal ruled that a withhold of adjudication is not sufficient to constitute a "conviction" for purposes of restricting convicted felons from firearms and that only an adjudication of guilt would suffice.

However, there are times when a withhold of adjudication for certain criminal offenses can result in negative consequences with regard to a person's ability to obtain or retain a CWFL. The following are examples of such difficulties that may result from persons receiving withholds of adjudication for certain criminal offenses:

(A) Florida Statute §790.06(2)(k)
Provides that the Florida Department of Agriculture and Consumer Services may not issue a CWFL if the applicant "had adjudication of guilt withheld or imposition of sentence suspended on any felony or misdemeanor crime of domestic violence unless 3 years have elapsed since probation or any other conditions set by the court have been fulfilled, or the record has been sealed or expunged."

(B) Florida Statute §790.06(3)
further provides that "[t]he [Florida] Department of Agriculture and Consumer Services shall deny a license if the applicant has been found guilty of, had adjudication of guilt withheld for, or had imposition of sentence suspended for one or more crimes of violence constituting a misdemeanor, unless 3 years have elapsed since probation or any other conditions set by the court have been fulfilled or the record has been sealed or expunged. The Department of Agriculture and Consumer Services shall revoke a license if the licensee has been found guilty of, had adjudication of guilt withheld for, or had imposition of sentence suspended for one or more crimes of violence within the preceding 3 years."

G. Suspension and revocation of a CWFL
1. What is the difference between suspension and revocation?
To begin, it is important to know that there is a difference between a suspension and a revocation of a person's CWFL. A suspension

is only temporary, and a person's license may be reinstated without the necessity of submitting a new application for a CWFL. This means that a person will not have to go through the rigors of the application process nor the classroom requirements again in order to regain their CWFL. On the other hand, a revocation means that the Florida Department of Agricultural and Consumer Services has decided that a person's CWFL shall be terminated and in order for the person to ultimately regain the CWFL, they must reapply from step one by submitting the application with the applicable fees.

2. Under what circumstances can the Florida Department of Agriculture and Consumer Services revoke or suspend a CWFL?

Florida Statute §790.06 governs CWFL revocations and states that a person's CWFL may be revoked for any of the following reasons:

a. Revoked if the "licensee has been found guilty of, had adjudication of guilt withheld for, or had imposition of sentence suspended for one or more crimes of violence within the preceding 3 years."

b. Revoked if the licensee is "convicted of a felony which would make the licensee in eligible to possess a firearm."

c. Revoked if the licensee is found guilty of a crime under the provisions of Florida's drug laws found in Florida Statute Chapter 893, or similar laws of any other state.

d. Suspended or revoked (the statute does not make it clear which) if the licensee is found to be ineligible under the criteria for issuing a CWFL found in Florida Statute §790.06(2).

e. Suspended or revoked (the statute does not make it clear which) if the licensee develops or sustains a physical infirmity which prevents the safe handling of a weapon or firearms. Presumably, whether the licensee is suspended or revoked may hinge upon whether the physical infirmity is temporary or permanent.

f. Suspended or revoked (the statute does not make it clear which) if the licensee is adjudicated an incapacitated person.

g. Suspended or revoked (the statute does not make it clear which) the licensee is committed to a mental institution.

h. Suspended or revoked (the statute does not make it clear which) the licensee is committed as a substance abuser or is deemed a habitual disorderly intoxication habitual offender pursuant to Florida Statute §856.011(3).

i. Suspended or revoked (the statute does not make it clear which) if the licensee is convicted of a second violation of Florida's driving under the influence law or a similar law of another state, within three years of a previous conviction for a driving under the influence charge, even if the first such conviction may have occurred prior to the date on which the licensee's CWFL application was submitted.

j. Suspended upon notification by a law enforcement agency, a court, or the Florida Department of Law Enforcement and subsequent written verification, if the licensee or applicant for a CWFL is arrested or formally charged with a crime that would disqualify such person from having a license until final disposition of the case.

k. Suspended if the licensee or applicant is issued an injunction that restrains the licensee or applicant from committing acts of domestic violence or acts of repeat violence.

3. What happens if my CWFL expires while it is suspended?

If you are unfortunate enough to have your Florida CWFL expire during your period of suspension, you must apply for a Florida CWFL as a new applicant once your suspension period ends.

4. Procedure for revocation or suspension of a CWFL

Suspension or revocation of a CWFL is governed by the Florida Administrative Procedures Act (the APA), which is contained in

Chapter Twelve of the Florida Statutes, and certain provisions of the Florida Administrative Code. Florida Administrative Code Rule 28-106.2015 specifies that:

> Prior to entry of a final order to suspend, revoke, or withdraw a license, to impose administrative fines, or to take other enforcement or disciplinary action against a licensee or person or entity subject to the agency's jurisdiction, the agency shall serve upon the licensee an administrative complaint. For purposes of this rule, an agency pleading or communication that seeks to exercise an agency's enforcement authority and to take any kind of disciplinary action against a licensee or other person shall be deemed an administrative complaint.

The administrative complaint to suspend or revoke a CWFL must contain the following information:

a. The name of the agency, the respondent or respondents against whom disciplinary action is sought and a file number;
b. The statutory sections, rules of the Florida Administrative Code or the agency order alleged to have been violated;
c. The facts or conduct relied on to establish the violation; and
d. A statement that the respondent has the right to request a hearing to be conducted in accordance with Florida Statutes §§120.569 and 120.57, and to be represented by counsel or other qualified representative.

Requests (petitions) for hearings, that are delivered to the agency involved, filed by the licensee contesting the suspension or revocation of their CWFL must include the following information:

a. The name, address, any e-mail address, telephone number and facsimile number, if any, of the licensee, if the licensee is not represented by an attorney or qualified representative;

b. The name, address, e-mail address, telephone number and facsimile number of the attorney or qualified representative of the licensee, if any, upon whom service of pleadings and other papers shall be made;

c. A statement requesting an administrative hearing identifying those material facts that are in dispute. If there are none, the petition must so indicate;

d. A statement of when the licensee received notice of the administrative complaint; and

e. A statement including the file number to the administrative complaint.

Licensees who request, via petitions, review of the suspension or revocation of their CWFL can, pursuant to Florida Statute §120.57(1), request formal hearings if there are material disputed facts. In contrast, licensees may, pursuant to §120.57(2), request informal hearings if there are no disputed material facts. If during an informal hearing, material disputed facts arise, unless the parties waive it, the informal hearing must be terminated and a formal hearing convened. Pursuant to Florida Administrative Code Rule 28-106.111(2), an aggrieved licensee must file a petition for a hearing to contest the suspension or revocation of their CWFL within 21 days of receipt of written notice of the decision. Failure to file a written request for a hearing within the 21-day limit, will waive the right to request a hearing. Requests for a hearing should be sent to the following address:

Florida Department of Agriculture and Consumer Services
P.O. Box 5708
Tallahassee, Florida 32314-5708

III. THE CWFL APPLICATION AND PROCESS
A. The CWFL application
The Division of Licensing has developed an application intake service at each of their eight regional offices located throughout the state of Florida, which allows applicants to complete the entire process quickly and conveniently by appointment. During the appointment, an electronic application form is submitted at a kiosk, reviewed by staff, fingerprints and photograph are taken, and payment is processed by staff. The eight regional offices are located in Ft. Walton Beach, Jacksonville, Doral, Orlando, Punta Gorda, Tallahassee, Tampa, and West Palm Beach. However, this intake service is also available at authorized tax collector's offices which are more numerous and also located throughout the state of Florida.

Individuals can also submit a written application package via mail to Tallahassee; specifically, to: Florida Department of Agriculture and Consumer Services, Division of Licensing, P.O. Box 6687, Tallahassee, Florida, 32314-6687.

The packet can be downloaded and printed out by visiting the Florida Department of Agriculture and Consumer Services website: www.freshfromflorida.com. The packet can also be delivered by mail upon request made by applicant through the same website.

Each application has an assigned identification and tracking number in order to provide applicants more accessibility to status information throughout the application process. The application itself, requires personally identifying information including a valid social security number or alien registration number, current demographic, address, and contact information, residential and employment information, place of birth, a valid email address, as well as personal background information including information regarding any mental health, drug, alcohol, domestic violence and/or criminal history from the applicant as described in Section 790.06 of the Florida Statutes. The application concludes with a required sworn oath affirming that the applicant is knowledgeable regarding the Firearms and Weapons section of the Florida Statutes (Chapter 790), that the applicant desires a legal means of carrying a weapon for lawful self-defense, that the applicant does not suffer from any physical infirmity that would prevent the safe handling of the weapon, and that all of the information provided in the application packet is true and correct. This portion must be notarized and sworn to by the applicant.

The process of applying for a CWFL requires a person to complete the application, submit fingerprints, take a photograph, and pay the application fee. The fingerprints are required as part of a background check; and can be submitted electronically during your appointment with the Division of Licensing or at any authorized tax collector's office.

B. CWFL class and shooting qualifications
In order to obtain a Florida CWFL, applicants must submit proof of competency with a firearm. A certificate of completion from any of the following sources will suffice:
1. Any hunter education or hunter safety course approved by the Florida Fish and Wildlife Conservation Commission;
2. Any National Rifle Association firearms safety or training course;
3. Any firearms safety or training course or class available to the general public offered by a law enforcement agency, junior college, college, or private or public institution or organization or firearms training school, utilizing instructors certified by the

National Rifle Association, the Criminal Justice Standards and Training Commission, or the Department of Agriculture and Consumer Services;

4. Any law enforcement firearms safety or training course or class offered for security officers, investigators, special deputies, or any division or subdivision of law enforcement or security enforcement; or

5. Any firearms training or safety course or class conducted by a state-certified instructor or by an instructor certified by the National Rifle Association.

Your copy of the training certificate or completion document from any of the above listed sources must be clear and legible in order to be accepted. Do not send in originals. The copy of the certificate must display your name, your instructor's name, and your instructor's credentials including your instructor's license/certification number. Other acceptable forms of competency documentation include: evidence of experience with a firearm obtained through participation in organized shooting competition; evidence of experience gained during military service for active-duty military personnel (for example: military orders including call to active-duty letter; a statement of military service signed by or at the direction of the adjutant, personnel officer or commander of your unit or higher headquarters which identifies you and provides your date of entry for your current active duty period); and former military can submit a DD Form 214 reflecting honorable discharge from military service.

LAW OF CONCEALED CARRY: PART II
CONCEALED WEAPONS OR FIREARMS
What, How, And Where You Can Legally Carry With A CWFL

I. CONCEALED HANDGUNS MUST BE CONCEALED!

First, it should be obvious that handguns or other weapons allowed to be carried under Florida Statute §790.06 – which is titled "License to carry concealed weapon or firearm" – must be concealed when carrying pursuant to a CWFL.

A. Improper exhibition of a deadly weapon or firearm is a crime

It is only a crime when a weapon or firearm becomes unconcealed if it is exhibited in a "rude, careless, angry, or threatening manner, not in necessary self-defense." Therefore, our discussion will focus on what is legal under this standard.

> **IMPROPER EXHIBITION OF A DANGEROUS WEAPON OR FIREARM; FLORIDA STATUTE §790.10**
>
> If any person having or carrying any dirk, sword, sword cane, firearm, electric weapon or device, or other weapon shall, in the presence of one or more persons, exhibit the same in a rude, careless, angry, or threatening manner, not in necessary self-defense, the person so offending shall be guilty of a misdemeanor of the first degree, punishable as provided in §775.082 or §775.083.

This is an area that rightfully concerns a lot of CWFL holders and is a very misunderstood area of the law. Florida law states that a CWFL holder commits a crime if they exhibit their firearm or other weapon in the presence of one or more people in a "rude, careless, angry or threatening manner." It is a defense to this crime if such weapon is displayed in self-defense. An unintentional, accidental, or inadvertent display is not a crime under Florida law so long as it was not done in a careless manner. *See* Florida Statute §790.10.

Obvious examples of intentionally displaying a concealed weapon would be in a heated verbal argument pulling up your shirt to reveal a portion or all of your handgun to another person, with the desire that they see it, or simply pulling your handgun out of its holster and waving it in the air in front of somebody in order to frighten them.

B. Unintentional displays of a handgun are not a crime

What do you do if a gust of wind picks up your shirt and shows off your 1911 handgun? What about when your pants accidentally split revealing your Spiderman underwear and your Sig Sauer? How about the time your purse accidentally opens, flashing your Desert Eagle? The good news is that none of these incidents are crimes under Florida law.

If a CWFL holder's concealed handgun becomes unconcealed inadvertently, such as by "flashing" or "printing," (see below) the CWFL holder is not breaking the law. Furthermore, under Florida law, a CWFL holder who is carrying a concealed firearm legally is allowed to briefly and openly display his or her firearm to the ordinary sight of another person so long as it is not done in an angry or threatening manner. Florida Statute §790.053(1). This means an accidental display is not a criminal offense.

C. What is "printing" and is it a crime?

What is printing? First, printing is not a legal term and it is not a crime. Further, the word printing does not appear anywhere in the Florida Statutes. Printing is a common street term that generally refers to the outline or characteristics of a handgun becoming visible under the clothing of a person. For example, someone may be wearing extremely tight fitting clothes, and carrying a full size Glock 9 mm under these clothes, as a result the outline of the gun would be clearly visible, however, since the gun is covered by a layer of clothing, the gun is still considered concealed under Florida law. It may be boorish behavior, bad taste, or even unwise, but under the plain meaning of the statute, it is not a crime.

II. WHERE CAN A CWFL HOLDER LEGALLY CARRY A CONCEALED HANDGUN?

A person in possession of a CWFL may legally carry their handgun concealed any place where it is not illegal for them to possess a concealed handgun under either state or federal law. The places prohibited under Florida law are located in Florida Statute §790.06(12)(a) and will be discussed below. In addition, because a CWFL is issued by the State of Florida and not the federal government, a CWFL holder may not legally carry their concealed handgun on federal property unless specifically authorized by federal law.

Prohibited places for CWFL holders

There are a number of places under Florida law where persons are prohibited from carrying a firearm or a concealed weapon, whether or not that person is a CWFL holder. We discuss these places in detail in Chapter Ten. We also discuss both state and federal "Gun Free School Zones" in Chapter Ten to explain the limits of carrying or possessing a firearm at or near a school. Specific to our discussion on CWFL holders, however, under Section 790.06, a CWFL holder may not legally carry a concealed handgun in the following places:

a. Any Place of Nuisance

A place of nuisance can be a building, booth, tent or place which tends to annoy the community, injure the health of the people, or corrupts the public morals. A place of nuisance can also be any location that is used by a criminal gang, criminal gang members, or criminal gang associates for the purpose of engaging in criminal gang-related activity on two or more occasions. Finally, a massage establishment that operates in violation of Florida law is also a place of nuisance. Florida Statute §823.05. Essentially, this means that firearms may not be taken into any place where prostitution, secret meetings, gambling, or criminal activity takes place.

CONCEALED HANDGUN PROHIBITED INTO ANY PLACE OF NUISANCE; FLORIDA STATUTE §790.06(12)(a)(b)

A CWFL holder commits a second-degree misdemeanor if the CWFL holder openly carries a handgun or carries a concealed weapon or firearm into a place of nuisance as defined in Florida Statute §823.05.

EXAMPLE

After spending the day helping a friend move into a new house, Gordon decides to get a massage. Gordon's friend tells him where to go and suggests that he ask for Bubbles. Gordon's friend then informs him for an extra tip Bubbles will do a lot more than just give a massage. Although Gordon is not looking for anything besides a massage, he decides to go to see Bubbles. Gordon is a CWFL holder and because it is late and the parlor is located in a bad area of town, he decides it is best to carry his gun for protection. When Gordon enters the establishment, he immediately notices all of the employees are young females wearing lingerie and that there is a sign on the front counter saying, "Cash Only". Gordon requests Bubbles and she leads him to a room. Once in the room, Bubbles informs Gordon that for an extra $100 she will make sure he leaves very happy. Gordon politely declines her solicitation and informs her he just wants a regular massage. Moments later the police raid the establishment. The police search Gordon and discover his gun at which time Gordon informs them he has a CWFL. During the police investigation, it is determined that Gordon did not commit solicitation. Unfortunately, Gordon could still be arrested and charged with a second-degree misdemeanor because he possessed a firearm in a place of nuisance.

b. Police, sheriff, or highway patrol station and any detention facility, prison, or jail

CONCEALED HANDGUN PROHIBITED AT ANY POLICE, SHERIFF, OR HIGHWAY PATROL STATION AND ANY DETENTION FACILITY, PRISON, OR JAIL; FLORIDA STATUTE §790.06(12)(a)(2),(3)

A CWFL holder commits a second-degree misdemeanor if the CWFL holder openly carries a handgun or carries a concealed weapon or firearm into any police, sheriff or highway patrol station. This also applies to any detention facility, prison, or jail.

A CWFL holder is not permitted to carry a concealed handgun into any police, sheriff or highway patrol station nor any detention facility, prison, or jail. However, a CWFL holder is not prohibited from carrying the concealed handgun in the parking lot of any police, sheriff or highway patrol station. Florida Statute §790.251, makes it illegal to possess a firearm in your vehicle at any state correctional facility. Anyone who possesses a firearm on the grounds of any state correctional facility commits a felony of the third degree. Florida Statute §944.47(2). Therefore, if you are visiting someone serving time in a state prison, you must either leave your firearm at home or park off the property of that prison.

c. Courthouses and Courtrooms

CONCEALED HANDGUN PROHIBITED AT ANY COURTHOUSE AND ANY COURTROOM; FLORIDA STATUTE §790.06(12)(a)(4),(5)

A CWFL holder commits a second-degree misdemeanor if the CWFL holder openly carries a handgun or carries a concealed weapon or firearm into any courthouse or any courtroom.

Individuals are not allowed to take firearms or other weapons into courthouses or courtrooms, except for the presiding judge or persons given permission to carry by the presiding judge. Florida Statute §790.06(12)(a)(4),(5). According to a Florida Attorney General's advisory opinion from 2012, "a presiding judge may determine who will carry a concealed weapon in his or her courtroom and such determination necessarily allows the individual to proceed through the courthouse in order to access the courtroom." Fla. Att'y Gen. Op. 2012-08 (2012).

d. Polling places, government meetings, and the Legislature or a committee of the Legislature.

> **CONCEALED HANDGUN PROHIBITED AT ANY POLLING PLACE; ANY MEETING OF THE GOVERNING BODY OF A COUNTY, PUBLIC SCHOOL DISTRICT, MUNICIPALITY, OR SPECIAL DISTRICT; OR ANY MEETING OF THE LEGISLATURE OR A COMMITTEE THEREOF; FLORIDA STATUTE §790.06(12)(a)(6)-(8)**
>
> A CWFL holder commits a second-degree misdemeanor if the CWFL holder openly carries a handgun or carries a concealed weapon or firearm into any polling place; any meeting of the governing body of a county, public school district, municipality, or special district; or any meeting of the Legislature or a committee thereof.

No firearms can be carried at any polling place in Florida. Florida Statute §790.06(12)(a)(6). Even if the location which one goes to vote may usually be a place that a CWFL holder may carry a concealed weapon or firearm, during polling times it is off limits.

Meetings of the governing body of a county, public school,

district, municipality, or special district are off-limits to carrying a concealed or openly-carried firearm. Florida Statute §790.06(12)(a)(7). This means that an individual cannot carry at school board, city council, and other types of meetings that involve local governments. Likewise, Florida law prohibits carrying a firearm at "any meeting of the Legislature or a committee thereof." Florida Statute §790.06(12)(a)(8). Therefore, Florida law prohibits the carrying of a firearm at all government meetings, whether local or state.

e. School, college, or professional athletic event not related to firearm

> **CONCEALED HANDGUN PROHIBITED AT ANY SCHOOL, COLLEGIATE, AND PROFESSIONAL ATHLETIC EVENT NOT RELATED TO FIREARMS;**
> **FLORIDA STATUTE §790.06(12)(a)(9)**
>
> A CWFL holder commits a second-degree misdemeanor if the CWFL holder openly carries a handgun or carries a concealed weapon or firearm into any school, college, or professional event, unless the CWFL holder is a participant in the event and a firearm is used in the event.

Firearms are prohibited at any school, college, or professional athletic event not related to firearms. This includes high school football games, elementary school "field days" and other non-firearms related school sports events. However, firearms are not prohibited for use at school-shooting clubs or marksmanship competitions. Florida Statute §790.06(12)(a)(9).

Examples of professional athletic events in Florida include

Jacksonville Jaguars or Miami Dolphins football games, Orlando City Soccer and Orlando Magic games. Firearms may not be carried anywhere on the premises where these events are held.

Private golf tournaments, sporting events, or rodeos

What about the scenario where a person decides to "host" a rodeo, golf tournament, or other sporting event on his private property? Are CWFL holders prohibited from carrying at such an event under the law? It depends on the manner in which the event takes place. If the hosted rodeo, golf tournament, or other sporting event is one of an amateur nature (and not collegiate or interscholastic), rather than professional, then the event likely falls outside the purviews of Florida Statute §790.06(12)(a)(9). On the other hand, if participants are persons who regularly compete in professional competitions; if there is a significant prize or purse associated with the event; if the event is sponsored completely or in-part by outside organizations and companies, then the event begins to look a lot more like a professional sporting event—even though it may not take place at a prominent public venue. It is worth pointing out that there is no case law on this subject, and it falls squarely within some of the legal "gray area" we see all-too-often in firearms law.

f. Elementary or secondary school facility or administration building

CONCEALED HANDGUN PROHIBITED AT ANY ELEMENTARY OR SECONDARY SCHOOL FACILITY OR ADMINISTRATION BUILDING; FLORIDA STATUTE §790.06(12)(a)(10)

A CWFL holder commits a second-degree misdemeanor if the CWFL holder openly carries a handgun or carries a concealed weapon or firearm into any elementary or secondary school facility or administration building.

g. Career centers

Career Centers are commonly referred to as technical schools. Section 1002.34(3)(a), of the Florida Statutes defines "charter technical career center" or "center" as a public school or a public technical center operated under a charter granted by a district school board or Florida College System Institution Board of Trustees or a consortium, including one or more district school boards and Florida College System Institution Boards of Trustees, that includes the district in which the facility is located that is nonsectarian in its programs, admission policies, employment practices and operations, and is managed by a board of directors.

h. Any portion of an establishment licensed to dispense alcoholic beverages for consumption on the premises, which portion of the establishment is primarily devoted to such purpose

> **CONCEALED HANDGUN PROHIBITED AT ANY PORTION OF AN ESTABLISHMENT LICENSED TO DISPENSE ALCOHOLIC BEVERAGES FOR CONSUMPTION ON THE PREMISES, WHICH PORTION OF THE ESTABLISHMENT IS PRIMARILY DEVOTED TO SUCH PURPOSE; FLORIDA STATUTE §790.06(12)(a)(12)**
>
> A CWFL holder commits a second-degree misdemeanor if the CWFL holder openly carries a handgun or carries a concealed weapon or firearm into any portion of an establishment licensed to dispense alcoholic beverages for consumption on the premises, which portion of the establishment is primarily devoted to such purpose.

Under Florida law, a person may not carry their firearm in "any portion of an establishment licensed to dispense alcoholic beverages for consumption on the premise, which portion of the establishment is primarily devoted to such purpose." This means that the carrying of firearms into pubs, taverns, and the like are barred. Florida Statute §790.06(12)(a)(12)

Unfortunately, this law is ambiguous and is subject to different interpretations as to whether restaurants with bars, casinos, and other places of entertainment, that are licensed to serve alcohol, but serve other purposes, are prohibited for CWFL firearms carriers. In a response letter U.S. Law Shield received from the Florida Department of Agriculture, it was stated that concealed weapons may be legally carried by a CWFL holder into a business that serves alcohol, so long as it is not their primary business. However, firearms may not be carried into portions of the business where the service of alcohol is the primary function – *e.g.* the bar area of a restaurant. What does a CWFL holder who is sitting in the dining area of the restaurant and has to use the restroom to do if the restroom is located in the bar area or passage through the bar is required to reach it? Unfortunately, there is no case law or authority regarding this situation. It seems that under Florida law, the CWFL holder would have to leave the restaurant, secure their firearm in their car, use the restroom, retrieve their firearm and return to the dinner table.

NOTE: Possession of a Firearm While Intoxicated Is NOT A CRIME
Florida Statute §790.151 prohibits a person from using a firearm when he or she is under the influence of alcoholic beverages, certain chemical substances, or any substance controlled under Chapter 893 of the Florida Statutes (dealing with Drug Abuse Prevention and Control), when affected to the extent that his or her normal faculties are impaired. The law does not require a person to be "drunk" or "intoxicated" but instead only requires a person's normal faculties to be diminished as a result of alcohol or a controlled substance.

NORMAL FACULTIES;

Normal faculties include, but are not limited to, the ability to see, hear, walk, talk, judge distances, drive an automobile, make judgments, act in emergencies, and, in general, normally perform the many mental and physical acts of daily life.

While the immediate meaning of "use" might seem to be shooting a firearm or displaying it, the statute defines use of a firearm as discharging a firearm or having a firearm readily accessible for immediate discharge. What does readily accessible mean? "Readily accessible for immediate discharge" means loaded and in a person's hand. Florida Statute §790.151(1)-(2)

Therefore, while a loaded and concealed firearm may be brought into a restaurant that serves alcohol, a person who has been drinking alcohol to the point of being impaired or intoxicated should not have the loaded firearm in their hand, much less discharge it! If police suspect that you have discharged a firearm or held a loaded firearm while under the influence, they can ask you to submit to a chemical test (*e.g.* a breath alcohol test) to determine the presence of alcohol or a controlled substance in your body.

i. Any college or university facility

CONCEALED HANDGUN PROHIBITED AT ANY COLLEGE OR UNIVERSITY FACILITY; FLORIDA STATUTE §790.06(12)(a)(13)

A CWFL holder commits a second-degree misdemeanor if the CWFL holder openly carries a handgun or carries a concealed weapon or firearm.

Although a CWFL holder is not allowed to carry a firearm on campus, the statute does provide an exception for stun guns or other non-lethal electric weapon. The stun gun or electric weapon cannot fire a dart or a projectile and it must be designed for self-defense purpose only. In order for a CWFL holder to carry a stun gun or non-lethal electric weapon, he or she must either be a registered student, faculty member, or employee of the college or university.

j. Airport terminals and sterile areas

> **CONCEALED HANDGUN PROHIBITED IN THE INSIDE OF THE PASSENGER TERMINAL AND STERILE AREA OF ANY AIRPORT; FLORIDA STATUTE §790.06(12)(a)(14)**
>
> A CWFL holder commits a second-degree misdemeanor if the CWFL holder openly carries a handgun or carries a concealed weapon or firearm into the inside of the passenger terminal and sterile area of any airport.

Firearms are not allowed inside the passenger terminal or sterile area of any airport. However, there is an exception for those looking to take a flight with their firearms. A person may carry an unloaded firearm that is in a locked hard sided case into the terminal, but not the sterile area, of an airport for the purpose of checking the firearm in as baggage. If a CWFL holder is dropping off or picking up a passenger from the airport, they cannot go into the terminal with their firearm.

k. Private and commercial property with NO GUN signs

Carrying a firearm on another person's property is not necessarily a crime. However, carrying a handgun while trespassing on another's property is a crime. Specifically, whoever is not authorized, licensed, or invited to enter or remain in any structure or conveyance, but stays on the property willingly is trespassing. If the property has a visible sign, indicating NO GUNS, then a person who actually sees the sign is put on notice that they are not invited on the property with a firearm. Unlike other states, Florida does not have any sign requirements such as specific sizes, locations for placement, specific language, etc. to make the sign effective notice. Further, if a person after having been authorized, licensed, or invited to first come onto the property is warned by the owner or lessee of the premises or by a person authorized by the owner/lessee to leave the property, and then refuses to do so, they are trespassing as well.

If the above actions occur while carrying a firearm or other dangerous weapon, the person will be committing the crime of "armed trespassing." Armed trespassing is a third-degree felony in Florida. If asked to leave while carrying your firearm, do so or risk losing not only your gun rights, but your freedom as well! *See* Florida Statute §810.09(1)(c).

l. Savannas Preserve State Park

It is unlawful for any person, except for a law enforcement or conservation officer, to have in their possession a firearm in the Savannas, except in compliance with a regulation established by the Fish and Wildlife Conservation Commission applying to lands within the described boundaries. Florida Statute §258.157(2).

m. Parking Lots

As a general rule, Florida business owners cannot prohibit a CWFL or non-CWFL holder from having a firearm securely encased in the car in the business parking lot. Florida Statute §790.251. However, there are some exceptions to this general rule found in Florida Statute §790.251(7).

These exceptions include the following:
• Any school property including school bus stops, a school sponsored event or a school bus. However, Florida Statute §790.115(2)(a)(3), does allow a person to have a firearm securely encased in their vehicle unless the school district adopted a written and published policy waiving this exception and prohibiting firearms

on their property. REMEMBER to check if there is such a written exception to this rule, before you decide to park your vehicle on school property with a firearm in it.

- Any correctional facility as discussed previously in this chapter.
- Any property where a nuclear power plant is located
- Any company property on which the company is engaged in national security, aerospace or homeland security.
- Any property of a company licensed to make, use or store explosives.

NOTE: It has been determined that this applies to all of Disney World's property.

III. AUTOMOBILES, WATERCRAFT, AND OTHER PLACES

A. Florida law on taking a firearm in your vehicle

A CWFL holder may carry a concealed handgun on their person inside their vehicle with no problem. Rifles and shotguns do not need to be concealed and may be carried anywhere in a private conveyance when such firearm is being carried for a lawful use, which includes activities such as self-defense and hunting. Florida Statute §790.25(5).

B. Can a person legally conceal a handgun on their body while they are in their vehicle?

If a person possesses a CWFL, he or she may have their firearm on their person inside the vehicle so long as it is concealed. Also, he or she may have it sitting anywhere in the vehicle that makes it readily accessible so long it is concealed. In essence, having a CWFL allows the holder to have it anywhere in the vehicle they would like and not encased in anything so long as the firearm is concealed from the ordinary sight of another person.

C. May a person legally carry a concealed handgun on public transportation?

Florida Statute §790.25(3)(l), restricts a person who is a CWFL holder to have firearms, other weapons, ammunition, and supplies on a public conveyance (which includes buses, trains, etc.) only if the weapon is securely encased and not in the person's manual possession. Manual possession means that the firearm in not on the person or in a bag that is under the person's control. An example would be a firearm in the luggage compartment under a bus that cannot be accessed from the interior of the bus.

D. May a person carry a concealed handgun on a boat or watercraft?

Yes, Florida law extends the same privileges a CWFL holder would have in his car to a boat or watercraft. However, it is worth noting that no firearms are allowed in restricted or secured Florida seaports. Florida Statute §311.12(3)(b). A person who possesses a concealed weapon or firearm on their person or in their motor vehicle at a secured seaport commits a first-degree misdemeanor. Each seaport is required by law to post appropriate signs and markers on the premises notifying individuals that firearms are prohibited.

E. May a person with a CWFL carry a concealed handgun in a state or municipal park?

Yes. State or municipal parks are subject to state law governing public places. A local municipality is preempted by state law from prohibiting the carrying of a concealed handgun by a CWFL holder and is, therefore, not authorized to prevent the legal carrying thereof. It is also permissible for a CWFL holder to possess a concealed handgun in a state park.

F. May a person legally carry a concealed handgun into a business that has a no firearm sign?

No. If the business has a no firearm sign on the entrance door it puts an individual on notice that people with firearms are not allowed inside the business. If a person does enter the business after seeing the sign, they have now become a trespasser. In fact, not only are they trespassing but they are committing an armed trespass, which is a third-degree felony, punishable up to five years in prison!

The key is knowledge. If a person sees the sign, then they know they are not wanted in the business with their firearm. Florida law is silent as to what a sign must look like to provide effective communication that CWFL holders are not allowed to carry in the business.

G. Federal Property

A Concealed Weapons and Firearms License and the rights it provides are a product of state law and convey no rights to the CWFL under federal law. However, in certain instances, the federal government has recognized these state given rights on certain federal property.

1. Federal buildings: firearms are prohibited

FIREARMS PROHIBITED IN FEDERAL FACILITIES;
18 U.S.C. §930(a)

...whoever knowingly possesses or causes to be present a firearm or other dangerous weapon in a Federal facility (other than a Federal court facility), or attempts to do so, shall be fined under this title or imprisoned not more than 1 year, or both.

Under this statute, a "federal facility" refers to any building or part of a building that is owned or leased by the federal government and is a place where federal employees are regularly present for the purpose of performing their official duties. *See* 18 U.S.C. §930(g)(1). However, this statute does not apply to "the lawful performance of official duties by an officer, agent, or employee of the United States, a State, or a political subdivision thereof, who is authorized by law to engage in or supervise the prevention, detection, investigation, or prosecution of any violation of law," nor does it apply to federal officials or members of the armed forces who are permitted to possess such a firearm by law, or the lawful carrying of a firearm incident to hunting or "other lawful purposes." 18 U.S.C. §930(d). This statute does not govern the possession of a firearm in a federal court facility.

2. National parks

CWFL holders are permitted to carry in National Parks located in Florida, but not buildings within those parks, such as ranger stations, because these are federal facilities. Under federal law, for firearms purposes, all federal parks are subject to the state law of the state in which the park is located. *See* 16 U.S.C. §1a-7b. A CWFL holder may, therefore, carry a handgun concealed in a federal park, but not in federal buildings in the park. Be sure to stay out of ranger stations, museums or gift shops with your firearm.

3. VA Hospitals: firearms prohibited

FIREARMS PROHIBITED AT VETERANS AFFAIRS HOSPITALS; 38 CFR §1.218(a)(13)

No person while on property shall carry firearms, other dangerous or deadly weapons, or explosives, either openly or concealed, except for official purposes.

One place where many law-abiding CWFL holders fall victim to federal firearm prohibitions is at the VA Hospital. The VA Hospital system is governed by federal law, which prohibits the carrying of any firearm while on VA property. This includes the parking lot, sidewalk, and any other area which is the property of the VA.

Under federal regulations, "no person while on property shall carry firearms, other dangerous or deadly weapons, or explosives, either openly or concealed, except for official purposes." 38 CFR §1.218(a)(13). The "official purposes" specified refer specifically to the VA Hospital Police. Significantly, the Department of Veterans Affairs has its own set of laws and guidelines and is not controlled strictly by the Gun Control Act of 1968 and the general provisions regarding the prohibition of firearms on federal property. The VA law is much more restrictive. Many law-abiding veterans have found themselves in trouble, for example, when they valet-park their vehicle and the valet discovers a concealed handgun in the console or door storage area. How rigidly this law is enforced is determined by the individual hospital administrators as described in 38 CFR §1.218(a). However, regardless of how strictly the law is enforced, firearms are still prohibited under the law and the VA police are very aggressive in enforcing them.

4. United States Post Offices: firearms prohibited

FIREARMS PROHIBITED AT POST OFFICES; 39 CFR §232.1(l)

Notwithstanding the provisions of any other law, rule or regulation, no person while on postal property may carry firearms, other dangerous or deadly weapons, or explosives, either openly or concealed, or store the same on postal property, except for official purposes.

Earlier in this chapter, we mentioned that parking lots, sidewalks, walkways, and other related areas are generally not included as places where firearms are prohibited even if the law or business owner prohibits entry into the building with a firearm. Under 39 CFR §232.1(l), firearms or other deadly weapons are prohibited on postal property including not only the building, but all property surrounding the building where a post office is located. This includes the parking lot (*e.g.*, a person's vehicle where a firearm may be stored), as well as the sidewalks and walkways. Like the VA Hospital, United States Post Offices are another exception to the rule. In 2013, there was a decision by a United States District Court addressing this issue in Colorado which allowed a license holder to bring his firearm into the parking lot of the Avon Colorado Post Office. However, in 2015, that case was reversed on appeal by the Tenth Circuit Court of Appeals. In 2016, the U.S. Supreme Court refused to review the Tenth Circuit's reversal. It should be noted that the Tenth Circuit does not include Florida, and therefore this case had no legal effect.

5. Military bases and installations: firearms generally prohibited
Military bases and installations are treated much like the VA Hospital and U.S. Post Offices in that they have, and are governed by, a separate set of rules and regulations with respect to firearms on the premises. On military installations or bases the carrying of firearms or other dangerous weapons is generally prohibited. Military installations are governed by federal law under Title 32 of the Code of Federal Regulations. Moreover, the sections covering the laws governing and relating to military bases and installations are exceedingly numerous. There are, in fact, sections which are dedicated to only certain bases, for example, 32 CFR §552.98 which only governs the possessing, carrying, concealing, and transporting of firearms on Fort Stewart/Hunter Army Airfield.

H. Can municipalities restrict firearms rights?

No, because municipalities and counties are restricted by the Florida Legislature from passing ordinances further restricting firearm rights. Specifically, municipalities cannot restrict the purchase, sale, transfer, ownership, manufacture, possession, storage, taxation, and trasportations of firearms. Florida Statute §790.33

IV. HOW BIG OF A HANDGUN CAN A CWFL HOLDER LEGALLY CARRY?

As we mentioned in Chapter Two, federal law dictates that any firearm which has any barrel with a bore of more than one-half inch in diameter (.50 caliber) is a "destructive device" and is subject to the National Firearms Act (except for certain shotguns). Possession of any such firearm without the proper paperwork associated with NFA firearms is illegal whether a person is a CWFL holder or not. For more information on destructive devices and the NFA, see Chapter Fourteen.

V. CWFL HOLDERS DEALING WITH LAW ENFORCEMENT

Do I legally have to present my CWFL to a police officer if they ask for my identification and I am carrying my gun?

There is no requirement in Florida to notify a police officer that you have a CWFL. However, anyone who is carrying a concealed firearm or weapon must at all times carry their CWFL and provide it to law enforcement upon request. Whether you voluntarily let the officer know you are carrying is a personal decision, however, from a practical standpoint, it may be a lot better for you to tell a police officer that you have a CWFL and a concealed weapon on you, than for them to find out on their own, as that might result in you seeing their firearm.

VI. CAN A POLICE OFFICER LEGALLY TAKE A CWFL HOLDER'S HANDGUN AWAY?

Yes, police are allowed to disarm CWFL holders in the interest of officer safety. A police officer can disarm a CWFL holder and confiscate the CWFL of a person whom he has arrested for a criminal offense. In addition, a police officer may disarm a CWFL holder during an encounter with the CWFL holder if the officer reasonably believes it is necessary to disarm them for the protection of the CWFL holder, the police officer, or any other individual.

At the conclusion of the encounter with the CWFL holder, the officer shall return the firearm to the CWFL holder, if he determines that the CWFL holder is not a threat and has not committed any violation of the law resulting in arrest. Keep in mind, however, that the law does not dictate the manner in which the officer must return the firearm. Many times, CWFL holders receive their firearm back unloaded, disassembled, or placed in an area of the car where it was not originally located.

PRACTICAL LEGAL TIP

Having a Concealed Weapon and Firearm License can make you feel safer as you are out and about. But remember, a CWFL is a license to protect against trouble—not to go looking for it! -James

VII. WHAT ARE PASSENGERS WITH A CWFL IN A VEHICLE LEGALLY OBLIGATED TO DO WHEN THE DRIVER IS STOPPED BY LAW ENFORCEMENT?

A passenger in a vehicle stopped by the police with a CWFL who is carrying a concealed weapon is only required to present their CWFL if they are asked for it by the officer.

VII. RECIPROCITY

A. Can I carry a concealed handgun in other states if I have a Florida CWFL?

Yes, in the following states that recognize a Florida CWFL:

Alabama	Alaska	Arizona+	Arkansas	Colorado*
Delaware+	Georgia	Idaho+	Indiana	Iowa+
Kansas	Kentucky+	Louisiana	Maine*+	Michigan*
Mississippi	Missouri+	Montana+	Nebraska	New Hampshire
New Mexico	North Carolina	North Dakota+	Ohio	Oklahoma
Pennsylvania*	South Carolina*	South Dakota	Tennessee	Texas
Utah	Vermont+	Virginia	West Virginia	Wyoming

*Indicates only recognizes Florida CWFLs for Florida residents
+Indicates all weapons covered by a CWFL are legal to carry in this state.

Reciprocity either exists between Florida and these states or they have unilaterally decided to recognize Florida CWFLs. Every state has the authority to determine whether or not their state will recognize a carry license or permit issued by another state. Reciprocity occurs when states enter into an agreement with each other, in this case, to recognize each other's carry licenses. However, states are not required to have reciprocity with one another nor are they required to recognize another state's carry license.

There are many states that issue their own licenses, but refuse to recognize a carry license from another state. Conversely, there are states that choose to recognize some or all other states' carry licenses. As of the date of writing, a Florida CWFL is recognized by 35 other states.

B. What out-of-state handgun licenses does Florida recognize?

Florida recognizes handgun licenses issued by the following states:

Alabama	Alaska	Arizona	Arkansas	Colorado
Delaware	Georgia	Idaho	Indiana	Iowa
Kansas	Kentucky	Louisiana	Maine	Michigan
Mississippi	Missouri	Montana	Nebraska	New Hampshire
New Mexico	North Carolina	North Dakota	Ohio	Oklahoma
Pennsylvania	South Carolina	South Dakota	Tennessee	Texas
Utah	Virginia	West Virginia	Wyoming	

A license holder from one of these states must be a resident of the state that issued the license and be at least 21 years old. An out-of-state handgun license holder must follow Florida law while in Florida just like a Florida CWFL holder must follow the laws of the state he or she is visiting.

IX. WHAT STATE'S LAWS APPLY WHEN USING MY FLORIDA CWFL IN ANOTHER STATE?

Anytime a CWFL holder is in another state, the laws of the state they are visiting apply. Even if that state recognizes a Florida CWFL, the law of the State the CWFL holder is in governs their possession and use of firearms and other weapons. If a person is traveling to another state, they must abide by that state's laws, just like a non-Floridian visiting Florida must follow Florida's law. Floridians who travel outside the state should make sure they are aware of the visited state's requirement to present a license and the places that are off-limits to firearms or other weapons, as these vary greatly from state to state. For example, a CWFL holder will only be allowed to carry a concealed or open handgun in Texas and not be legally allowed to carry other forms of weapons which they would be allowed to carry in Florida pursuant to Florida's CWFL.

X. CAN PERSONS WHO ARE NOT FLORIDA RESIDENTS OBTAIN A FLORIDA CWFL?

Yes. Florida Statute §790.06 authorizes the Florida Department of Agriculture and Consumer Services to issue CWFL to persons who are legal residents of the United States and are citizen of the United States or are permanent resident aliens of the United States, as determined by the United States Bureau of Citizenship and Immigration Services, or a consular security official of a foreign government that maintains diplomatic relations and treaties of commerce, friendship, and navigation with the United States and are certified as such by the foreign government and by the appropriate embassy in this country. Florida Statute §790.06(2)(a). There is no specific requirement that a CWFL applicant be a resident of the state of Florida. Therefore, the other states have many residents who carry Florida non-resident CWFLs.

CHAPTER THIRTEEN

UNDERSTANDING FIREARMS
FIREARMS WITHOUT A CWFL
Possessing, Carrying, And Transporting

I. WHERE CAN I CARRY MY FIREARM WITHOUT A LICENSE?

Florida law allows a person to carry a handgun or other type of firearm concealed or open in a few select places. First, you can carry a firearm at your home or place of business. Additionally, the carry of firearms is also allowed when traveling to and from places where firearms are typically used – for example, it is lawful to possess or use a firearm for fishing, hunting, or camping and when going to or returning from such an expedition; as well as while going to or from shooting if you are a regularly enrolled member of a target, skeet, or trap shooting club. Also, if you are firing weapons for testing or target practice under safe conditions, you may carry a firearm. Florida Statute §790.25(3) (g),(h),(j),(k). Significantly, if you stop to get gas or eat while on your way to fishing, hunting or camping, you are no longer on your way to fishing, hunting or camping. Rather, under the law, you are now considered to be on your way to get gas or eat. As a result, you cannot carry a handgun openly, but a non-license holder may still carry a handgun in a motor vehicle as long as it is concealed and securely encased. However, long guns used for hunting may be open in the vehicle.

Regularly enrolled members of a modern or antique firearms collecting club can carry openly or concealed going to or from a collector's gun show, convention, or exhibit. If you are engaged in manufacturing, repairing, or dealing in firearms, you or your representative can carry while engaged in the lawful course of the business. Lastly, an unloaded pistol can be carried in a secure wrapper from a place of purchase to home or to a place of business, or it may be carried back and forth between a place of repair and your home or place of business. Florida Statute §790.25(3)(g), (i), (m).

Openly carrying a firearm in public is not legal in Florida, except as mentioned above. Florida Statutes §§790.053 and 790.25(3)(a)(q).

II. WHERE ARE FIREARMS PROHIBITED IN FLORIDA?
Under Florida law, concealed firearms, as well as any other type of concealed weapon that may be carried with a CWFL (*e.g.* electronic weapons, tear gas guns, knives, etc.) are specifically prohibited in a number of places, as set out in Florida Statute §790.06(12). This means that holders of a CWFL may not carry in the following locations.

A. Places Where Firearms are Prohibited

1. Florida guns in schools laws

The possession of a firearm on school grounds is generally illegal, with few exceptions. Florida Statute §790.06, contains a number of subsections that explicitly prohibit the carrying and possession of firearms on school grounds. Firearms are not allowed at any school or college athletic event not related to firearms. Florida Statute §790.06(12)(9). Florida Statute §790.115 broadens this prohibition by applying it to all school-sponsored events and school property. A person may not possess a firearm or other weapon at a school-sponsored event or on the property of any school, school bus, or school bus stop subject to the exception explained below, found in Florida Statute §790.115. This includes the grounds of any elementary or secondary school facility or administration building, and career centers. Florida Statute §790.06(12)(a)(10)-(11).

Florida does not allow for the concealed or open carry of firearms on university or college campuses. However, if an individual is a registered student, employee, or faculty member of the college or university, they may carry a stun gun or nonlethal electric weapon or device designed solely for defensive purposes, if it does not fire a dart or projectile. Florida Statute §790.06(12).

As mentioned above, a person may carry, under one of the few exceptions laid out in Florida Statute §790.115(2)(a). A firearm can be carried in a case to a firearms program, class or function that has been approved in advance by the principal or chief administrative officer of the school as a program or class to which a firearm can be carried, or carried in a case to a career center having a firearms training range. Florida Statute §790.115(2)(a)(1)-(2).

NOTE: SCHOOL PARKING LOTS

Concealed firearms can be carried without a license, in a vehicle, under Florida law as long as a person is 18 or older, and the firearm is securely encased or otherwise not readily accessible for immediate use. Florida Statute §790.25(5). This extends to the carry of a firearm in a person's vehicle on the grounds of a school or at a school activity; however, school districts are free to adopt written and published policies that waive this exception for purposes of student and campus parking privileges. Florida Statute §790.115(2)(a)(3). This means that, while firearms in vehicles on school parking lots are legal under state law, an individual school may have a policy that makes it illegal to have one on the lot. Further, provided that a school does not have a policy prohibiting firearms on the property, they still may not be taken outside of the vehicle or into a school building.

NOTE: CHURCHES WITH SCHOOLS

Whether or not one may carry a firearm with a CWFL to church will depend on whether or not the church has a school component or day care component. Florida Statute §790.115 defines schools to include preschools. A child care facility includes any child care center or child care arrangement which provides child care for more than five children unrelated to the operator and which receives a payment, fee, or grant for any of the children receiving care, wherever operated, whether or not operated for profit. Florida Statute §402.302(2). *See* also Fl. Ad. Code §65C-22. Therefore, if your church has a school, daycare or child care facility with more than five children, you are not going to be able to carry a firearm to church services. This applies even if the school is not in the same building as the services you are attending and still applies even if the school is closed on the day you are attending services.

2. Federal Gun-Free School Zone Law: 18 U.S.C. §922(q)

The federal "Gun Free School Zone" law is found in the United States Code, 18 U.S.C. §922(q). Under this law, it is a federal crime for an individual to possess a firearm that has moved through interstate commerce (which includes virtually every firearm), on the grounds of or within 1,000 feet of a public, parochial, or private school. This takes the prohibition on carrying a firearm to a school one step further than Florida state law – even making the mere possession of a firearm by an occupant of a motor vehicle driving past a school or dropping their child off a federal crime!

However, seven exceptions are provided:

1. Exception one

If the possession is on private property which is not part of the school grounds. This means that a person living within 1,000 feet of a school can keep a firearm in their house.

2. Exception two

If the individual possessing the firearm is licensed to do so by the state in which the school zone is located or a political subdivision of the state, and the law of the state or political subdivision requires that, before an individual obtains such a license, the law enforcement authorities of the state or political subdivision verify that the individual is qualified under law to receive the license. This means that a CWFL holder may legally carry a concealed firearm into a "gun free school zone." However, there is one important note about the statute: a person can only lawfully carry in a school zone located in the state that issued the firearms license. Therefore, if a person has a Florida CWFL, they can only carry through Florida school zones. If that Florida CWFL holder is traveling through another state, the exception under federal law does not apply to them, and they will be violating the law if they travel through a school zone in that state. It also means that a Florida resident, who holds a non-resident, non-Florida concealed carry license or permit, does not benefit from this exception and will be in violation of the law if they take a firearm into a school zone.

3. Exception three

If the firearm is not loaded, and is in a locked container, or a locked firearms rack that is on a motor vehicle. This means that if a firearm is unloaded and carried in a locked case - a glove box or trunk, for example - there is no violation of the federal law.

4. Exception four

If the firearm is carried by an individual for use in a program approved by a school in the school zone. This exception covers school-sponsored shooting activities, such as an ROTC program.

5. Exception five

If the firearm is carried by an individual in accordance with a contract entered into between a school in the school zone and the individual or an employer of the individual. This means that school security guards can carry firearms while on the job.

6. Exception six

If the firearm is carried by a law enforcement officer acting in his or her official capacity. This exception covers police officers while on-duty only. It does not appear to cover them while they are off-duty, even if they are required by state law to carry while off-duty.

7. Exception seven

If the firearm is unloaded and is in the possession of an individual while traversing school property for the purpose of gaining access to public or private lands open to hunting, if the entry on school premises is authorized by school authorities. This means that if a hunter must cross school property to get to a lawful hunting ground, they must have the permission of the school, and the firearm must be unloaded.

3. Reconciling Florida and federal laws on gun-free school zones
Fortunately, Florida state law and federal law are similar in their allowances for firearms in school parking lots. Florida state law allows a firearm to be carried in a school parking lot if it is concealed, and either in a secure, locked container or otherwise not readily accessible for immediate use, and exception three to the Gun Free School Zone Act above allows an unloaded firearm to be carried in a locked container or locked firearms rack.

The lesson from this is that if you intend to carry a firearm in your vehicle onto a school parking lot while in your vehicle, the firearm should be unloaded and in a locked container or gun rack, thus satisfying the requirements of both state and federal law. This includes rifles and shotguns, which do not otherwise require storage in a locked container under Florida law. A rifle or shotgun stored in the vehicle according to Florida law is not necessarily legal under the Gun Free School Zone Act.

B. Traveling with your firearm (or other weapon)
1. Florida law on taking a firearm in your vehicle
Concealed handguns may be carried in an individual's vehicle in Florida without a license if the driver is over 18 years of age, and the handgun is either "securely encased" or otherwise "not readily accessible for immediate use." Florida Statute §790.25(5). A CWFL

holder may carry a concealed handgun on their person inside their vehicle with no problem. Rifles and shotguns do not need to be concealed and may be carried "anywhere in a private 'conveyance' when such firearm is being carried for a lawful use, which includes activities such as self-defense and hunting. Id.

2. When is a concealed handgun "securely encased" or "not readily accessible for immediate use" so as to allow it in a vehicle?

Florida Statute §790.001(17) defines "securely encased" as "in a glove compartment, whether or not locked; snapped in a holster; in a gun case, whether or not locked; in a zippered gun case; or in a closed box or container which requires a lid or cover to be opened for access."

"Readily accessible for immediate use" means "that a firearm or other weapon is carried on the person or within such close proximity and in such a manner that it can be retrieved and used as easily and quickly as if carried on the person." Florida Statute §790.001(16). Therefore, a firearm not readily accessible for immediate use would be one that is not on an individual's person or in such close proximity that they can use it as easily as if it they were carrying it.

EXAMPLE

Joe, a non-CWFL holder, was stopped for speeding. When he went to open his glove compartment to get his registration, the officer noticed a handgun concealed by a newspaper on the passenger's seat. Although the handgun had been concealed it was not securely encased and was readily accessible for immediate use. Instead of getting a speeding ticket, Joe was arrested.

3. Can a person legally conceal a handgun with their body while they are in their vehicle?

A person who does not have a CWFL may not have a concealed handgun on their person while in their vehicle. Florida Statute §790.25(5). While the statute says a concealed firearm can be carried in a vehicle, it goes on to say "[n]othing herein contained shall be construed to authorize the carrying of a concealed firearm or other weapon on the person." Florida Statute §790.25(5). Thus, you can have the gun in the car, but you cannot carry it on your body if you do not have a CWFL. What about having a handgun on the floor of the vehicle, underneath the driver's seat, so it is easily accessible in case of an emergency? Having the handgun so close and presumably not in a case will make it readily accessible for immediate use, therefore not allowed.

4. Is it legal for the owner of a vehicle to possess a handgun when a passenger in the vehicle is a felon or is otherwise disqualified from possessing firearms?

Yes, as long as the felon (or person disqualified from ownership) never possesses the firearm. Florida law focuses on who has possession of the gun. Possession can be either actual or constructive – actual possession is where a person has physical possession of the gun and knowledge of the possession. Constructive possession is where a person who does not have physical possession of the gun nevertheless knows of its presence and has the ability to maintain control over it. *Wilcox v. State*, 522 So. 2d 1062, 1063 (Fla. 3rd 1988). If the felon or disqualified person either does not know about the firearm, or does not have the ability to exercise control over it (because it is in a locked glove compartment or case, for example), then they are not in constructive or actual possession of the firearm.

5. May I keep a firearm in my vehicle if there are children in the car?

Yes, however, it is a third-degree felony crime for a person to expose another to personal injury by negligently storing or leaving a loaded firearm within the reach or easy access of a minor if the minor obtains the firearm and then uses it to inflict injury or death on him or herself or someone else. Florida Statute §784.05(1),(3). Subsection (3)(a) provides an exception for firearms stored or left in securely locked boxes or containers, or in locations where a reasonable person would have believed the firearm to be secure, or if the firearm was securely locked with a trigger lock.

6. May I possess a firearm while riding in another person's vehicle?

A firearm can be carried in another person's vehicle if it is otherwise legally carried by a CWFL holder, securely encased, etc.

7. Possessing a firearm on public transportation

Florida Statute §790.25(3)(l), allows a person to have firearms, other weapons, ammunition, and supplies on a public conveyance (which includes buses, trains, etc.) if the weapon is securely encased and not in the person's manual possession, for instance, in the luggage compartment of a bus.

C. Traveling across state lines with a firearm

1. Federal law: qualifying for firearms "Safe Passage"

If a person wants to travel across state lines with a firearm, they may need to make use of the federal "Safe Passage" provision. This law allows individuals who are legally in possession of firearms in their state (the starting point of their travel) to travel through states that may not be as friendly to firearms owners. This protection is only available when transporting firearms across state lines for lawful purposes, and as long as the individual complies with the requirements of the Firearm Owners Protection Act, 18 U.S.C. §926A, which is another name for the "Safe Passage" law. The first requirement to qualify for "safe passage" is that throughout the duration of the trip through an anti-firearm state, any firearm must be unloaded and locked in the trunk or in a container that is out of reach or not readily accessible from the passenger compartment (where the occupants of the vehicle sit). Any ammunition must also be locked in the trunk or container. Note that for the storage of both firearms and ammunition, the glove box and center console are prohibited places of storage under the statute.

2. "Safe Passage" requires legal start to legal finish

To get protection under federal law, a gun owner's journey must start and end in states where the traveler's possession of the firearm is legal. For example, let's say Joe can legally possess a Glock 17 in both Oklahoma and Vermont. Joe starts his trip in Oklahoma, planning to end it in Vermont. Even though Joe must drive through New York or Massachusetts to get to Vermont, because his starting point, Oklahoma, and his ending destination, Vermont, both allow the possession of the firearm, Joe will qualify under the Safe Passage provision. However, if the start point is Oklahoma, and the end point is New York (a place where the handgun would be illegal), there is no protection under the federal law. Safe passage requires legal start and legal finish.

Although traveling across state lines naturally invokes federal law, it is important to remember that whenever a person completes their journey and reaches their destination, the laws of that state control the possession, carry, and use of the firearm. Federal law does not make it legal or provide any protection for possessing a firearm that is illegal under the laws of the destination state.

3. What is the definition of "traveling" for purposes of Safe Passage?

The final requirement for protection under the federal law is that individuals MUST be "traveling" while in a firearm hostile state. The legal definition of "traveling" is murky, but has historically been interpreted narrowly by the courts. Generally speaking, if a person stops somewhere for too long, they cease to be "traveling" and, therefore, lose their safe passage protection. How long this time limit is has not been determined either statutorily or by case law with any definitiveness.

4. Protection under federal law does not mean protection from prosecution in unfriendly states.

To make matters worse for traveling gun owners, even if a person qualifies for protection under the federal Safe Passage provision, New Jersey and New York treat this protection as a mere affirmative defense. This means that a person can be arrested in those states even though he or she met all of the requirements of the federal statute. The person's only recourse is to go to court and assert federal safe passage as a defense. This becomes even more troublesome in the case where someone is legally flying with their firearms, and then due to flight complications, must land in New Jersey or New York. Travelers in this position have been arrested or threatened with arrest in the past.

Once again, the Safe Passage provision only applies while a person is traveling. As soon as they arrive at their destination and cease their travels, the laws of that state control the carry and possession of a firearm. Remember: check all applicable state firearms laws before you leave for your destination.

5. May a person keep a firearm in their hotel room?

Yes. A hotel or motel room is considered to be the private dwelling of an occupant as long as he or she is legally there, has paid or arranged to pay rent, and has not been requested to leave by management. *Wassmer v. State*, 565 So. 2d 856, 857 (Fla. 2nd DCA 1990). Because Florida law allows the possession of a firearm in a person's home (dwelling for these purposes), a person may also possess one in a hotel room if they meet the requirements above.

One other consideration to keep in mind is that a hotel, or any other private business, has the right and ability to prohibit entry onto their property by anyone possessing a firearm. A person who has actual knowledge that they are not permitted to enter onto or remain on private property who refuses to leave may be committing a trespass.

6. Can I keep a firearm in my RV?

Yes, an RV is considered a "conveyance" under Florida law. If you choose to take a firearm in your RV, it must be securely encased or otherwise not readily accessible for immediate use, just like any other vehicle, unless you have a CWFL.

7. Traveling with other weapons (billies, knives, etc.)

In Florida, local municipalities are not allowed to make laws regarding firearms (see preemption elsewhere in this book). Florida Statutes §790.33. Local laws concerning other weapons such as knives, billie clubs, tasers, etc. are not preempted by state law, and therefore, any city or county may have their own laws concerning the carry and possession of these weapons. For example, Miami-Dade County has a section in their code of ordinances that explicitly prohibits the concealed carry of "any deadly weapon," which includes bowie knives, razors, dirks, daggers, or any knife resembling a bowie knife.

D. Air travel with a firearm

1. How do I legally travel with a firearm as a passenger on a commercial airline?

It is legal under both federal and Florida state law to travel with firearms on commercial airlines as long as they are unloaded and in a locked, hard-sided container as checked baggage. Florida Statute §790.06(12)(a)(14). Under federal law, the container must be completely inaccessible to passengers. Further, under U.S. Homeland Security rules, firearms, ammunition, and firearm parts – including frames, receivers, clips, and magazines – are prohibited in carry-on baggage. The Transportation Security Administration (TSA) also requires realistic replicas of firearms to be packed in checked baggage, but they do allow rifle-scopes to be carried in both carry-on and checked bags.

2. Firearms must be inaccessible

Federal law makes it a crime punishable by fine, imprisonment up to 10 years, or both, if a person "[is] on, or attempting to get on, an aircraft in, or intended for operation in, air transportation or intrastate air transportation, has on or about the individual or the property of the individual a concealed dangerous weapon that is or would be accessible to the individual in flight." 49 U.S.C. §46505(b). In other words, if you are getting on a plane to travel or are traveling, you better not have a firearm accessible to you. Additionally, under 49 U.S.C. §46303(a), you could also be liable to the United States Government for a civil penalty of up to $10,000.

3. Firearms must be checked in baggage

The TSA has issued the following guidelines for those looking to travel with firearms on airlines:

- All firearms must be declared to the airline during the ticket counter check-in process.
- The term firearm includes:
  - □ Any weapon (including a starter gun) which will, or is designed to, or may readily be converted to expel a projectile by the action of an explosive.
  - □ The frame or receiver of any such weapon.
  - □ Any firearm muffler or firearm silencer.
  - □ Any destructive device.
- The firearm must be unloaded.
  - □ As defined 49 CFR §1540.5, 'A loaded firearm means a firearm that has a live round of ammunition, or any component thereof, in the chamber or cylinder or in a magazine inserted in the firearm.'
- The firearm must be in a hard-sided container that is locked. A locked container is defined as one that completely secures the firearm from being accessed. Locked cases that can be pulled open with little effort cannot be brought aboard the aircraft.
- If firearms are not properly declared or packaged, TSA will provide the checked bag to law enforcement for resolution with the airline. If the issue is resolved, law enforcement will release the bag to TSA so screening may be completed.
- TSA must resolve all alarms in checked baggage. If a locked container containing a firearm alarms, TSA will contact the airline, who will make a reasonable attempt to contact the owner and advise the passenger to go to the screening location. If contact is not made, the container will not be placed on the aircraft.
- If a locked container alarms during screening and is not marked

as containing a declared firearm, TSA will cut the lock in order to resolve the alarm.

- Travelers should remain in the area designated by the aircraft operator or TSA representative to take the key back after the container is cleared for transportation.
- Travelers must securely pack any ammunition in fiber (such as cardboard), wood or metal boxes or other packaging specifically designed to carry small amounts of ammunition.
- Firearm magazines and ammunition clips, whether loaded or empty, must be securely boxed or included within a hard-sided case containing an unloaded firearm.
- Small arms ammunition, including ammunition not exceeding .75 caliber for a rifle or pistol and shotgun shells of any gauge, may be carried in the same hard-sided case as the firearm, as long as it follows the packing guidelines described above.
- TSA prohibits black powder or percussion caps used with black-powder.
- Rifle scopes are not prohibited in carry-on bags and do not need to be in the hard-sided, locked checked bag."

See www.tsa.gov

4. May I have a firearm while operating or as a passenger in a private aircraft flying just in Florida?

Yes. The provisions of Florida law allowing a person to have a concealed handgun or other firearm in their vehicle also allow a person to have a firearm in their private aircraft under the same conditions. The definition of conveyance includes aircraft as well as motor vehicles. Florida Statute §810.011(3).

5. May I have a firearm in a private aircraft that takes off from Florida and lands in another state?

In situations when a private aircraft is taking off from one state and landing in another, the law will view this in the same way it views traveling interstate with firearms in a vehicle. Where no other statutes apply to the person's flight, the person will be subject to the provisions of 18 U.S.C. §926A regarding the interstate transportation of a firearm: "any person who is not otherwise prohibited by this chapter from transporting, shipping, or receiving a firearm shall be entitled to transport a firearm for any lawful purpose from any place where he may lawfully possess and carry such firearm to any other place where he may lawfully possess and carry such firearm, if during such transportation the firearm is unloaded, and neither the firearm nor any ammunition being transported is readily accessible or is directly accessible from the passenger compartment of such transporting vehicle."

This statute allows a person to transport firearms between states subject to the following conditions: that the person can lawfully possess the firearm at his or her points of departure and arrival, and that the firearm remain unloaded and inaccessible during the trip. However, what if the person is a CWFL holder and wants to carry concealed between states? Fortunately, 18 U.S.C. §927 states that Section 926A does not preempt applicable state law. Thus, if a person can lawfully carry a concealed weapon in the state in which he or she boards the aircraft and in the state in which he or she lands, the CWFL holder is not subject to the unloaded and inaccessible restrictions of Section 926A.

For operations of private aircraft within a single state other than that person's home state, a person will only be subject to the laws of the state within which he or she is in operation. A person will need to review the state's statutes where they will be flying to determine whether they impose any restrictions on possession of firearm within non-secure areas of airports. The person will also need to be familiar with the airports he or she will be visiting to determine whether each airport has any restrictions (*e.g.* a posting notifying of the prohibition of concealed carry, etc.).

III. FIREARMS AND BOATING IN THE SUNSHINE STATE
A. Can I take my firearm on waters in Florida?
Unlike many other states, Florida is fortunate to have hundreds of miles of beaches and beautiful waters for boating. Fortunately for Floridians, it is lawful for a person without a CWFL to have a concealed handgun, rifle, or shotgun in their boat or ship. The definition of conveyance discussed above includes not only motor vehicles and aircraft, but also any ship or vessel. Again, the same conditions apply when carrying a concealed handgun in a boat or other vessel as when carrying in a vehicle or private aircraft – a concealed handgun must be securely encased or otherwise not readily accessible for immediate use unless you have a CWFL. Florida Statute §810.011(3).

There is an exception allowing concealed carry for those legally hunting or fishing in the state. If an individual is legally hunting or fishing from their boat, they may have their firearm accessible. Additionally, if the boater or passenger has a valid CWFL, or a recognized concealed carry license from another state, they may carry a handgun concealed on their person. Florida Statute §790.25(3)(h).

However, it is worth noting that no firearms are allowed in restricted or secured Florida seaports. Florida Statute §311.12(3)(b). "Any person in a restricted area who has in his or her possession a concealed weapon, or who operate or has possession or control of a vehicle in or upon which a concealed weapon is placed or stored, commits a misdemeanor of the first degree..." Each seaport is required by law to post appropriate signs and markers on the premises notifying individuals that firearms are prohibited.

B. What about boating with a firearm in the waters of another state or country?

It is important to realize that state laws differ, so it is wise to contact the law enforcement agency local to where you will be boating to get more information. The same applies to other countries if you intend to dock in a foreign port, you should contact that country's consulate in advance to find out what their laws say regarding the possession of firearms in your boat or vessel. Many countries have very strict firearms laws, with potentially severe consequences that come along with violating them.

In international waters, the laws of the boat's "Flag of Origin" govern. Therefore, Florida law will regulate a ship that is registered in Florida. The Coast Guard may board an individual's vessel at any time and perform random searches. If this happens, a person should immediately inform officers that they are in possession of a firearm. The standard Coast Guard procedure is to document the serial number of any firearm the person has on board.

> CHAPTER FOURTEEN ◄

RESTORATION OF FIREARMS RIGHTS
FIREARMS RIGHTS
The Law Of Pardons
And Expungements

I. IS IT POSSIBLE TO RESTORE A PERSON'S RIGHT TO BEAR ARMS?

What chapter deals with when and where a pershat happens after a person has been convicted of a crime, is it possible to later clear their name and/or criminal record? If possible, what is the process for removing a conviction and restoring a person's right to purchase and possess firearms? This chapter will explain how a person under very limited circumstances can have arrest records, criminal charges, and even criminal convictions removed or nullified. But success in this arena is rare. Further, each state has different rules concerning these issues as well as a completely different set of rules under federal law. Before we begin a meaningful discussion, it is important to explain two terms and concepts: clemency and expungement.

A. What is clemency?

Clemency is the action the government, usually the chief executive (*e.g.*, the President on the federal level or a governor on the state level), takes in forgiving or pardoning a crime or canceling the penalty of a crime, either wholly, or in part. Clemency can include full pardons after a conviction, full pardons after completion of deferred adjudication community supervision, conditional pardons, pardons based on innocence, commutations of a sentence, emergency medical reprieves, and family medical reprieves. Clemency can be granted at both the federal and state level.

B. What is expungement?

Expungement is the physical act of destroying or purging

government criminal records, unlike sealing which is simply hiding the records from the public. Under certain circumstances, a person may have their criminal record either expunged or sealed.

II. FEDERAL LAW

A. Presidential pardon

Under Article II, Section 2 of the United States Constitution, the President of the United States has the power "to grant reprieves and pardons for offenses against the United States, except in cases of impeachment." The President's power to pardon offenses has also been interpreted to include the power to grant conditional pardons, commutations of sentence, conditional commutations of sentence, remission of fines and forfeitures, respites, and amnesties. However, the President's clemency authority only extends to federal offenses; the President cannot grant clemency for a state crime.

1. How does a person petition for federal clemency or a pardon?

Under federal law, a person requesting executive clemency must petition the President of the United States and submit the petition to the Office of the Pardon Attorney in the Department of Justice. The Office of the Pardon Attorney can provide petitions and other required forms necessary to complete the application for clemency. *See* 28 CFR §1.1. Petition forms for commutation of sentence may also be obtained from the wardens of federal penal institutions. In addition, a petitioner applying for executive clemency with respect to military offenses should submit his or her petition directly to the Secretary of the military branch that had original jurisdiction over the court-martial trial and conviction of the petitioner.

The Code of Federal Regulations requires an applicant to wait five years after the date of the release of the petitioner from confinement, or in a case where no prison sentence was imposed, an applicant is required to wait five years after the date of conviction prior to submitting a petition for clemency. The regulation further states that "generally, no petition should be submitted by a person who is on probation, parole, or supervised release." *See* 28 CFR §1.2. With that in mind, the President can grant clemency at any time, whether an individual has made a formal petition or not. For example, President Gerald Ford granted a full and unconditional pardon to former President Richard Nixon prior to any indictment or charges being filed related to his involvement in Watergate.

2. What should a petition for clemency include?

Petitions for executive clemency should include the information required in the form prescribed by the United States Attorney General.

This includes information:

1. that the person requesting clemency must state specifically the purpose for which clemency is sought, as well as attach any and all relevant documentary evidence that will support how clemency will support that purpose;
2. that discloses any arrests or convictions subsequent to the federal crime for which clemency is sought;
3. that discloses all delinquent credit obligations (whether disputed or not), all civil lawsuits to which the applicant is a party (whether plaintiff or defendant), and all unpaid tax obligations (whether local, state, or federal);
4. that includes three character affidavits from persons not related to the applicant by blood or marriage.

In addition, acceptance of a Presidential pardon generally carries with it an admission of guilt. For that reason, a petitioner should include in his or her petition a statement of the petitioner's acceptance of responsibility, an expression of remorse, and atonement for the offense. All of the requirements are contained in 28 CFR §§1.1-1.11.

3. What happens after a petition for executive clemency is submitted?

All petitions for federal clemency are reviewed by the Office of the Pardon Attorney in the Department of Justice. A non-binding recommendation on an application is made to the President. Federal regulations also provide for guidelines and requirements to notify victims of the crimes, if any, for which clemency is sought. The President will either grant or deny a pardon. There are no hearings held on the petition, and there is no appeal of the President's decision.

4. What is the effect of a Presidential Pardon?

A pardon is the forgiveness of a crime and the cancellation of the penalty associated with that crime. While a Presidential Pardon will restore various rights lost as a result of the pardoned offense, it will not expunge the record of your conviction. This means that even if a person is granted a pardon, the person must still disclose their conviction on any form where such information is required, although the person may also disclose the fact that the offense for which they were convicted was pardoned.

B. Expungement of federal convictions

1. No law exists for general federal expungement

Congress has not provided federal legislation that offers any comprehensive authority or procedure for expunging criminal offenses. There exist only statues that allow expungement in certain cases for possession of small amounts of controlled substances (see below) and interestingly, a procedure to expunge DNA samples of certain members of the military wrongfully convicted. Because there is no statutory guidance, federal courts have literally made up the rules and procedures themselves, often coming to different conclusions. Some federal court circuits have stated they have no power to expunge records. However, other federal courts have indicated that they do have the power to expunge. The federal Fifth Circuit has held that under certain limited circumstances, federal courts may order expungement both of records held by other branches of the government (*e.g.*, executive branch), and its own court records. *See Sealed Appellant v. Sealed Appellee*, 130 F.3d 695 (5th Cir. 1997). Florida is within the federal Eleventh Circuit. However, pre-1981 it was part of the Fifth Circuit, therefore, Fifth Circuit decisions have authority as precedent in the Eleventh Circuit [*See Bonner v. City of Prichard*, 661 F.2d 1206, 1209 (11th Cir. 1981) (en banc)]. Also, in *Severson v. Duff*, 322 F.Supp. 4 (M.D. FL. 1970), the Middle District of Florida ordered that State records regarding a conviction for a constitutionally vague statute be expunged. The Supreme Court has passed on hearing cases that would have resolved the split between the circuits. This issue remains legally murky.

2. Possible procedure for federal expungement

There are no statutory guidelines for how to seek an expungement under federal law, however, the place to start would be to file a motion with the federal court that issued the conviction that a person wants to be expunged. However, federal judges very rarely grant these types of motions. Some circuits, including the Fifth Circuit, have adopted a balancing test to decide if a record held by the court may be expunged: "if the dangers of unwarranted adverse consequences to the individual outweigh the public interest in maintenance of the records, then expunction is appropriate." Further, these same courts have freely stated that this balancing test "rarely tips in favor of expungement," and that expungement should be granted in only the most extreme cases. *United States v. Flowers*, 389 F.3d 737 (7th Cir. 2004). Some of the areas where expungement has worked are in incidents of extreme police misconduct, or where the conviction is being misused against the person. Unless there exist compelling reasons, a federal judge is highly unlikely to grant expungement.

3. Expungement for drug possession: statutory authority

Under a federal law entitled "special probation and expungement procedures for drug possessors," certain persons are allowed to request a federal court to issue an expungement order from all public records. See 18 U.S.C. §3607. Congress intended this order to restore the person to the status he or she "occupied before such arrest or institution of criminal proceedings." 18 U.S.C. §3607(c).

In order to qualify for the expungement, you must have been under the age of 21 when you were convicted, you must have no prior drug offenses, and your conviction must have been for simple possession of a small amount of a controlled substance.

4. How does a person have firearms rights restored under federal law?

Under the Gun Control Act of 1968 (GCA), a person who has received a Presidential pardon is not considered convicted of a crime preventing the purchase and possession of firearms subject to all other federal laws. See 18 U.S.C. §§921(a)(20) and (a)(33). In addition, persons who had a conviction expunged or set aside, or who have had their civil rights restored are not considered to have been convicted for purposes of the GCA "unless the pardon, expungement, or restoration of civil rights expressly provides the person may not ship, transport, possess, or receive firearms." 18 U.S.C. §§921(a)(20) and (a)(33).

The GCA also provides the United States Attorney General with the authority to grant relief from firearms disabilities where the Attorney General determines that the person is not likely to act in a manner dangerous to the public safety and where granting relief would not be contrary to the public interest. See 18 U.S.C. §925(c). The Attorney General has delegated this authority to the ATF. Unfortunately, the ATF reports that it has been prohibited from spending any funds in order to investigate or act upon applications from individuals seeking relief from federal firearms disabilities. This means that until the ATF's prohibition has been lifted, a person's best—and most likely—option to have their firearms rights restored is through a Presidential pardon. See www.atf.gov.

III. FLORIDA LAW

A. Clemency by Governor and Board of Pardons and Paroles

The Governor of Florida possesses the authority to grant executive clemency under Article IV, Section 8(a) of the Florida Constitution of 1968, except in cases of treason and impeachment. Unlike federal clemency where the President is free to pardon whomever the President chooses, the Governor of Florida can only grant clemency if two members of the Clemency Board approves such recommendation. However, the Governor has full discretion to deny clemency for any reason without the approval of the Clemency Board. Furthermore, the Governor and the Clemency Board may grant executive clemency on a conditional basis, requiring an individual to perform various conditions. If an individual receives a conditional clemency and violates one of the conditions, the Clemency Board can revoke the clemency.

1. Are there different types of clemency in Florida?

There are eight different types of clemency in the State of Florida.

A. Full Pardon

This completely forgives a person for any convictions they received in Florida. A full Pardon restores all rights as they were prior to conviction. Most importantly these restored rights include the right to own, possess or use a firearm.

B. Pardon Without Firearm Authority

This allows an individual the same relief as a Full Pardon except the right to own, possess or use a firearm.

C. Pardon for Misdemeanor

This forgives anyone who has been convicted of a misdemeanor.

D. Commutation of Sentence

This allows an individual to have his penalty lowered to a less severe penalty. However, this type of clemency does not restore any of the individual's civil rights including the right to own, possess or use firearms.

E. Remission of Fines and Forfeitures

This form of clemency only suspends, reduces, or removes a fine or forfeiture. There is no restoration of civil rights including the right to own, possess or use firearms.

F. Specific Authority to Own, Possess or Use Firearms

This allows an individual who has been convicted of a felony to have his or her right to own, possess or use a firearm. In cases involving a federal conviction, the Clemency Board will only consider a request for this type of clemency if a Presidential Pardon or a Relief of Disability from the Bureau of Alcohol, Tobacco and Firearms has been granted. If the individual has a conviction from another state, then a pardon or restoration of civil rights with no restrictions on firearms is a prerequisite for this type of clemency.

G. Restoration of Civil Rights in Florida
This allows an individual to have his or her civil rights restored except for the right to own, possess or use firearms. Although the individual's civil rights are restored, he or she will still have to comply with all the registration and notifications requirements or any other obligations and restrictions imposed by law upon sexual predators or sexual offenders.

H. Restoration of Alien status under Florida Law
This gives a non-citizen of the United States, his or her civil rights under the authority of the State of Florida that he or she had prior to receiving a felony conviction. However, his or her right to own, possess or use firearms will not be restored.

2. Who is eligible for executive clemency in Florida?
Anyone seeking clemency in Florida must meet the requirement of the specific clemency they are seeking to obtain. However, individuals wanting to be able to own, possess or use a firearm must either receive a Pardon or Specific Authority to Own, Possess or Use Firearms.

The eligibility requirements for these two types of clemency are listed in the table below.

TYPE OF CLEMENCY	ELIGIBILITY REQUIREMENT
Pardons	• completed all sentences imposed for applicant's most recent felony conviction • at least 10 years has passed since the completion of all the conditions of supervision imposed for the applicant's most recent felony • satisfied all outstanding detainers, or any pecuniary penalties or liabilities which total more than $1,000.00 and result from any criminal conviction or traffic infractions • satisfied all outstanding restitution owed to any victim, including but not limited to restitution pursuant to a court order, civil judgment, or obligations pursuant to Chapter 960, Florida Statutes
Specific Authority to Own, Possess or Use Firearms	• completed all sentences imposed for applicant's most recent felony conviction • at least 8 years has passed since the completion of all the conditions of supervision imposed for the applicant's most recent felony • satisfied all outstanding detainers, or any pecuniary penalties or liabilities which total more than $1,000.00 and result from any criminal conviction or traffic infractions • satisfied all outstanding restitution owed to any victim, including but not limited to restitution pursuant to a court order, civil judgment, or obligations pursuant to Chapter 960, Florida Statutes • no prior federal, military, or out-of-state convictions

3. How does a person seek executive clemency in Florida?

A person seeking executive clemency in Florida is required to complete an application, which is available from the Office of Executive Clemency. Each applicant must attach a certified copy of the charging instrument and certified copy of the judgment and sentence for each conviction for which he or she is seeking clemency. Although not required, an applicant may include with their application character references, letters of support, and any other relevant documents. Once properly submitted, the file of any applicant eligible for clemency is forwarded to the Office of Clemency Investigation, which assigns the case to an examiner in the field offices.

Upon completion of the investigation by the Office of Clemency, a report is generated and submitted to the Clemency Board for a decision. The Clemency Board meets in the months of March, June, September and December of each year. The Governor may also call a special meeting at any time during the year. An applicant is not required to attend the hearing. If the Clemency Board grants clemency, a certificate of Restoration of Civil Rights will be mailed to the applicant

Applicants are not able to appeal the decision of the Clemency Board, but applicants may re-apply for clemency after at least two years has passed from the date of the final order denying clemency. For more information on the process, please visit www. fcor.state.fl.us.

4. What is the effect of executive clemency in Florida?

A person who received an executive clemency may have their civil rights restored, but unfortunately the criminal conviction will remain on his or her criminal record. Anyone convicted of a felony is not eligible to have their record sealed or expunged under Florida law regardless if he or she received a clemency.

B. Florida expungement

Florida Statute §943.0585 controls expungement under Florida law. This statute provides for when a person is entitled to expungement. Note that the technical term under Florida law is expunction, but we will use these terms interchangeably. This section allows a person to expunge their record if he or she were acquitted, had charges dismissed or were no-billed by a grand jury or the State Attorney's Office.

However, not all individuals are entitled to an expungement of their record. For instance, if a person was acquitted of one offense, but was convicted or remains subject to prosecution for another offense relating to or arising out of the charge for which they were acquitted, that person is not entitled to an expungement of their record. Anyone who has a prior conviction for any crime will not be eligible to have their record expunged. Additionally, if an adult was previously adjudicated a deliquent as a minor, he or she will not be eligile for expungement. A person is only allowed one expungement.

To obtain an expunction, a petitioner must first obtain a Certificate of Eligibility from Florida Department of Law Enforcement (FDLE). In order to obtain a Certificate of Eligibility, the petitioner must fill out an application which must be signed by the State Attorney's Office, provide fingerprints, a certified copy of the disposition and provide a $75 check or money order made out to FDLE. Once a Certificate of Eligibility is obtained, the petitioner must file a Petition for Expungement in the county in which the charge(s) originated in. A hearing on the Petition for Expungement may or not be required depending on the State Attorney's position and the Judge's preference.

➢ CHAPTER FIFTEEN ◄

I'M BEING SUED FOR WHAT?
CIVIL LIABILITY
If You Have Used Your Gun

I. WHAT DOES IT MEAN TO BE SUED?

The term "lawsuit" refers to one party's assertion in a written filing with a court that another party has violated the law. In the context of firearms, typically the party suing has been injured and wants a ruling or judgment from the court that will entitle the person suing to receive money.

A. What is a civil claim or lawsuit?

A civil "lawsuit" or "suit" refers to the actual filing of written paperwork with a court (1) asserting that another party violated the law, and (2) seeking some type of redress. A "claim" can exist without the filing of a lawsuit. A claim is simply the belief or assertion that another party has violated the law. Many parties have claims they never assert, or sometimes parties informally assert the claim in hopes of resolving the disputes without the filing of a lawsuit. Also, another term commonly used is "tort" or "tort claim." A tort is a civil claim arising out of a wrongful act, not including a breach of contract or trust, that results in injury to another's person, property, reputation, or the like. The claims described below are all tort claims.

B. Difference between "civil claims" and "criminal charges"

To start with the basics, there are two different arenas in the legal system that gun owners may face after the use of a firearm: criminal and civil. There are several names and descriptive terms used for each (e.g., civil lawsuit, criminal actions, civil claims, criminal proceedings, etc.), but regardless of the terms, the same breakdown applies; most cases are either criminal or civil. There is another subgroup of proceedings called administrative actions. Those actions are not covered by this chapter but can sometimes impact CWFL holders. For example, appealing the denial of a CWFL is an administrative act. See Chapter Eight for more information.

With that said, the three primary differences between a criminal action and a civil proceeding are: (1) who or what is bringing the action or lawsuit, (2) what they are seeking, and (3) what is the burden of proof? These differences are fairly straightforward:

1. State versus individual bringing claims

In a criminal case, the party bringing the action is the "sovereign," meaning the United States, state, municipality, county, etc. that believes that a person violated their laws. Even if an individual calls the police, fills out a criminal complaint, or even asks the state attorney to file charges, the party that actually brings a criminal action is the state, county, etc., not the individual.

However, a civil action may be filed by any individual, business, or other entity (partnership, LLC, trust, etc.). The entity bringing the claim is called the "plaintiff." Even governmental entities can bring civil claims; i.e., if you negligently shoot a county propane tank causing a fire, the county can sue you civilly for those damages. The typical gun case, though, will involve an individual filing a lawsuit against another individual for damages caused by the firearm. If the incident occurs at a place of business, the plaintiff may also sue the business claiming that it is in some way at fault for the incident. The party being sued is typically called the "defendant."

2. Relief sought/awarded

In a criminal case, the entity prosecuting the case is usually seeking to imprison or fine the person who they bring the action against. Most crimes are punishable by "X" number of days/months/years in prison or jail, and a fine not to exceed "X" dollars.

By contrast, the plaintiff in the civil case is almost always seeking a monetary award. Several other types of relief are available (declaratory, injunctive, specific performance), but for the most part, gun cases will involve the plaintiff seeking monetary damages.

3. Burden of proof

In a criminal case, the standard is "beyond a reasonable doubt." In civil cases, however, a plaintiff must prove a person is liable for damages by a "preponderance of the evidence" standard. A preponderance of the evidence is a much lower standard than the criminal standard of beyond a reasonable doubt. It generally means that the party with the greater weight of credible evidence wins that issue. The preponderance of the evidence has been described as more than half, that is, if the evidence demonstrates that something "more likely occurred than not," this meets the burden of proof. Whereas in a criminal case, if there exists any "reasonable doubt," the burden of proof is not met. It does not mean the party with the most exhibits or greater number of witnesses will prevail. One highly credible witness can prevail over the testimony of a dozen biased, shady witnesses.

EXAMPLE

John mistakes a utility meter reader for a burglar due to his disheveled appearance, tool bag, and because he looks to be snooping around John's house. John fires a shot without warning and injures the meter reader.

Possible criminal liability: the State of Florida could bring criminal charges against John for a number of crimes (aggravated assault, attempted murder, aggravated battery or with a firearm, and so forth). The State would be seeking to imprison or fine John for his conduct, and it would be required to prove that John committed the crime at issue "beyond a reasonable doubt."

Possible civil liability: the meter reader could also file a civil lawsuit against John alleging that John was negligent or committed the tort of assault. The meter reader would seek monetary damages and be required to prove his claims by a "preponderance of the evidence."

C. Impact of result in one court upon the other
1. Can a result in a criminal trial be used in a civil trial?
Yes, because of the legal doctrines of res judicata and collateral estoppel. These two legal doctrines govern the impact of a ruling or judgment in one case, upon a separate case involving the same set of facts and circumstances. For the present discussion, if a person is found guilty of a crime in a criminal proceeding, because that court uses a higher standard of "beyond a reasonable doubt" than the civil requirement of "preponderance of the evidence," the finding of the criminal court may be used for purposes of establishing civil liability. Entire chapters in law books have been written on these topics, so, suffice to say, this section is a brief overview of these laws.

The criminal concept of nolo contendere or "no contest" often generates confusion in this area. In a criminal case, a plea of nolo contendere or no contest means that the defendant does not admit guilt. The plea, however, still results in a judgment that the defendant is guilty of the crime and that judgment can be used to establish the defendant's liability in a separate civil case.

EXAMPLE

Phil and Jeremy become involved in a road rage incident and an altercation follows. Phil shoots Jeremy, wounding him. When all is sorted out, Phil is found guilty of criminal assault and receives punishment from the court (remember, criminal trials use the "beyond a reasonable doubt" standard).

If Jeremy later sues Phil from the injuries he received when Phil shot him, Jeremy, in his civil action, will very likely be allowed to use the finding of guilt in the criminal case (because it used the higher standard of beyond a reasonable doubt) to establish his burden in the civil case (the lower preponderance of the evidence standard) that he is owed damages or money in the civil case. This is an example of collateral estoppel; Phil will not be permitted to re-litigate his guilt in the civil case.

Both doctrines are based on the concept that a party to a legal proceeding should not be able to endlessly litigate issues that have already been decided by the legal system. At its most basic level, it means that a party to a legal proceeding who receives a final ruling on a particular issue, win or lose, cannot attempt to have another trial court or even the same court decide the same issue.

Note about appeals: this is a different concept than an appeal, or asking the court in the first proceeding to reconsider its ruling, or grant a new trial. An appeal is a request to a higher court to review the decision of a lower court. Likewise, in any given case, the parties will have numerous opportunities to ask the current court to reconsider its rulings, or even ask for a new trial after a trial is completed. Collateral estoppel and res judicata come into play after a final judgment that is no longer subject to appeal or revision by the trial court.

EXAMPLE

Michele is sued for accidentally shooting Nancy. Nancy wins a judgment of $350 against Michele, much less than Nancy believed she was damaged.

In that case, Nancy can appeal the decision, or even ask that trial court for a new trial. However, Nancy cannot file another, or new, lawsuit regarding the same incident and attempt to recover more in the second case because of the doctrine of res judicata. In order for the doctrine to apply, the facts, circumstances, and issues must be the same.

EXAMPLE

Justin fires his hunting rifle from his deer blind, hitting Peter with one round. Peter files a civil suit against Justin and loses at trial. The court awards Peter no damages. Peter appeals and loses the appeal also.

Peter is legally barred from recovering in another lawsuit against Justin involving the same incident. However, Peter is not barred from filing suit against Justin for damages arising out of another set of facts and circumstances, for example, if the two are involved in a car wreck on a different day.

2. Civil case result impact on criminal case

Suppose you lose a civil suit and a judgment is entered against you arising out of a shooting incident. Can that judgment be used to establish that you committed a crime? No. The burden of proof is much higher in the criminal context than the civil case. The plaintiff proved his civil case by a "preponderance of the evidence." This does not mean that he proved his case "beyond a reasonable doubt," meaning a separate criminal trial is required to make that determination.

The one area where a civil case can impact a criminal case is the potential overlapping use of evidence and testimony. Your admission in one case can almost always be used against you in another case. Meaning, your sworn testimony in the civil case ("Yes, I shot the guy") can almost always be used against you in the criminal case, and vice versa.

II. WHAT MIGHT YOU BE SUED FOR? GUN RELATED CLAIMS IN CIVIL COURTS

A. Liability for unintentional discharge

This section deals with accidental or unintentional discharges of your firearm. Common unintentional discharges are associated with hunting and cleaning accidents or the mishandling of a weapon. Intentional shootings are addressed in the following section.

With that said, the following are the types of civil claims that may be asserted in connection with an unintentional discharge:

1. Negligence/gross negligence

Most civil cases for damages resulting from an accidental discharge will include a negligence or gross negligence claim. What does this mean and what does a plaintiff have to prove before they can win? Under Florida law, negligence is defined as the failure to use ordinary care, that is, failing to do that which a person of ordinary prudence would have done under the same or similar circumstances, or doing that which a person of ordinary prudence would not have done under the same or similar circumstances. If a person fails to use ordinary care, then they have acted negligently and will be liable for damages resulting from their conduct. "Ordinary care" means that degree of care that would be used by a person of ordinary prudence under the same or similar circumstances. This is an "objective standard," meaning, the test is not whether you believed you acted prudently, but whether the judge or jury believes you acted as a person of ordinary prudence would have acted. Of course, this is the definition of negligence in the civil context. There is actually a different definition of criminal negligence, which is beyond the scope of this book's discussion.

What is gross negligence and how is it different than "regular" negligence? Many gun cases will include a claim for "gross negligence" by the plaintiff. The primary reason for this is that if a plaintiff establishes gross negligence by a defendant, the plaintiff may be entitled to additional types or amounts of money that are legally available than if mere negligence is established. In fact, Florida Statutes §768.72(2) states:

A defendant may be held liable for punitive damages only if the trier of fact, based on clear and convincing evidence, finds that the defendant was personally guilty of intentional misconduct or gross negligence. As used in this section, the term:

(a) **"Intentional misconduct"** means that the defendant had actual knowledge of the wrongfulness of the conduct and the high probability that injury or damage to the claimant would result and, despite that knowledge, intentionally pursued that course of conduct, resulting in injury or damage.

(b) **"Gross negligence"** means that the defendant's conduct was so reckless or wanting in care that it constituted a conscious disregard or indifference to the life, safety, or rights of persons exposed to such conduct.

The defendant's state of mind is also a key difference between negligence and gross negligence. Negligence involves an objective standard—how would a reasonable person have acted? Gross negligence applies a subjective component—was this defendant's conduct so reckless or wanting in care that it constituted a conscious disregard or indifference to the life, safety, or rights of persons exposed to it.

EXAMPLE

Jessica has practiced her shooting at a private range on her country property for 20 years, without incident. Jessica shoots towards an area where she has never seen another person, and she believes the range of her guns cannot reach her property line. One day, a neighbor is hit by a shot as he is strolling through the woods just off of Jessica's property.

Result: Jessica might be liable for negligence if a jury determines, for example, that a reasonably prudent person would have acted differently, tested the range of her guns, or built a different type of back stop or berm, etc. However, Jessica was not subjectively aware of an extreme degree of risk so there would be no evidence of gross negligence. However, change Jessica's awareness and it changes the result.

EXAMPLE

Jessica has received several complaints over the years about bullets leaving her property and hitting her neighbor's property. Nevertheless, Jessica ignores the complaints and continues practicing in the direction that she typically shoots. One day while practicing, her bullet leaves her property and hits her neighbor. She is later sued by the neighbor for gross negligence.

Result: Jessica may very well be liable for gross negligence because she was subjectively aware that her shots were reaching the neighbor's property and that there were people in the same area (i.e., the folks who reported the shots), and despite that knowledge, she continued to shoot without changing direction or building a back stop or berm and someone was injured as a result. This would evidence conduct so reckless or wanting in care that it constituted a conscious disregard or indifference to the life, safety, or rights of persons exposed to it.

2. Negligent entrustment of a firearm

Florida recognizes a claim for entrusting (e.g., giving, lending, transferring) a firearm to another person. To prove that a person or entity negligently entrusted a firearm, the plaintiff must show that (1) the owner entrusted the gun, (2) whom the owner knew or should have known, (3) to a person who was incompetent, reckless, careless, intoxicated or had a propensity to commit crime.

EXAMPLE

Shaun lets his adult grandson Gordon borrow a shotgun to take on a fishing trip because he knows there are water moccasins in the spot where they plan to fish. Gordon has never been in trouble with the law, has repeatedly been trained in firearms safety, and has never had an incident with a gun. However, while on the trip, Gordon accidentally shoots a fellow fishing buddy with Shaun's shotgun. The fishing buddy, now turned plaintiff, sues Gordon for negligence and Shaun for negligent entrustment of a firearm.

Can the plaintiff win his claim for negligent entrustment? Probably not; Shaun might get sued for giving the shotgun to his grandson, but the facts described do not meet the elements necessary to establish negligent entrustment under Florida case law; and Shaun should prevail in any lawsuit. First, there are no facts that suggest Gordon was incompetent or reckless, careless, intoxicated, incompetent or had a propensity to misuse a firearm. Further, there are no facts showing knowledge by Shaun that Gordon was likely to misuse the firearm. Thus, the negligent entrustment claim would legally fail.

In Florida, the owner of an automobile is strictly liable for damages caused by their automobile, even when someone else is driving. Thus far, Florida has not enacted a similar law for firearms.

3. Is negligent storage of a firearm recognized in Florida?

A question commonly asked by gun owners is "if someone steals my gun, am I liable if they shoot someone?" In other words, if I store my gun and a criminal or another less-than-responsible person gets the gun, am I liable if they shoot someone? As of the date of this publication, the answer in Florida is "probably not." There is a difference in Florida if a thief steals your firearm, or if someone in the home legally who should not have possession of a firearm gets a hold of it. Florida law looks to see if your conduct created a foreseeable zone of harm. If it does, then you have a duty to take action to prevent that harm. Further, if you have a duty, then you look to see if the harm caused by you violating that duty (failing to secure your firearm) was foreseeable. For example, if you have a house full of neighborhood children and you place your loaded firearm out in the open, you would be liable for negligent storage if someone got harmed. First, you would look to see if leaving a loaded firearm out in a room full of children created a foreseeable zone of harm. Once it was determined that it did, you would look to see if the harm actually caused was foreseeable.

As discussed previously, there are also potential criminal consequences for storing your gun where it can be accessed by a minor. See Florida Statute §790.174. As a result, it remains extraordinarily important to exercise care in the storage of your firearms.

B. Intentional discharge: a person intended to shoot

1. Negligence/gross negligence

Just because you intend to shoot someone, or otherwise "use" your gun, does not necessarily mean that the plaintiff will not assert negligence or gross negligence claims. In other words, you may have fully intended to pull the trigger, but the plaintiff may claim that you were negligent for any number of reasons; for example, you mistook the mailman for a burglar, or the criminal was retreating and you were negligent in using deadly force. The negligence and gross negligence claims, as defined above, can be brought even if you intended to pull the trigger. Another reason a person may sue for negligence when you intended to shoot them is that most homeowner's policies do not cover intentional acts. Therefore, to go after the deep pockets of the insurance company claims of negligence are often brought even when the homeowner intended to shoot.

2. Assault and battery

Unlike many states, Florida has no Civil Code that specifies definitions of various claims available in the civil area of law. This leaves an injured party to look to the common law for avenues to seek relief. Common law is based on decisions in previous cases also known as case law. Under the common law, an assault is an act intended to cause fear of harm or offensive contact that does cause fear or apprehension of the threatened contact.

Civil battery is defined as an intentional and voluntary unwanted harmful or offensive touching with another person. The definition also includes the offensive touching of an object in contact with the person. For instance, knocking a hat off someone's head can still be a battery even though no touching occurred to the person.

If a person has shot at or shot someone, if they are sued, it may include a claim for assault and battery. This is an intentional act, not an accident or a claim based on a deviation from a standard of care.

EXAMPLE

Bill is startled while driving. Martha is standing next to his passenger window at a light screaming that he cut her off in traffic, but taking no action to indicate she intends to harm Bill or do anything besides verbally lodge her complaints. In response, Bill fires a shot at Martha to make her go away, and hits her in the leg.

Bill has committed a civil battery. He intended to and did cause serious bodily injury to Martha with no legal justification. Therefore, a civil jury would likely find Bill liable and award damages to Martha.

EXAMPLE

Bill is startled while driving. Martha is standing next to his passenger window at a light screaming that he cut her off in traffic, but taking no action to indicate she intends to harm Bill or do anything besides verbally lodge her complaints. In response, Bill points his gun at Martha and says "You're dead!" He fires his gun but misses.

Bill has committed a civil assault. He knowingly threatened Martha with imminent bodily injury with no legal justification.

3. False imprisonment: being sued for detaining people

What if a gun owner detains someone at gun point? If the person who was detained later decides to sue, it will likely include a claim for "false imprisonment." Florida recognizes a civil claim for false imprisonment. This claim can arise when someone detains persons waiting for police, e.g. homeowners detaining burglars, etc. However, it can also come up commonly in shoplifting cases (see Chapter Seven). In Florida, false imprisonment is defined as "the unlawful restraint of a person, against his will, the gist of which action is the unlawful detention of the plaintiff and the deprivation of his liberty." Escambia County School Board v. Bragg, 680 So.2d 571 (Fla 1st DCA 1996).

> **EXAMPLE**
>
> Emily fears she is about to be attacked in a grocery store parking lot by Randall. Randall follows her step-by-step through the parking lot and stops right next to Emily's car. Emily draws her .380 and tells Randall to "stay right there while I call the police." Randall complies, and Emily holds him at gunpoint until the police arrive. When the police arrive, they determine that Randall was an out-of-uniform store employee tasked with rounding up the grocery carts in the parking lot and was no threat to Emily.

If a jury determines that Emily acted without justification (i.e., she was not reasonably in fear of death or bodily injury), Emily could be civilly liable for falsely imprisoning Randall and owe him damages, if any.

4. Wrongful death

If a person is in the unfortunate position that they have shot and killed another individual and a civil suit occurs because of the shooting, it likely will include a claim for wrongful death. According to Florida Statute §768.19 a cause of action for wrongful death can arise "when the death of a person is caused by the wrongful act, negligence, default, or breach of contract or warranty of any person, including those occurring on navigable waters, and the event would have entitled the person injured to maintain an action and recover damages if death had not ensued, the person or watercraft that would have been liable in damages if death had not ensued shall be liable for damages as specified in this act notwithstanding the death of the person injured, although death was caused under circumstances constituting a felony."

A wrongful death claim can be proven by establishing that one of the other claims described in this chapter caused the death of another person. In other words, the "wrongful act, neglect, carelessness, unskillfulness, or default" needed to establish a wrongful death claim, can be established by proving that the defendant was liable for a tort such as battery or negligence and that the tort caused the death of a person.

III. WHAT CAN THE PLAINTIFF RECOVER?

If a person is sued in civil court and the plaintiff convinces a jury that the defendant was liable for damages, what and how much can a plaintiff get? There are scores of cases discussing the details of each category of damages that a plaintiff can recover in a civil lawsuit. The following is a brief description of two very important concepts: (1) "proximate cause," which is essential to recover damages in most circumstances, and (2) the basic types of damages that a plaintiff may typically seek in a gun case.

A. Proximate cause

One basic concept that is important to most civil claims, and is usually required to recover damages, is "proximate cause." Virtually every tort claim will require the plaintiff to prove that his damages were proximately caused by the defendant. "Proximate cause" is defined as cause that was a substantial factor in bringing about an event and without which the event would not have occurred. This concept has few bright-line tests.

For a gun owner, the most obvious cases of proximate cause are pulling the trigger on a firearm and hitting the person or thing you aimed at. The law will hold that your action proximately caused whatever physical damage the bullet did to persons or property. But what about those circumstances where the use of the gun is so far removed from the damages claimed? This is where the doctrine of proximate cause will cut off liability. If the damage is too far removed from the act, then the act cannot be a proximate cause of that damage.

EXAMPLE

Anthony is cleaning his AR-15 one night in his apartment and is negligent in his handling of the rifle. He has an accidental discharge and the bullet goes through the wall of his apartment and strikes his neighbor, Ray, in the leg. Ray, although in massive pain, received prompt medical care from his wife, Gail, and made a speedy recovery.

If Anthony is later sued by Ray and his wife Gail, Anthony's negligence undoubtedly "proximately caused" damages for things like Ray's medical bills, hospital stay, and perhaps even lost wages. But what if Gail claims that because of her having to treat Ray's wounds that she missed a big job interview and lost out on a big raise in pay and that she wants Anthony to pay that as a component of damages? The law would hold that Gail likely could not recover damages for her lost raise in pay because the loss would not be "proximately caused" by the act being sued for. To put it another way, it is reasonably foreseeable that the negligent discharge of a firearm will cause medical bills, etc., for someone struck by a bullet. Therefore, this is recoverable. However, the law would say that the loss of a possible job opportunity for the wife who treated the person who was actually shot is not a reasonably foreseeable consequence of negligently discharging a firearm and, therefore, was not proximately caused by the act of negligence. In that case, there will be no recovery for the plaintiff, Gail. Proximate cause must be established in every case and may appear to be an arbitrary legal line drawing, because it is.

As discussed below, Florida law also recognizes a doctrine that unforeseen criminal conduct breaks the causal link between an action and a third-party's injuries. However, Florida courts have been clear that foreseeability is almost always a question for the jury. "The key to proximate cause is foreseeability." Vining v. Avis Rent-A-Car Systems, Inc., 354 So. 2d 54, 56 (Fla. 1977). "If an intervening cause is foreseeable the original negligent actor may still be held liable. The question of whether an intervening cause is foreseeable is for the trier of fact." Gibson v. Avis Rent-A-Car System, Inc., 386 So. 2d 520, 522 (Fla. 1980). Further Florida courts have held a foreseeable criminal act does not break the causal link between action and injury. See Nicholas v. Miami Burglar Alarm Co., 339 So. 2d 175, 177 (Fla. 1976); Holley v. Mt. Zion Terrace Apartments, Inc., 382 So. 2d 98, 100 (Fla. 3d D.C.A. 1980); Werndli v. Greyhound Corp., 365 So. 2d 177 (Fla. 2d D.C.A.

1978); Rosier v. Gainesville Ins. Associates, Inc., 347 So. 2d 1100 (Fla. 1st D.C.A. 1977); Rotbart v. Jordan Marsh Co., 305 So. 2d 255 (Fla. 3d D.C.A. 1974).

B. What types of damages can a plaintiff recover?

The following is merely a brief snapshot of the types of damages that are recoverable in a firearms case. To recover any of the damages below, the plaintiff must first prove one of the claims above by a preponderance of the evidence. For example, if the jury determines a defendant was not negligent, a plaintiff cannot recover his or her medical costs, no matter how severe the plaintiff's injuries. Some of the damages a plaintiff can try to recover include:

• Lost Wages
• Medical Costs
• Disability
• Pain & Suffering (Physical, Mental & Emotional)
• Funeral and Burial Costs
• Disfigurement
• Loss of Companionship
• Loss of Household Services
• Lost Future Wages
• Future Medical Costs
• Punitive or exemplary damages (Note, the standard of proof for punitive/exemplary damages is "clear and convincing evidence," which is higher than a "preponderance of the evidence." Punitive damages are also only available in cases of intentional or reckless conduct, or gross negligence.)

A court can find the defendant 100% at fault, but award no damages because the plaintiff failed to prove damages by a preponderance of the evidence. For example, a plaintiff who seeks reimbursement for medical expenses but has no evidence that they ever went to a doctor or hospital, will very unlikely be able to recover those medical expenses.

IV. HOW GOOD ARE FLORIDA CIVIL IMMUNITY LAWS FOR GUN OWNERS?

A. No immunity from lawsuits

There is a common misunderstanding that there exists a law that if you are legally justified in using your gun that you can't be sued. This is just not the case. First, if a person has the filing fee, anyone can sue anyone else in the State of Florida. There is no one stopping anyone from filing a lawsuit. Winning a lawsuit is a different issue entirely. If someone files the lawsuit, no matter how frivolous, it still must be dealt with, and it still must be shown to the court that there is a defense that bars the lawsuit. This process can t. significant time, money, and legal energy even for the most loser of cases. In short, lawyers get paid and even if you beat the "rap," you still have to take the civil "ride." So, if there is no immunity to lawsuits being filed for gun owners, what protection is there?

IMMUNITY FROM DAMAGES; FLORIDA STATUTE § 776.032

(1) A person who uses or threatens to use force as permitted in s. 776.012, s. 776.013, or s.776.031 is justified in such conduct and is immune from criminal prosecution and civil action for the use or threatened use of such force by the person, personal representative, or heirs of the person against whom the force was used or threatened, unless the person against whom force was used or threatened is a law enforcement officer, as defined in s. 943.10(14), who was acting in the performance of his or her official duties and the officer identified himself or herself in accordance with any applicable law or the person using or threatening to use force knew or reasonably should have known that the person was a law enforcement officer. As used in this subsection, the term "criminal prosecution" includes arresting, detaining in custody, and charging or prosecuting the defendant.

(2) A law enforcement agency may use standard procedures for investigating the use or threatened use of force as described in subsection (1), but the agency may not arrest the person for using or threatening to use force unless it determines that there is probable cause that the force that was used or threatened was unlawful.

urt shall award reasonable attorney's fees, court costs, nsation for loss of income, and all expenses incurred by the defendant in defense of any civil action brought by a plaintiff if the court finds that the defendant is immune from prosecution as provided in subsection (1).

(4) In a criminal prosecution, once a prima facie claim of self-defense immunity from criminal prosecution has been raised by the defendant at a pretrial immunity hearing, the burden of proof by clear and convincing evidence is on the party seeking to overcome the immunity from criminal prosecution provided in subsection (1).

B. Immunity for certain claims

Most important for gun owners if they find themselves included in a civil suit after a justified use of force will be Florida Statute §776.032. This section provides in relevant part that:

1. A person who uses or threatens to use force as permitted in §776.012, §776.013 or §776.031 is justified in such conduct and is immune from criminal prosecution including arresting, detaining in custody, and charging or prosecuting the defendant and civil action for the use or threatened use of such force by the person, personal representative, or heirs of the person against whom the force was used or threatened

2. (Intentionally omitted deals with criminal investigations and is discussed elsewhere in this book.)

3. The court shall award reasonable attorney's fees, court costs, compensation for loss of income, and all expenses incurred by the defendant in defense of any civil action brought by a plaintiff

if the court finds that the defendant is immune from prosecution as provided in subsection (1).
4. (Intentionally omitted. See discussion regarding criminal prosecution elsewhere in this book.)

Unfortunately, this statute does not prevent lawsuits; it just makes the ones filed harder to win. Immunity from liability is more than just another affirmative defense. A defendant may raise an immunity challenge at any time before trial and again in trial as an affirmative defense. Florida courts have held that in this hearing it is the Defendant's burden to show by a preponderance of evidence that he was acting in accordance with the law before immunity will be granted.

Florida's immunity statute is a very strong one. Unlike a purely criminal immunity statute found in many states, Florida's immunity statute also applies to civil cases. The language of the immunity statute acts to discourage plaintiffs from risking a questionable lawsuit. The law provides that the court shall award the defendant his attorney's fees, court costs, and even compensation for loss of income, if the defendant is found to be immune. In this case, there is no discretion left to the court about awarding these damages to a defendant. The statutory language of "shall" makes it mandatory that a judge award these damages, as opposed to the term may, that would allow a judge to award them in some instances, but refuse to award damages to the defendant in other instances.

C. Justification
All of the justifications under the immunity statute and Florida's use of force laws can also be asserted as affirmative defenses in a civil action. This means, for example, if you shoot someone in defense

of yourself, others, or your property and are sued as a result, you may assert the applicable sections of the statutes as a defense to the civil claims in a trial, not just in a pretrial immunity hearing. If the judge or jury agrees that you acted in self-defense, or properly used force to defend others or property, the plaintiff will be barred from recovery. See Chapters Four through Seven.

D. Statute of limitations for civil claims

The statute of limitations is a doctrine in Florida (and almost every other jurisdiction) that requires civil claims to be brought within a certain period of time after the incident. If the claim is not brought within the statute of limitations period, it is barred. There are a number of issues relating to when the statute of limitations starts to run in many cases, but for the most part, limitations will start to run immediately after a shooting incident. The statute of limitations can vary from claim to claim, most, however, are between one and four years. In Florida, the limitations period most likely to apply to gun cases is going to be four years. Assault and battery, negligence, and false imprisonment claims all provide four-year limitations periods. However, wrongful death has a much shorter limitation period. In fact, at only two years, it is half of the time allowed for the other claims mentioned.

What does this mean for gun owners? If you "use" your gun, the plaintiff must bring a civil suit against you within four years of the incident in almost all cases or else the claim will be barred.

E. Superseding or intervening criminal conduct

Florida law recognizes a doctrine that absolves someone from responsibility for conduct that might otherwise be a tort (e.g., negligence) if a criminal act breaks the causal connection between the tort and the injury. Generally, a third party's criminal conduct is a superseding cause which relieves the negligent actor from liability. However, "If an intervening cause is foreseeable the original negligent actor may still be held liable. The question of whether an intervening cause is foreseeable is for the trier of fact." Gibson v. Avis Rent-A-Car System, Inc., 386 So. 2d 520, 522 (Fla. 1980). Further Florida courts have held a foreseeable criminal act does not break the causal link between action and injury. See Nicholas v. Miami Burglar Alarm Co., 339 So. 2d 175, 177 (Fla. 1976); Holley v. Mt. Zion Terrace Apartments, Inc., 382 So. 2d 98, 100 (Fla. 3d D.C.A. 1980); Werndli v. Greyhound Corp., 365 So. 2d 177 (Fla. 2d D.C.A. 1978); Rosier v. Gainesville Ins. Associates, Inc., 347 So. 2d 1100 (Fla. 1st D.C.A. 1977); Rotbart v. Jordan Marsh Co., 305 So. 2d 255 (Fla. 3d D.C.A. 1974).

EXAMPLE

Justin allows his nephew Randall to use his handgun for protection. Justin knows Randall has been in trouble with the law repeatedly and has been accused of armed robbery. While Randall has the handgun, his apartment is burglarized, and the gun is stolen and used in a crime spree. During the crime spree, Melanie is shot and injured.

Melanie would not likely be able to recover from Justin, even though Justin may have been negligent in giving his gun to Randall, because the criminal act of burglarizing Randall's apartment and subsequent crime spree were superseding causes that broke the link between Justin's actions and the resulting injuries.

F. Comparative negligence
Florida uses a doctrine called comparative fault. Florida Statute

§768.81 (2) explains this doctrine, saying, "In a negligence action, contributory fault chargeable to the claimant diminishes proportionately the amount awarded as economic and noneconomic damages for an injury attributable to the claimant's contributory fault, but does not bar recovery." The Statute goes on to explain how damages are calculated against each party by explaining that, "In a negligence action, the court shall enter judgment against each party liable on the basis of such party's percentage of fault and not on the basis of the doctrine of joint and several liability." In plain English this can be explained by thinking about a pie. Let's say the pie is worth $100,000. If the pie is divided into 10 pieces, each piece is worth $10,000. In a negligence lawsuit, think of the awarded damages as the pie. A plaintiff who suffers $100,000 in damages sues a defendant to recover his loses. It is determined that the Defendant was 90% at fault in causing the loss, but that the plaintiff shared 10% of the responsibility. From that $100,000 pie, one tenth (10%), or one slice would be removed because that was the portion of damages caused by the plaintiff and he would be able to recover $90,000 in damages from the Defendant, which equals 90% of the damages, the percentage caused by the defendant. Although many states do not allow recovery by a plaintiff who is equally or more at fault for his own injuries that the defendant or defendants, Florida has no such rule. A person who causes 99% of their own damage, can still recover in Florida for the 1% of damages against the person who caused them.

EXAMPLE

Richard is a young adult trick-or-treater. He uses a fake gun as a part of his costume and knocks loudly on Nancy's door at 11:30 p.m. on October 31. Nancy, having forgotten about Halloween, is frightened by the knock, the fake gun, and the late hour of Richard's arrival. She fires through the door, injuring Richard.

In the civil suit that follows by Richard against Nancy, the jury will be permitted to consider whether Richard's negligence, if any, contributed to cause the resulting injuries. The court could determine that Richard was 0% at fault, 100% at fault, or anything in between. By way of example only, if the jury awarded Richard $100,000 in damages, but the court determined that he was 30% at fault, and Nancy 70%, Richard would only be able to recover $70,000 of his damages. Of course, Nancy would also likely raise an immunity challenge, but for this example assume she lost that challenge.

V. WHAT ABOUT THIRD-PARTIES?

Florida law provides a different standard when it comes to injuries to third parties. In this section, a "third-party" generally means someone who is not a party to the encounter with the firearm; e.g., bystanders, witnesses, folks nearby who were not the intended target, etc.

The public policy and laws of the State of Florida have always allowed a person to protect themselves and their property. However, when acts of self-defense or defense of property are undertaken, if these acts create an unreasonable risk of causing harm to innocent third-parties, the actor may be subject to civil liability. Further, the Florida criminal case law tells us that if a person is justified in killing in self-defense and a third-party gets injured, the justification transfers to the third party. In Brown v. State, 84 Fla. 660, 94 So. 874, 874 (1922), the Florida Supreme Court held that "[i]f the killing of the party intended to be killed would, under all the circumstances, have been excusable or justifiable homicide upon the theory of self-defense, then the unintended killing of a bystander, by a random shot fired in the proper and prudent exercise of such self-defense, is also excusable or justifiable." See also Foreman v. State, 47 So.2d 308 (Fla.1950)

This means that even if you defend yourself, others, or property lawfully, but you create an unreasonable risk to others while doing so, you can be liable if one of those third parties is injured.

EXAMPLE

Mel shoots Anthony as he unlawfully breaks into Mel's occupied home at night. She fires a single shot with her .22 that narrowly misses Anthony but hits a man washing his car down the street.

Mel is probably not liable to the man down the street, because her conduct did not unreasonably place third parties at risk.

EXAMPLE

Ben shoots at Anthony as he unlawfully breaks into Ben's occupied home at night. Ben fires 30 shots with his fully-automatic M-16, missing with the initial burst. Anthony turns and runs. Ben continues to fire haphazardly at Anthony as he runs down the street. One shot hits a man washing his car four houses away.

Ben could very likely be liable to the man washing his car because he unreasonably placed third-parties at risk by firing a fully automatic weapon down a neighborhood street.

VI. TRAPS AND SPRING GUNS

Florida law does not have an explicit trap or spring gun prohibition. However, Florida law does not allow the use of deadly force to protect solely property. Florida Statute §776.031(1) states:

A person is justified in using or threatening to use force, except deadly force, against another when and to the extent that the person reasonably believes that such conduct is necessary to prevent or terminate the other's trespass on, or other tortious or criminal interference with, either real property other than a dwelling or personal property, lawfully in his or her possession or in the possession of another who is a member of his or her immediate family or household or of a person whose property he or she has a legal duty to protect. A person who uses or threatens to use force in accordance with this subsection does not have a duty to retreat before using or threating to use such force.

Visitors upon the private property of others fall within one of three classifications: they are either trespassers, licensees, or invitees. The classification is important because it determines the duty of care owed the visitor by the property owner or occupier. He must not willfully and wantonly injure a trespasser; he must not willfully and wantonly injure a licensee, or intentionally expose him to danger; and, where the visitor is an invitee, he must keep his property reasonably safe and protect the visitor from dangers of which he is, or should be aware. Post v. Lunney 261 So.2d 146 (Fla. 2007). Under these standards it appears that setting a trap for a trespasser is not permissible under Florida law.

What types of "devices" could lead to civil liability under Florida law? As with almost all questions, in this area, the reasonableness under the circumstances will control.

1. Barbed wire around a business in the warehouse district of town

Likely permitted. Barbed wire is typically a reasonable security measure and usually not capable of, or designed to, cause death or serious bodily injury.

2. Razor wire around a playground across from an elementary school

Likely not permitted. While probably not designed to cause death, it is arguably unreasonable to install such a "device" near an elementary school, particularly around a playground likely to attract children.

VII. WILL INSURANCE COVER IT IF I SHOOT SOMEONE?

A. Homeowners' insurance

With few exceptions, almost every homeowner's insurance policy excludes coverage for intentional acts. The act of using your firearm in self-defense is almost always an intentional act. You intended to stop the threat. Plaintiffs' attorneys will very likely assert a negligence claim against a homeowner in an attempt to fall within the coverage, but at the end of the day, if the only evidence is that you intentionally shot the plaintiff because you intended to stop a threat, it is likely that any policy with an intentional act exclusion will not provide coverage for any damages awarded.

B. Auto insurance

Scores of cases around the country exist where the parties allege that a gun incident is covered by automobile insurance merely because the use of the firearm occurs in the auto or involves an auto. Almost universally, courts have held that these incidents are not covered merely because the discharge occurs in a car or involves a car.

EXAMPLE

Justin is cleaning his 9mm handgun in the car. It accidentally discharges causing his passenger Edwin severe injuries.

This event will almost certainly not be covered by auto insurance.

EXAMPLE

Justin discharges his 9mm handgun in the car at Edwin during an attempted carjacking, causing Edwin severe injuries and also hitting a bystander.

This event will almost certainly not be covered by auto insurance.

For an injury to fall within the "use" coverage of an automobile policy (1) the accident must have arisen out of the inherent nature of the automobile, as such, (2) the accident must have arisen within the natural territorial limits of an automobile, and the actual use must not have terminated, (3) the automobile must not merely contribute to cause the condition which produces the injury, but must itself produce injury.

VIII. WHAT CIVIL LIABILITY DOES A PERSON FACE IF THEIR CHILDREN ACCESS THEIR FIREARMS?

A. Parents are not responsible for minor children's actions merely because they are parents!

The Florida Supreme Court has ruled that a parent is not liable for the torts committed by his or her children unless (1) the parent entrusts the child with a dangerous instrumentality; (2) the child is acting as the parent's agent in committing the tortious act; (3) the parent knows of and consents to the child's tortious act; or (4) the parent fails to exercise control over the child when injury to another is a possible consequence. See Snow v. Nelson, 475 So.2d 225 (Fla. 1985); Gissen v. Goodwill, 80 So.2d 701 (Fla. 1955)

Therefore, as a general rule, minors are civilly liable for their own torts (that is, their wrongful actions such as negligence, gross negligence, assault, etc.). The mere fact of paternity or maternity does not make a parent liable to third parties for the torts of his or her minor children. Under this general rule, parents are not responsible for their minor children's tortious actions when the minor child commits a tort and the parent had no direct relationship to the child's action, such as providing a firearm in a negligent manner, failing to supervise the child, or allowing the child to engage in behavior the parent knows is dangerous or risky.

B. Parents who fail to "parent" may become responsible for minor children's actions

While a parent who has no direct relationship to a minor child's tortious actions is generally not liable for that child's actions, if the parent negligently allows his child to act in a manner likely to harm another, if he gives his child a dangerous instrumentality, or if he does not restrain a child known to have dangerous tendencies, the parent may be liable.

Another issue related to negligent storage is whether or not the storage of a gun in violation of Florida Statutes could result in civil liability, in addition to the criminal penalties in the statute.

As a reminder, Florida Statue §790.174 provides criminal sanction for a gun owner who, "(1) [fails] to store or leave a firearm in the required manner and as a result thereof a minor gains access to the firearm, without the lawful permission of the minor's parent or the person having charge of the minor, and possesses or exhibits it, without the supervision required by law:

(a) In a public place; or

(b) In a rude, careless, angry, or threatening manner."

As with all civil matters, the reasonableness of your actions under the circumstances will determine whether liability attaches.

EXAMPLE

Jon, your 17-year-old son, has been hunting since he was 11 and has taken several firearms training courses.

If you take Jon hunting, and for some reason Jon accidentally discharges his shotgun, injuring another person, it is highly unlikely that you, the parent, will be civilly liable for an accident that occurs while hunting.

EXAMPLE

Gordon, your 12-year-old son, has never handled a gun or taken a firearms training course. You decide to take him to the range for the first time, but you are both asked to leave the range after Gordon repeatedly fires into the ceiling and the floor. Fed up, you take Gordon to another range with no additional instruction or training.

If Gordon shoots and injures someone at the second range, it is likely that you will be liable, because you allowed him to act in a manner likely to harm another, and you did not restrain him despite his dangerous conduct.

In preparation for the annual family hunting trip, Frank took his 16-year-old son Billy to the outdoor shooting range. As happens every year, while at the range, Billy was haphazard and intentionally unsafe in his handling of his firearm. Billy, who refuses to take anything seriously, repeatedly pointed his firearm in the direction of other persons, and even discharged his gun into the air three times while hooting and hollering. Frank scolded Billy by telling him that it is "not nice" to point guns at other people. During the hunting trip, Billy randomly fired his shotgun for no apparent reason at all into the trees. Billy's last shot hit a fellow hunter standing among the trees.

Is Frank liable for his minor son Billy's acts? Probably yes. Frank was well-aware of the fact that Billy handles firearms in a dangerous manner, and Frank failed to take any reasonable measures to prevent Billy injuring another person. The law would very likely find that Frank's failure to reasonably discipline and supervise his child proximately caused the injury to the other hunter.

> CHAPTER SIXTEEN ◄

OTHER LAWS
BEYOND FIREARMS
Knives, Chemical Weapons, And Tasers

I. INTRODUCTION

In addition to Florida's many firearms laws, there also exist state laws governing the manufacture, sale, possession, and use of "other weapons." This includes any object that is not a firearm, but could be used as a weapon. This chapter will briefly discuss the laws governing these other weapons, including weapons that are absolutely illegal under the law, weapons that are illegal to carry, and exceptions to the laws prohibiting the carrying of illegal weapons.

II. ABSOLUTELY PROHIBITED WEAPONS

A. What is an absolutely prohibited weapon?

Some laws merely prohibit the possession of or certain uses of weapons. In contrast, other laws prohibit all dealings with certain weapons.

B. What weapons are absolutely prohibited under Florida law?

The list of absolutely prohibited weapons under Florida law is rather short. Florida Statute §790.225 makes it unlawful for any person to manufacture, display, sell, own, possess, or use a ballistic, self-propelled knife, which is a device that propels a knifelike blade as a projectile and which physically separates the blade from the device by means of a coil spring, elastic material, or compressed gas. A ballistic self-propelled knife is declared to be a dangerous or deadly weapon and a contraband item. However, §790.225 does not prohibit 1) any device from which a knifelike blade opens, where such blade remains physically integrated with the device when open; or 2) any device which propels an arrow, a bolt, or a dart by means of any common bow, compound bow, crossbow, or underwater spear gun.

Florida Statute §790.161 addresses destructive devices. It is unlawful under that statute for a person to willfully and unlawfully make, possess, throw, project, place, discharge, or attempt to make, possess, throw, project, place, or discharge any destructive device. Florida Statute §790.001(4) defines a "destructive device" as:

any bomb, grenade, mine, rocket, missile, pipe bomb, or similar device containing an explosive, incendiary, or poison gas and includes any frangible container filled with an explosive, incendiary, explosive gas, or expanding gas, which is designed or so constructed as to explode by such filler and is capable of causing bodily harm or property damage; any combination of parts either designed or intended for use in converting any device into a destructive device and from which a destructive device may be readily assembled; any device declared a destructive device by the Bureau of Alcohol, Tobacco, Firearms and Explosives; any type of weapon which will, is designed to, or may readily be converted to expel a projectile by the action of any explosive and which has a barrel with a bore of one-half inch or more in diameter; and ammunition for such destructive devices, but not including shotgun shells or any other ammunition designed for use in a firearm other than a destructive device. "Destructive device" does not include:

(a) A device which is not designed, redesigned, used, or intended for use as a weapon;

(b) Any device, although originally designed as a weapon, which is redesigned so that it may be used solely as a signaling, line-throwing, safety, or similar device;

(c) Any shotgun other than a short-barreled shotgun; or

(d) Any non-automatic rifle (other than a short-barreled rifle) generally recognized or particularly suitable for use for the hunting of big game.

Florida Statute §790.001(5) defines "Explosive" as:

any chemical compound or mixture that has the property of yielding readily to combustion or oxidation upon application of heat, flame, or shock, including but not limited to dynamite, nitroglycerin, trinitrotoluene, or ammonium nitrate when combined with other ingredients to form an explosive mixture, blasting caps, and detonators; but not including:

(a) Shotgun shells, cartridges, or ammunition for firearms;

(b) Fireworks as defined in s. 791.01;

(c) Smokeless propellant powder or small arms ammunition primers, if possessed, purchased, sold, transported, or used in compliance with s. 552.241;

(d) Black powder in quantities not to exceed that authorized by chapter 552, or by any rules adopted thereunder by the Department of Financial Services, when used for, or intended to be used for, the manufacture of target and sporting ammunition or for use in muzzle-loading flint or percussion weapons.

EXAMPLE

Adam has a sealed gas can filled with gasoline in his garage for the purpose of running his lawn mower. While the can has a combustible material in it (gasoline), the container is not designed to cause the gasoline to combust. In comparison, Bob has a gas can filled with gasoline that has been sealed and he has placed ball bearings in the can to act as shrapnel, with a single fuse leading into the can. Should the fuse be lit, the gasoline within the can would be ignited and the resulting gases would overcome the tensile strength of the container thereby causing an explosion. Therefore, Bob's gas can would be a destructive device and violate Florida law.

III. RESTRICTED WEAPONS

A. Slungshots and "metallic knuckles" (commonly known as "brass knuckles"

As opposed to Florida Statute §790.225, which strictly prohibits the possession, manufacture, use, or sale of ballistic self-propelled knives, other sections merely place limited restrictions regarding certain weapons. Florida Statute §790.09 does not prohibit slungshots or metallic knuckles in all respects, but it does prohibit the manufacture, sale or exposure for sale of any instrument or weapon of the kind usually known as a slungshot or metallic knuckles.

Definition of a "slungshot"

What is a "slungshot"? Florida Statute §790.01(12) defines a "slungshot" as a mass of metal, stone, sand or similar material fixed on a flexible handle, strap or the like that is used as a weapon.

Definition of "metallic knuckles"
The Florida Statutes do not clearly define metallic knuckles. Likewise, there appears to be no Florida case law delineating what "metallic" or "brass" knuckles are. The image immediately below reflects typical brass knuckles:

B. Chemical dispensing devices
Florida Statute §790.001(3)(b) states that a "tear gas gun" or "chemical weapon or device" means any weapon of that type (*i.e.,* a gun that fires tear gas or a weapon that dispenses a chemical), except a device known as a "self-defense chemical spray" (which can be carried openly pursuant to Florida Statute §790.053). "Self-defense chemical spray" means a device carried solely for purposes of lawful self-defense that is compact in size, designed to be carried on or about the person, and contains not more than two ounces of chemical. Florida Statute §790.001(3)(a) states that a "concealed weapon" means any dirk, metallic knuckles, slungshot, billie, tear gas gun, chemical weapon or device, or other deadly weapon carried on or about a person in such a manner as to conceal the weapon from the ordinary sight of another person.

Florida Statute §790.01 provides that it is a crime to carry a concealed weapon without a license. Thus, one must have a concealed weapons license to carry a concealed "chemical weapon or device".

C. Tasers and similar devices

Florida Statute §790.001(14) states that an "electric weapon or device" means any device which, through the application or use of electrical current, is designed, redesigned, used, or intended to be used for offensive or defensive purposes, the destruction of life, or the infliction of injury.

Florida Statute §790.01 provides that it is a crime to carry a concealed electric weapon or device without a license. Thus, one must have a concealed weapons license to carry a concealed "electric weapon or device".

Pursuant to Florida Statute §790.053, one may openly carry an "electric weapon or device" only if it is a "nonlethal stun gun or dart-firing stun gun or other nonlethal electric weapon or device that is designed solely for defensive purposes." The key seems to the nonlethal and defensive quality of the device.

Handheld "Stun Gun"   Cartridge Taser

IV. WEAPONS AND MINORS

Pursuant to Florida Statute §790.22(1), the use for any purpose whatsoever of BB guns, air or gas-operated guns, or electric weapons or devices, by any minor under the age of 16 years is prohibited unless such use is under the supervision and in the presence of an adult who is acting with the consent of the minor's parent. Florida Statute §790.22(2) further provides that any adult responsible for the welfare of any child under the age of 16 years who knowingly permits such child to use or have in his or her possession any BB gun, air or gas-operated gun, electric weapon or device in violation of that statute commits a misdemeanor of the second degree.

EXAMPLE

Adam allows his neighbor's 13-year-old son to play with his BB gun without first getting the neighbor's permission or without supervising the him by staying in his presence, Adam will have committed a misdemeanor crime under Florida law.

Florida Statute §790.17 provides that a person who sells, hires, barters, lends, transfers, or gives any minor under 18 years of age any dirk, electric weapon or device, or other weapon, other than an ordinary pocketknife, without permission of the minor's parent or guardian, or sells, hires, barters, lends, transfers, or gives to any person of unsound mind an electric weapon or device or any dangerous weapon, other than an ordinary pocketknife, commits a misdemeanor of the first degree.

EXAMPLE

Adam has a large KABAR knife that his friend's 16-year-old son has always liked. As a kind gesture, Adam one day gives the KABAR knife to his friend's, neglecting to ask his friend if doing so was acceptable. Adam will have committed a misdemeanor crime under Florida law.

V. FELONS AND DELINQUENTS – POSSESSION OF WEAPONS

Many are aware that convicted felons cannot possess or purchase firearms. However, there are also restrictions as to other weapons.

Florida Statute §790.23 provides that it is unlawful for any person to own or to have in his or her care, custody, possession, or control any electric weapon or device, or to carry a concealed weapon, including a tear gas gun or chemical weapon or device, if that person has been:

1. Convicted of a felony in the courts of Florida;
2. Found, in the courts of Florida, to have committed a delinquent act that would be a felony if committed by an adult and such person is under 24 years of age;
3. Convicted of or found to have committed a crime against the United States which is designated as a felony;
4. Found to have committed a delinquent act in a state, territory, or country other than Florida that would be a felony if committed by an adult and which was punishable by imprisonment for a term exceeding 1 year and such person is under 24 years of age; or
5. Found guilty of an offense that is a felony in a state, territory, or country other than Florida and which was punishable by imprisonment for a term exceeding 1 year.

VI. THE COMMON POCKET KNIFE

Florida Statute §790.001(13) exempts from the definition of "weapon" the "common pocket knife". However, the statute does not define the parameters of a "common pocket knife". That task has been left to the courts.

In *L.B. v. State*, 700 So.2d 370, (Fla. 1997), the Florida Supreme

Court held that a folding knife with a 3¾ inch blade and an approximate overall length of 8½ inches was a "common pocket knife" and was, therefore, not a weapon. Some case law has suggested that the manner in which the knife is carried can be an important factor. For example, in *Walls v. State*, 730 So.2d 294 (Fla. 1st DCA 1999), the court held that whether a folding knife with a blade of approximately four inches when carried locked in the open position was a question for the jury to decide and was not per se a common pocket knife. A similar decision was reached in *Porter v. State*, 798 So. 2d 855 (Fla. 5th DCA 2001).

CHAPTER SEVENTEEN

OTHER WEAPONS
THE NATIONAL FIREARMS ACT
Silencers, Short-Barreled Weapons, And Machine Guns

C an an individual in Florida legally own a silencer or suppressor, short-barreled shotgun, short-barreled rifle, machine gun, or "destructive device"? Yes, if all NFA regulations are satisfied. This chapter deals with the laws regarding the possession and use of firearms that are subject to the provisions of the National Firearms Act (NFA) codified in 26 U.S.C. Chapter 53, specifically, silencers, short-barreled firearms, machine guns, and firearms that are otherwise illegal. These firearms are illegal to purchase or possess without possessing the proper paperwork and a "tax stamp." In this chapter, we will discuss the purpose behind the NFA, what firearms are regulated by the Act, as well as the process and procedure for legally possessing weapons that are subject to the Act's provisions.

I. WHAT IS THE NATIONAL FIREARMS ACT?

The National Firearms Act was enacted in 1934 in response to gangster crimes. Prior to the Act's passage, any person could go to the local hardware store and purchase a Thompson Submachine Gun or shorten the barrel on their rifle or shotgun. President Roosevelt pushed for the passage of the NFA in an attempt to diminish a gangster's ability to possess and carry dangerous and/ or easily concealable firearms, such as machine guns and short-barreled rifles and shotguns.

NFA is firearms regulation using a registration and tax requirement

The NFA requires both the registration of and tax on the manufacture and transfer of certain firearms. The law created a tax of $200 on the transfer of the following firearms: short-barreled shotguns, short-barreled rifles, machine guns, silencers, and destructive devices. The tax is only $5 for firearms that are classified as "Any Other Weapons" or AOWs. Back in 1934, a $200 tax was the approximate equivalent to about $3,500 today!

Five years after the NFA's passage, the Supreme Court held in *United States v. Miller* that the right to bear arms can be subject to federal regulation. Miller defended himself against a criminal charge by the government stating that the NFA infringed upon his Constitutional right to bear arms under the Second Amendment. While the Court agreed that the Constitution does guarantee a right to bear arms, it held that the right does not extend to every firearm. See *United States v. Miller*, 307 U.S. 174 (1939).

II. WHAT FIREARMS DOES THE NFA REGULATE?

A. Short-barreled rifles and shotguns

In order to be legal, short-barreled shotguns and rifles must be registered, and a tax paid on the firearm. What is a short-barreled shotgun? Under both federal and Florida law, short-barreled shotguns have one or more barrels less than 18 inches in length and the overall length of the shotgun is less than 26 inches. What is a short-barreled rifle? It is any rifle with one or more barrels less than 16 inches in length, and the overall length of the rifle is less than 26 inches. See 27 CFR §478.11 and Florida Statutes §790.001(10), (11).

Short-barreled shotguns and rifles may be purchased from an FFL who deals in NFA items. Also, short-barreled firearms are very popular for individuals to build and/or modify on their own. This is legal if the person has properly registered the firearm to be modified into a short-barreled firearm with the ATF and paid the tax before it is modified. Once approved, a person may alter or produce a short-barreled firearm and must engrave legally required information on the receiver of the firearm such as manufacturer, location, etc. See discussion later in this chapter for detailed requirements.

B. Machine guns

Machine guns are illegal under federal and state law. However, if the requirements of the NFA are satisfied, machine guns may be legally owned by individuals. First, what is a machine gun? Federal law defines a machine gun as "any weapon which shoots, is designed to shoot, or can be readily restored to shoot, automatically more than one shot, without manual reloading, by a single function of the trigger. The term shall also include the frame or receiver of any such weapon, any part designed and intended solely and exclusively, or combination of parts designed and intended, for use in converting a weapon into a machine gun, and any combination of parts from which a machine gun can be assembled if such parts are in the possession or under the control of a person." 27 CFR §478.11. As a result of this definition, the individual metal components that make up a whole machine gun, such as a full-auto sear, individually meet the federal definition of machine gun. The parts for the machine gun do not have to be assembled.

Similarly, under Florida law, a machine gun is defined as "any firearm, as defined herein, which shoots, or is designed to shoot, automatically more than one shot, without manually reloading, by a single function of the trigger." Florida Statute §790.001(9). In other words, if more than two bullets come out of a firearm with only one pull of the trigger, the firearm is a machine gun. Florida law lists machine guns as prohibited weapons under Section 790.221(1) of the Florida Statutes unless the possessor holds the proper paperwork under the NFA. See Florida Statute §790.221(3).

No new manufacturing of machine guns for private ownership
Because of a federal law that effectively disallows private ownership (not military, police department, etc.) of any machine guns manufactured after May 19, 1986, machine guns available for private ownership are limited to the legally registered machine guns that existed prior to May 19, 1986. Thus, the private market is very limited and prices, as a result, are very high.

C. Firearm suppressors

What is a suppressor? It is just a muffler for a firearm and is legal if all NFA requirements are met. In legal terms, a firearm suppressor is defined in 27 CFR §478.11 as "any device for silencing, muffling, or diminishing the report of a portable firearm, including any combination of parts, designed or redesigned, and intended for use in assembling or fabricating a firearm silencer or firearm muffler, and any part intended only for use in such assembly or fabrication."

Firearm suppressors are very practical instruments. They are great for hunting and recreational shooting not only because it suppresses gunshots in a way so as to not alarm other animals being hunted nearby, but also because it lessens the impact on the shooter's ears. However, firearms owners should be carefully aware that the definition of a suppressor is very broad under federal law. Suppressors do not need to be items manufactured specifically for use as a suppressor. There are some ordinary, everyday items that could be easily converted into a suppressor such as a water bottle or an automotive oil filter. Possession of otherwise legal items when used or modified to be used as a suppressor is illegal.

D. Destructive devices

The term "destructive device" is a legal term given to certain firearms, objects, and munitions that are illegal under the NFA.

The "destructive devices" as defined in the statute are effectively broken down into three categories: explosive devices, large caliber weapons, and parts easily convertible into a destructive device

---

DESTRUCTIVE DEVICES – PART A;
27 C.F.R. §478.11

Any explosive, incendiary, or poison gas (1) bomb, (2) grenade, (3) rocket having a propellant charge of more than 4 ounces, (4) missile having an explosive or incendiary charge of more than one-quarter ounce, (5) mine, or (6) device similar to any of the devices described in the preceding paragraphs of this definition.

The first portion of the definition of a destructive device deals with explosive, incendiary and poison gas munitions. The definition specifies that any explosive, incendiary, or poison gas bomb, grenade, mine or similar device is a destructive device. In addition, the definition includes a rocket having a propellant charge of more than four ounces and a missile (projectile) having an explosive or incendiary charge of more than one-quarter ounce. These topics and the regulations thereof are beyond the scope of this book's discussion.

DESTRUCTIVE DEVICES – PART B;
27 C.F.R. §478.11

Any type of weapon (other than a shotgun or shotgun shell which the Director finds is generally recognized as particularly suitable for sporting purposes) by whatever name known which will, or which may be readily converted to, expel a projectile by the action of an explosive or other propellant, and which has any barrel with a bore of more than one-half inch in diameter.

The second section of the definition addresses large caliber weapons and states that any type of weapon that has a bore diameter of more than one-half inch in diameter is a destructive device with the exception of shotguns (and shotgun shells) that are suitable for sporting purposes. Thus, any caliber in a rifle or handgun more than .5 inches or fifty caliber is classified as a destructive device. Shotguns are exempt from this prohibition on size unless the ATF rules it is not for "sporting purposes." How do you know if a shotgun is suitable for sporting purposes? The ATF keeps a list, and has issued rulings classifying specific shotguns as destructive devices because they are not considered to be particularly "suitable for sporting purposes" including the USAS-12, Striker-12, Streetsweeper, and 37/38mm Beanbags. The ATF does not provide any specific definition of what constitutes being "suitable for sporting purposes" nor does it specify the methodology in which it determines what makes a particular shotgun suitable for sporting purposes. Ultimately, one will have to check with the ATF lists to see whether a particular shotgun with a larger bore-diameter is classified as a destructive device or not.

DESTRUCTIVE DEVICES – PART C; 27 C.F.R. § 478.11

Any combination of parts either designed or intended for use in converting any destructive device described in [part] (A) and (B) of this section and from which a destructive device may be readily assembled.

Finally, a destructive device does not need to be a completed and assembled product to fall under the federal definition and regulation under the NFA. Much like machine guns, if a person possesses parts that can be readily assembled into a destructive device, then whether or not the device has actually been constructed is irrelevant—by law it's already a destructive device.

Although these firearms, munitions, and devices are prohibited by the law on its face pursuant to the National Firearms Act, a person may nevertheless receive permission to possess them so long as they possess the correct legal authorization.

E. "Any Other Weapons" or AOWs

The AOW category under the NFA pertains to firearms and weapons that may not fit the traditional definition of some of the firearms discussed elsewhere in this book due to the way in which they are manufactured or modified. Under federal law, an AOW is "any weapon or device capable of being concealed on the person from which a shot can be discharged through the energy of an explosive, a pistol or revolver having a barrel with a smooth bore designed or redesigned to fire a fixed shotgun shell, weapons with combination shotgun and rifle barrels 12 inches or more, less than 18 inches in length, from which only a single discharge can be made from either barrel without manual reloading, and shall include any such weapon which may be readily restored to fire. Such term shall not include a pistol or a revolver having a rifled bore, or rifled bores, or weapons designed, made, or intended to be fired from the shoulder and not capable of firing fixed ammunition." 26 U.S.C. §5845(e).

1. Concealable weapons and devices

Weapons which are capable of being concealed from which one shot can be discharged are AOWs. This includes such weapons as a pen gun, knife gun, or umbrella gun. Florida law does not use the term AOW but rather makes any weapon designed "to expel a projectile by the action of an explosive; the frame or receiver of any such weapon; any firearm muffler or firearm silencer; any destructive device; or any machine gun" a firearm within the meaning of our laws. See Florida Statute §790.001(6).

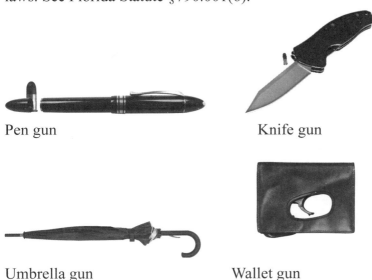

Pen gun

Knife gun

Umbrella gun

Wallet gun

2. Pistols and revolvers having a smooth-bore barrel for firing shotgun shells

Pistols and revolvers that have a smooth bore (no rifling) that are designed to shoot shotgun ammunition are defined as an AOW. The ATF cites firearms such as the H&R Handy Gun or the Ithaca Auto & Burglar Gun as firearms which fall under the AOW category. Note: handguns with partially rifled barrels such as The Judge do not fall under this category due to the rifling of the barrel.

H&R Handy Gun

Ithaca Auto & Burglar Gun

3. Weapons with barrels 12 inches or longer and lengths 18 inches or shorter

The definition of Any Other Weapon also includes any weapon which has a shotgun or rifle barrel of 12 inches or more but is 18 inches or less in overall length from which only a single discharge can be made from either barrel without manual reloading. The ATF identifies the "Marble Game Getter" as the firearm most commonly associated with this definition (excluding the model with an 18" barrel and folding shoulder stock).

4. Pistols and revolvers with vertical handgrips

If a pistol is modified with a vertical grip on the front, it will now be legally classified as an AOW and require registration and a paid tax. Note, vertical grips are readily available and are legal to own as long as they are not placed on a handgun. The definition of a handgun is a weapon which is intended to be fired by one hand; the addition of the vertical foregrip makes it so the weapon now is intended to be used with two hands to fire. This modification changes the weapon from a handgun to what is known as an "AOW" and is now a prohibited weapon without the proper documentation.

F. Antique firearms

Firearms that are defined by the NFA as "antique firearms" are not regulated by the NFA. The NFA definition of antique firearm is found in 26 U.S.C. §5845(g) as "any firearm not designed or redesigned for using rim fire or conventional center fire ignition with fixed ammunition and manufactured in or before 1898 (including any matchlock, flintlock, percussion cap, or similar type of ignition system or replica thereof, whether actually manufactured before or after the year 1898) and also any firearm using fixed ammunition manufactured in or before 1898, for which ammunition is no longer manufactured in the United States and is not readily available in the ordinary channels of commercial trade." Under this statute and for NFA purposes, the only firearms that are antiques are firearms which were both actually manufactured in or before 1898 and ones for which fixed ammunition is no longer manufactured in the United States and is not readily available in the ordinary channels of commercial trade.

With this in mind, the ATF states in its NFA guidebook that "it is important to note that a specific type of fixed ammunition that has been out of production for many years may again become available due to increasing interest in older firearms. Therefore, the classification of a specific NFA firearm as an antique can change if ammunition for the weapon becomes readily available in the ordinary channels of commerce."

G. NFA curio firearms and relics

Under federal law, curios or relics are defined in 27 CFR §478.11 as "firearms which are of special interest to collectors by reason of some quality other than is associated with firearms intended for sporting use or as offensive or defensive weapons." Persons who collect curios or relics may do so with a special collector's license although one is not required. The impact of an NFA item being classified as a curio or relic, however, is that it allows the item to be transferred interstate to persons possessing a collector's license. The collector's license does not allow the individual to deal in curios or relics, nor does it allow the collector to obtain other firearms interstate as those transactions still require an FFL.

PRACTICAL LEGAL TIP

Some of the items regulated by the NFA simply don't make as much sense as other things it regulates. Suppressors are really nothing more than mufflers for your firearm—they aren't really firearms themselves (notwithstanding the legal definition). Thinking about the utility of the suppressor, if the firearm was invented today, you can be sure that not only would the government not prohibit them, OSHA would probably require them for safety purposes! -David

To be classified as a curio or relic, federal law states that the firearm must fall into one of the following three categories:

1. Firearms which were manufactured at least 50 years prior to the current date, but not including replicas thereof;
2. Firearms which are certified by the curator of a municipal, State, or Federal museum which exhibits firearms to be curious or relics of museum interest; or
3. Any other firearms which derive a substantial part of their monetary value from the fact that they are novel, rare, bizarre, or because of their association with some historical figure, period, or event.

See 27 CFR §478.11.

The ATF maintains a list of firearms that are classified as curios or relics.

H. How can some after-market gun parts make your firearm illegal?

A number of companies manufacture and sell gun products or parts that alter the appearance or utility of a firearm (*i.e.*, shoulder stocks, forward hand grips, etc.). However, some of these after-market products can actually change the firearm you possess from one type of a weapon to another type of weapon for legal purposes whether you realize it or not. As a result, many individuals make the modifications to their firearms thinking that because there was no special process for purchasing the accessory, any modification would be in compliance with the law. Unfortunately, this is not always the case. Consider the example of short-barreled uppers for AR-15s: selling, buying, or possessing AR-15 "uppers" with barrels less than 16 inches is legal. However, it is illegal to put the upper on a receiver of an AR-15 because this would be the act of manufacturing a short-barreled rifle and is legally prohibited. This is equally true of vertical forward grips on a handgun. Vertical foregrips are legal to buy or possess, however, if you actually install one on a handgun, you have manufactured an AOW, and it is illegal, unless registered and a tax paid. Note: there are other types of braces that are permissible in their proper application and illegal in any application or adaptation that would alter the classification of the weapon. For example, the Sig Arm Brace is legal to attach to an AR Pistol when used as an arm brace, but illegal when used as a shoulder stock.

III. PROCESS AND PROCEDURE FOR OBTAINING NFA FIREARMS
A. Who can own and possess an NFA firearm?

Any person may own and possess an NFA firearm as long as they are legally not disqualified to own or possess firearms and live in a state that allows possession of NFA items. See Chapters 2 and 3. The ATF also allows for a non-person legal entity to own these items, such as corporations, partnerships, and trusts, etc.

B. What are the usual steps for buying or manufacturing NFA items?

Whether a person is buying or making (manufacturing) an NFA firearm, there are several steps in the process. The transfer or manufacture of an NFA firearm requires the filing of an appropriate transfer form with the ATF, payment of any federally-mandated transfer tax, approval of the transfer by the ATF, and registration of the firearm to the transferee. Only after these steps have occurred may a buyer legally take possession of the NFA item, or may a person legally assemble or manufacture the NFA item. In this section, we will walk through the process, step-by-step, of (1) purchasing an NFA item that already exists, and (2) manufacturing an NFA firearm.

PRACTICAL LEGAL TIP

Even if you don't own a machine gun today, that doesn't mean you won't be the intended owner of one later. A person could always leave you their NFA items in a will. If this happens, you must file the appropriate paperwork with the ATF as soon as possible, or at least before probate is closed. -David

Steps for buying an existing NFA item (for example, a suppressor)

1. Select and purchase the item (suppressor) from a dealer;
2. Assemble appropriate paperwork (ATF Form 4, see Appendix B) and money order for the tax stamp ($200);
   a. If the buyer is an individual, the individual must secure

Chief Law Enforcement Officer signature on ATF Form 4, a photograph, and fingerprints (though after July 13, 2016, only CLEO notification is required, not certification);

b. If the buyer is a corporation/trust, no Chief Law Enforcement Officer signature, photograph, or fingerprints are required. Note that this step changes due to ATF Rule 41f, effective July 13, 2016. Once effective, the ATF will require that for each application, all "responsible persons" of the trust submit fingerprints and photographs as well as notify their CLEO (though no certification or approval is required).

c. After July 13, 2016, all applicants will also have to complete and send in a copy of ATF Form 5320.23 for each responsible person. Form 5320.23 requires certain identifying information for each responsible person. This information will allow the ATF to conduct background checks on each responsible person.

3. Submit paperwork, fingerprints, and money order for the tax stamp to the ATF → ATF review and approval;

4. ATF sends approval (tax stamp affixed to Form 4) to the dealer;

5. Pick up suppressor from the dealer.

Steps for manufacturing an NFA item (such as a short-barreled rifle)

1. Select the item to manufacture or modify, *i.e.*, short-barreled AR-15;

2. Assemble appropriate paperwork (ATF Form 1, see Appendix B) and a money order for the tax stamp ($200);

a. If the maker is an individual, the individual must secure Chief Law Enforcement Officer signature on ATF Form 1, a photograph, and fingerprints (though after July 13, 2016, only CLEO notification is required, not certification).

b. If the maker is a corporation/trust, no Chief Law Enforcement

Officer signature, photograph, or fingerprints are required. Note that this step changes due to ATF Rule 41f, effective July 13, 2016. Once effective, the ATF will require that for each application, all "responsible persons" of the trust submit fingerprints and photographs as well as notify their CLEO (though no certification or approval is required).

   c. After July 13, 2016, all applicants will also have to complete and send in a copy of ATF Form 5320.23 for each responsible person. Form 5320.23 requires certain identifying information for each responsible person. This information will allow the ATF to conduct background checks on each responsible person.

3. Submit paperwork and tax to the ATF → ATF review and approval;

4. ATF sends you the approval (tax stamp affixed to Form 1);

5. Maker may then legally assemble the AR-15, *i.e.*, put upper with a barrel length of less than 16 inches on a lower receiver, etc. The item must now be engraved and identified, see below.

When purchasing an NFA firearm from a dealer, the dealer is required to have the purchaser fill out ATF Form 4473 when the purchaser goes to pick up the item from the dealer. There is a background check for a firearm, but not for a suppressor.

Who is a "responsible person" under the new ATF rule?

The ATF defines a "responsible person" as "anyone with the power or authority to direct the management of the trust to receive, possess, ship, transport, deliver, transfer, or dispose of the NFA firearm." In other words, pretty much everybody in a trust, except for the beneficiaries (unless they also have the power listed above), or anyone who is allowed to possess the items in a corporation.

Do I have to send photographs and fingerprints for every single item I purchase?

According to the ATF's rule, for applications submitted after July 13, 2016, while you will have to provide this information for each responsible person, if nothing has changed since a previous purchase where you provided this information, you can send a certification that there have been no changes instead of having to send along the photographs and fingerprints.

C. How must an NFA item be engraved and identified if I make it myself?

Once you receive ATF approval to manufacture your own NFA item (such as the short-barreled AR-15 in the previous section), federal law requires that you engrave, cast, stamp, or otherwise conspicuously place or cause to be engraved, cast, stamped, or placed on the frame, receiver, or barrel of the NFA item the following information:

1. The item's serial number;
2. The item's model (if so designated);
3. Caliber or gauge;
4. The name of the owner whether individual, corporation, or trust; and
5. The city and state where the item was made.

D. Which way should I own my NFA item? Paperwork requirements for individuals, trusts, or business entities to own NFA items

Form 4 and Form 1

The appropriate paperwork that must be assembled and submitted to the ATF under the NFA varies depending on whether an individual, or a legal entity such as a trust, corporation, or partnership is purchasing or manufacturing the NFA item. The paperwork generally starts either with an ATF Form 4 (used for purchasing an existing item), or an ATF Form 1 which is used if a person wishes to manufacture a new NFA item. All relevant portions of the Form must be completed. Both Form 4 and Form 1 have a requirement that a Chief Law Enforcement Officer for the applicant must sign the ATF Form. However, this requirement only applies to living, breathing individuals; it does not apply to applicants who are legal entities like trusts, corporations, etc. Therefore, a Chief Law Enforcement Officer signature is not necessary. The signature of the Chief Law Enforcement Officer may be difficult or impossible to obtain for an individual in Florida. There is no law that says the Chief Law Enforcement Officer must sign off on the Form 1 or Form 4.

Note that this is the law until ATF Rule 41f goes into effect, July 13, 2016. After July 13, 2016, the ATF will require that for each application, all "responsible persons" of the trust submit fingerprints and photographs, as well as notify their CLEO by sending a copy of the Form 1 or 4 respectively, or a copy of the 5320.23 (though no certification or approval is required). Under the ATF's new rule, all applicants will also have to complete and send in a copy of ATF Form 5320.23 for each responsible person. Form 5320.23 requires certain identifying information for each responsible person. This information will allow the ATF to conduct background checks on each responsible person.

Who may sign a Form 4 or Form 1 as a Chief Law Enforcement Officer?

For the purposes of Form 4, "the chief law enforcement officer is considered to be the Chief of Police for the transferee's city or town of residence, the Sheriff for the transferee's county of residence; the

Head of the State Police for the transferee's State of residence; a State or local district attorney or prosecutor having jurisdiction in the transferee's area of residence; or another person whose certification is acceptable to the Director, Bureau of Alcohol, Tobacco and Firearms." ATF Form 1, Instructions. Keep in mind, this step will no longer be required for applications submitted after July 13, 2016.

Photograph and fingerprints only required for individual applicants
In addition, if an individual is purchasing or manufacturing an NFA item, the applicant must submit an appropriate photograph and their fingerprints. Neither fingerprints nor photographs are required if the applicant is not an individual. Conversely, an entity such as a trust or corporation must submit the appropriate documents showing its existence, such as the trust or corporate formation documents. Note that this only applies to applications submitted prior to the July 13, 2016; for trusts and corporations that attempt to purchase items after July 13, 2016, both photographs and fingerprint cards are necessary for every responsible person in a trust or corporation.

Does the new ATF rule, Rule 41f, grandfather in existing items or submitted applications?
If you have a tax stamp prior to the new rule, or have already submitted your paperwork, the ATF will grandfather in all such applicants. However, any application submitted after the effective date of 41f, July 13, 2016, even if the trust already existed, you will have to comply with the regulations of Rule 41f.

E. Why are trusts so popular to own NFA items?
There are four major reasons trusts are very popular to own NFA items: turnaround time, paperwork, control, and ease of ownership. A trust is a legal entity that can hold property.

The turnaround time for NFA approvals with the ATF varies. For example, in 2014, we were seeing wait times on Form 4 approval for individuals as long as 10 months or longer. In 2014, we were seeing wait times on Form 1 approval for individuals as long as 5 months or longer. In the first quarter of 2015, we saw these times reduced quite a bit. However, one important aspect to note is that the wait time for Form 1 or Form 4 approvals for trusts are reduced by several months when compared to approval times for individuals.

On the paperwork side, trusts are beneficial because they, as of the time of writing, do not require the signature of the Chief Law Enforcement Officer on Form 1 or Form 4. In addition, unlike individuals seeking ownership of an NFA item, no fingerprints or photographs are required (though after July 13, 2016, fingerprints and photographs will be required for every responsible person in a trust). The only paperwork required to own an NFA item under a trust is the trust agreement and the appropriate ATF form or forms.

A third major reason for having a trust own an NFA item is that it makes owning and using the NFA item easier if more than one person wishes to use the item. If an individual owns the item, then only the individual can ever "possess" it. On the other hand, if the item is owned by a trust, all trustees, including co-trustees, are able to possess and use the items contained in the trust. Therefore, co-trustees may be added or removed. [Note: non-trustees and non-owners may still use a properly registered NFA firearm, but only when in "the presence" of the owner.]

Finally, unlike other entities such as corporations, LLCs, etc., a trust requires no filings with a government to create, which saves expenses and even preserves privacy. Further, these expense savings continue because there are no continuing government fees or compliance requirements. Thus, trusts are one of the best ways currently to own an NFA item.

F. The Tax Stamp

Once the ATF has an applicant's materials in hand, they will be reviewed and checked by NFA researchers and an examiner. The application will then either be approved or denied. A denial will be accompanied by an explanation of why the application was denied and how to remedy it, if possible. If the application is approved, the examiner will affix a tax stamp on one of the submitted Form 1 or Form 4 and send the newly-stamped Form to the applicant.

This tax stamp on the appropriate form is a person's evidence of compliance with the NFA's requirements and is a very important document. A copy should always be kept with the NFA item.

G. What documents should I have with me when I am in actual possession of my suppressor, short-barreled firearm, or other NFA item?

If you have an NFA item, always have the proper documentation with you to prove that you legally possess the item. Again, if you are in possession of your suppressor, short-barreled firearm, destructive device, or if you are lucky enough, your machine gun, always have your paperwork showing you are legal, or it may be a long day with law enforcement. To show you are legal, always keep a copy of your ATF Form 4 or Form 1 (whichever is applicable) with the tax stamp affixed for every NFA item in your possession, personal identification, and if the item is held in a trust or corporation, a copy of the trust or articles of incorporation, and the authorization for your possession. Care should be given to make sure these documents name the individual so as to show legal ownership, *i.e.*, trust and/or amendments showing the person is a co-trustee or an officer of the corporation.

Practically, individuals should not carry around the original documents as they could be destroyed by wear and tear, rain, or be misplaced, effectively destroying the required evidence of compliance. Photocopies of the stamp and any other pertinent documents are generally enough to satisfy inquisitive law enforcement officials. The more technologically advanced may take pictures on their phone or other mobile device, or even upload them to a cloud database. Keep in mind that if the phone dies or the cloud cannot be reached, and you have no way to access the documents, your proof is gone and you may have a very bad day ahead of you! We recommend keeping photocopies of the ATF form with the tax stamp affixed and appropriate documents to avoid any problems with technology.

H. Why is the paperwork necessary?

According to Florida Statute §790.221, short-barreled rifles, short-barreled shotguns, and machine guns are illegal to possess. However, Florida Statute §790.221(3) states that "Firearms in violation hereof which are lawfully owned and possessed under provisions of federal law are excepted." In other words, if you own and possess one of these weapons and are in compliance with the NFA, you have not violated the law in Florida and cannot be arrested.

APPENDIX A
Selected Florida Statutes

FLORIDA STATUTES TITLE XLVI, CHAPTER 776: JUSTIFIABLE USE OF FORCE

776.012 USE OR THREATENED USE OF FORCE IN DEFENSE OF PERSON.— JUSTIFICATION AS A DEFENSE.

(1) A person is justified in using or threatening to use force, except deadly force, against another when and to the extent that the person reasonably believes that such conduct is necessary to defend himself or herself or another against the other's imminent use of unlawful force. A person who uses or threatens to use force in accordance with this subsection does not have a duty to retreat before using or threatening to use such force.

(2) A person is justified in using or threatening to use deadly force if he or she reasonably believes that using or threatening to use

such force is necessary to prevent imminent death or great bodily harm to himself or herself or another or to prevent the imminent commission of a forcible felony. A person who uses or threatens to use deadly force in accordance with this subsection does not have a duty to retreat and has the right to stand his or her ground if the person using or threatening to use the deadly force is not engaged in a criminal activity and is in a place where he or she has a right to be.

776.013

(current law as amended July 2017) Home protection; use or threatened use of deadly force; presumption of fear of death or great bodily harm.—

(1) A person who is in a dwelling or residence in which the person has a right to be has no duty to retreat and has the right to stand his or her ground and use or threaten to use:

    (a) Nondeadly force against another when and to the extent that the person reasonably believes that such conduct is necessary to defend himself or herself or another against the other's imminent use of unlawful force; or

    (b) Deadly force if he or she reasonably believes that using or threatening to use such force is necessary to prevent imminent death or great bodily harm to himself or herself or another or to prevent the imminent commission of a forcible felony.

(2) A person is presumed to have held a reasonable fear of imminent peril of death or great bodily harm to himself or herself or another when using or threatening to use defensive force that is intended or likely to cause death or great bodily harm to another if:

    (a) The person against whom the defensive force was used or threatened was in the process of unlawfully and forcefully entering, or had unlawfully and forcibly entered, a dwelling, residence, or occupied vehicle, or if that person had removed or was attempting to remove another against that person's will from the dwelling, residence, or occupied vehicle; and

(b) The person who uses or threatens to use defensive force knew or had reason to believe that an unlawful and forcible entry or unlawful and forcible act was occurring or had occurred.

(3) The presumption set forth in subsection (2) does not apply if:

(a) The person against whom the defensive force is used or threatened has the right to be in or is a lawful resident of the dwelling, residence, or vehicle, such as an owner, lessee, or titleholder, and there is not an injunction for protection from domestic violence or a written pretrial supervision order of no contact against that person; or

(b) The person or persons sought to be removed is a child or grandchild, or is otherwise in the lawful custody or under the lawful guardianship of, the person against whom the defensive force is used or threatened; or

(c) The person who uses or threatens to use defensive force is engaged in a criminal activity or is using the dwelling, residence, or occupied vehicle to further a criminal activity; or

(d) The person against whom the defensive force is used or threatened is a law enforcement officer, as defined in s. 943.10(14), who enters or attempts to enter a dwelling, residence, or vehicle in the performance of his or her official duties and the officer identified himself or herself in accordance with any applicable law or the person using or threatening to use force knew or reasonably should have known that the person entering or attempting to enter was a law enforcement officer.

(4) A person who unlawfully and by force enters or attempts to

enter a person's dwelling, residence, or occupied vehicle is presumed to be doing so with the intent to commit an unlawful act involving force or violence.

(5) As used in this section, the term:

    (a) "Dwelling" means a building or conveyance of any kind, including any attached porch, whether the building or conveyance is temporary or permanent, mobile or immobile, which has a roof over it, including a tent, and is designed to be occupied by people lodging therein at night.

    (b) "Residence" means a dwelling in which a person resides either temporarily or permanently or is visiting as an invited guest.

    (c) "Vehicle" means a conveyance of any kind, whether or not motorized, which is designed to transport people or property.

776.013

(No longer valid, included for comparison to above current law) Home protection; use or threatened use of deadly force; presumption of fear of death or great bodily harm.–

(1) A person is presumed to have held a reasonable fear of imminent peril of death or great bodily harm to himself or herself or another when using or threatening to use defensive force that is intended or likely to cause death or great bodily harm to another if:

    (a) The person against whom the defensive force was used or threatened was in the process of unlawfully and forcefully entering, or had unlawfully and forcibly entered, a dwelling, residence, or occupied vehicle, or if that person had removed or was attempting to remove another against that person's will from the dwelling, residence, or occupied vehicle; and

    (b) The person who uses or threatens to use defensive force knew or had reason to believe that an unlawful and forcible entry or unlawful and forcible act was occurring or had occurred.

(2) The presumption set forth in subsection (1) does not apply if:

(a) The person against whom the defensive force is used or threatened has the right to be in or is a lawful resident of the dwelling, residence, or vehicle, such as an owner, lessee, or titleholder, and there is not an injunction for protection from domestic violence or a written pretrial supervision order of no contact against that person; or

(b) The person or persons sought to be removed is a child or grandchild, or is otherwise in the lawful custody or under the lawful guardianship of, the person against whom the defensive force is used or threatened; or

(c) The person who uses or threatens to use defensive force is engaged in a criminal activity or is using the dwelling, residence, or occupied vehicle to further a criminal activity; or

(d) The person against whom the defensive force is used or threatened is a law enforcement officer, as defined in s. 943.10(14), who enters or attempts to enter a dwelling, residence, or vehicle in the performance of his or her official duties and the officer identified himself or herself in accordance with any applicable law or the person using or threatening to use force knew or reasonably should have known that the person entering or attempting to enter was a law enforcement officer.

(3) A person who is attacked in his or her dwelling, residence, or vehicle has no duty to retreat and has the right to stand his or her ground and use or threaten to use force, including deadly force, if he or she uses or threatens to use force in accordance with s. 776.012(1) or (2) or s. 776.031(1) or (2).

(4) A person who unlawfully and by force enters or attempts to

enter a person's dwelling, residence, or occupied vehicle is presumed to be doing so with the intent to commit an unlawful act involving force or violence.

(5) As used in this section, the term:

    (a) "Dwelling" means a building or conveyance of any kind, including any attached porch, whether the building or conveyance is temporary or permanent, mobile or immobile, which has a roof over it, including a tent, and is designed to be occupied by people lodging therein at night.

    (b) "Residence" means a dwelling in which a person resides either temporarily or permanently or is visiting as an invited guest.

    (c) "Vehicle" means a conveyance of any kind, whether or not motorized, which is designed to transport people or property.

776.031

Use or threatened use of force in defense of property.–

(1) A person is justified in using or threatening to use force, except deadly force, against another when and to the extent that the person reasonably believes that such conduct is necessary to prevent or terminate the other's trespass on, or other tortious or criminal interference with, either real property other than a dwelling or personal property, lawfully in his or her possession or in the possession of another who is a member of his or her immediate family or household or of a person whose property he or she has a legal duty to protect. A person who uses or threatens to use force in accordance with this subsection does not have a duty to retreat before using or threatening to use such force.

(2) A person is justified in using or threatening to use deadly force only if he or she reasonably believes that such conduct

is necessary to prevent the imminent commission of a forcible felony. A person who uses or threatens to use deadly force in accordance with this subsection does not have a duty to retreat and has the right to stand his or her ground if the person using or threatening to use the deadly force is not engaged in a criminal activity and is in a place where he or she has a right to be.

776.032

(current law as amended July 2017) Immunity from criminal prosecution and civil action for justifiable use or threatened use of force.—

(1) A person who uses or threatens to use force as permitted in s. 776.012, s. 776.013, or s. 776.031 is justified in such conduct and is immune from criminal prosecution and civil action for the use or threatened use of such force by the person, personal representative, or heirs of the person against whom the force was used or threatened, unless the person against whom force was used or threatened is a law enforcement officer, as defined in s. 943.10(14), who was acting in the performance of his or her official duties and the officer identified himself or herself in accordance with any applicable law or the person using or threatening to use force knew or reasonably should have known that the person was a law enforcement officer. As used in this subsection, the term "criminal prosecution" includes arresting, detaining in custody, and charging or prosecuting the defendant.

(2) A law enforcement agency may use standard procedures for investigating the use or threatened use of force as described in subsection (1), but the agency may not arrest the person for using or threatening to use force unless it determines that there is probable cause that the force that was used or threatened was unlawful.

(3) The court shall award reasonable attorney's fees, court costs, compensation for loss of income, and all expenses incurred by the defendant in defense of any civil action brought by a plaintiff if the court finds that the defendant is immune from prosecution as provided in subsection (1).

(4) In a criminal prosecution, once a prima facie claim of self-defense immunity from criminal prosecution has been raised by the defendant at a pretrial immunity hearing, the burden of proof by clear and convincing evidence is on the party seeking to overcome the immunity from criminal prosecution provided in subsection (1).

776.032

(No longer valid, included for comparison to above current law)Immunity from criminal prosecution and civil action for justifiable use or threatened use of force.–

(1) A person who uses or threatens to use force as permitted in s. 776.012, s. 776.013, or s. 776.031 is justified in such conduct and is immune from criminal prosecution and civil action for the use or threatened use of such force by the person, personal representative, or heirs of the person against whom the force was used or threatened, unless the person against whom force was used or threatened is a law enforcement officer, as defined in s. 943.10(14), who was acting in the performance of his or her official duties and the officer identified himself or herself in accordance with any applicable law or the person using or threatening to use force knew or reasonably should have known that the person was a law enforcement officer. As used in this subsection, the term "criminal prosecution" includes arresting, detaining in custody, and charging or prosecuting the defendant.

(2) A law enforcement agency may use standard procedures for investigating the use or threatened use of force as described in subsection (1), but the agency may not arrest the person for using or threatening to use force unless it determines that there is probable cause that the force that was used or threatened was unlawful.

(3) The court shall award reasonable attorney's fees, court costs, compensation for loss of income, and all expenses incurred by the defendant in defense of any civil action brought by a plaintiff if the court finds that the defendant is immune from prosecution as provided in subsection (1).

776.041

Use or threatened use of force by aggressor.—The justification described in the preceding sections of this chapter is not available to a person who:

(1) Is attempting to commit, committing, or escaping after the commission of, a forcible felony; or

(2) Initially provokes the use or threatened use of force against himself or herself, unless:

    (a) Such force or threat of force is so great that the person reasonably believes that he or she is in imminent danger of death or great bodily harm and that he or she has exhausted every reasonable means to escape such danger other than the use or threatened use of force which is likely to cause death or great bodily harm to the assailant; or

    (b) In good faith, the person withdraws from physical contact with the assailant and indicates clearly to the assailant that he or she desires to withdraw and terminate the use or threatened use of force, but the assailant continues or resumes the use or threatened use of force.

776.05

Law enforcement officers; use of force in making an arrest.—A law enforcement officer, or any person whom the officer has summoned or directed to assist him or her, need not retreat or desist from efforts to make a lawful arrest because of resistance or threatened resistance to the arrest. The officer is justified in the use of any force:

(1) Which he or she reasonably believes to be necessary to defend himself or herself or another from bodily harm while making the arrest;

(2) When necessarily committed in retaking felons who have escaped; or

(3) When necessarily committed in arresting felons fleeing from justice. However, this subsection shall not constitute a defense in any civil action for damages brought for the wrongful use of deadly force unless the use of deadly force was necessary to prevent the arrest from being defeated by such flight and, when feasible, some warning had been given, and:

(a) The officer reasonably believes that the fleeing felon poses a threat of death or serious physical harm to the officer or others; or

(b) The officer reasonably believes that the fleeing felon has committed a crime involving the infliction or threatened infliction of serious physical harm to another person.

776.051

Use or threatened use of force in resisting arrest or making an arrest or in the execution of a legal duty; prohibition.–

(1) A person is not justified in the use or threatened use of force to resist an arrest by a law enforcement officer, or to resist a

law enforcement officer who is engaged in the execution of a legal duty, if the law enforcement officer was acting in good faith and he or she is known, or reasonably appears, to be a law enforcement officer.

(2) A law enforcement officer, or any person whom the officer has summoned or directed to assist him or her, is not justified in the use of force if the arrest or execution of a legal duty is unlawful and known by him or her to be unlawful.

776.06

Deadly force by a law enforcement or correctional officer.–

(1) As applied to a law enforcement officer or correctional officer acting in the performance of his or her official duties, the term "deadly force" means force that is likely to cause death or great bodily harm and includes, but is not limited to:

(a) The firing of a firearm in the direction of the person to be arrested, even though no intent exists to kill or inflict great bodily harm; and

(b) The firing of a firearm at a vehicle in which the person to be arrested is riding.

(2)

(a) The term "deadly force" does not include the discharge of a firearm by a law enforcement officer or correctional officer during and within the scope of his or her official duties which is loaded with a less-lethal munition. As used in this subsection, the term "less-lethal munition" means a projectile that is designed to stun, temporarily incapacitate, or cause temporary discomfort to a person without penetrating the person's body.

(b) A law enforcement officer or a correctional officer is not liable in any civil or criminal action arising out of the use of any less-lethal munition in good faith during and within the scope of his or her official duties.

776.07
Use of force to prevent escape.–

(1) A law enforcement officer or other person who has an arrested person in his or her custody is justified in the use of any force which he or she reasonably believes to be necessary to prevent the escape of the arrested person from custody.

(2) A correctional officer or other law enforcement officer is justified in the use of force, including deadly force, which he or she reasonably believes to be necessary to prevent the escape from a penal institution of a person whom the officer reasonably believes to be lawfully detained in such institution under sentence for an offense or awaiting trial or commitment for an offense.

776.08
Forcible felony

"Forcible felony" means treason; murder; manslaughter; sexual battery; carjacking; home-invasion robbery; robbery; burglary; arson; kidnapping; aggravated assault; aggravated battery; aggravated stalking; aircraft piracy; unlawful throwing, placing, or discharging of a destructive device or bomb; and any other felony which involves the use or threat of physical force or violence against any individual.

776.085

Defense to civil action for damages; party convicted of forcible or attempted forcible felony.–

(1) It shall be a defense to any action for damages for personal injury or wrongful death, or for injury to property, that such action arose from injury sustained by a participant during the commission or attempted commission of a forcible felony. The defense authorized by this section shall be established by evidence that the participant has been convicted of such forcible felony or attempted forcible felony, or by proof of the commission of such crime or attempted crime by a preponderance of the evidence.

(2) For the purposes of this section, the term "forcible felony" shall have the same meaning as in s. 776.08.

(3) Any civil action in which the defense recognized by this section is raised shall be stayed by the court on the motion of the civil defendant during the pendency of any criminal action which forms the basis for the defense, unless the court finds that a conviction in the criminal action would not form a valid defense under this section.

(4) In any civil action where a party prevails based on the defense created by this section:

(a) The losing party, if convicted of and incarcerated for the crime or attempted crime, shall, as determined by the court, lose any privileges provided by the correctional facility, including, but not limited to:

1. Canteen purchases;
2. Telephone access;
3. Outdoor exercise;
4. Use of the library; and
5. Visitation.

(b) The court shall award a reasonable attorney's fee to be paid to the prevailing party in equal amounts by the losing party and the losing party's attorney; however, the losing party's attorney is not personally responsible if he or she has acted in good faith, based on the representations of his or her client. If the losing party is incarcerated for the crime or attempted crime and has insufficient assets to cover payment of the costs of the action and the award of fees pursuant to this paragraph, the party shall, as determined by the court, be required to pay by deduction from any payments the prisoner receives while incarcerated.

(c) If the losing party is incarcerated for the crime or attempted crime, the court shall issue a written order containing its findings and ruling pursuant to paragraphs (a) and (b) and shall direct that a certified copy be forwarded to the appropriate correctional institution or facility.

776.09

Retention of records pertaining to persons found to be acting in lawful self-defense; expunction of criminal history records.–

(1) Whenever the state attorney or statewide prosecutor dismisses an information, indictment, or other charging document, or decides not to file an information, indictment, or other charging document because of a finding that the person accused acted in lawful self-defense pursuant to the provisions related to the justifiable use of force in this chapter, that finding shall be documented in writing and retained in the files of the state attorney or statewide prosecutor.

(2) Whenever a court dismisses an information, indictment, or other charging document because of a finding that the person

accused acted in lawful self-defense pursuant to the provisions related to the justifiable use of force in this chapter, that finding shall be recorded in an order or memorandum, which shall be retained in the court's records.

(3) Under either condition described in subsection (1) or subsection (2), the person accused may apply for a certificate of eligibility to expunge the associated criminal history record, pursuant to s. 943.0585(5), notwithstanding the eligibility requirements prescribed in s. 943.0585(1)(b) or (2).

FLORIDA STATUTES TITLE XLVI, CHAPTER 790: WEAPONS AND FIREARMS

790.001   DEFINITIONS.

As used in this chapter, except where the context otherwise requires:

(1) "Antique firearm" means any firearm manufactured in or before 1918 (including any matchlock, flintlock, percussion cap, or similar early type of ignition system) or replica thereof, whether actually manufactured before or after the year 1918, and also any firearm using fixed ammunition manufactured in or before 1918, for which ammunition is no longer manufactured in the United States and is not readily available in the ordinary channels of commercial trade.

(2) "Concealed firearm" means any firearm, as defined in subsection (6), which is carried on or about a person in such a manner as to conceal the firearm from the ordinary sight of another person.

(3)

    (a) "Concealed weapon" means any dirk, metallic knuckles, slungshot, billie, tear gas gun, chemical weapon or device, or other deadly weapon carried on or about a person in such a manner as to conceal the weapon from the ordinary sight of another person.

(b) "Tear gas gun" or "chemical weapon or device" means any weapon of such nature, except a device known as a "self-defense chemical spray." "Self-defense chemical spray" means a device carried solely for purposes of lawful self-defense that is compact in size, designed to be carried on or about the person, and contains not more than two ounces of chemical.

(4) "Destructive device" means any bomb, grenade, mine, rocket, missile, pipe bomb, or similar device containing an explosive, incendiary, or poison gas and includes any frangible container filled with an explosive, incendiary, explosive gas, or expanding gas, which is designed or so constructed as to explode by such filler and is capable of causing bodily harm or property damage; any combination of parts either designed or intended for use in converting any device into a destructive device and from which a destructive device may be readily assembled; any device declared a destructive device by the Bureau of Alcohol, Tobacco, and Firearms; any type of weapon which will, is designed to, or may readily be converted to expel a projectile by the action of any explosive and which has a barrel with a bore of one-half inch or more in diameter; and ammunition for such destructive devices, but not including shotgun shells or any other ammunition designed for use in a firearm other than a destructive device. "Destructive device" does not include:

(a) A device which is not designed, redesigned, used, or intended for use as a weapon;

(b) Any device, although originally designed as a weapon, which is redesigned so that it may be used solely as a signaling, line-throwing, safety, or similar device;

(c) Any shotgun other than a short-barreled shotgun; or

(d) Any non-automatic rifle (other than a short-barreled rifle) generally recognized or particularly suitable for use for the hunting of big game.

(5) "Explosive" means any chemical compound or mixture that has the property of yielding readily to combustion or oxidation upon application of heat, flame, or shock, including but not limited to dynamite, nitroglycerin, trinitrotoluene, or ammonium nitrate when combined with other ingredients to form an explosive mixture, blasting caps, and detonators; but not including:

(a) Shotgun shells, cartridges, or ammunition for firearms;

(b) Fireworks as defined in s. 791.01;

(c) Smokeless propellant powder or small arms ammunition primers, if possessed, purchased, sold, transported, or used in compliance with s. 552.241;

(d) Black powder in quantities not to exceed that authorized by chapter 552, or by any rules adopted thereunder by the Department of Financial Services, when used for, or intended to be used for, the manufacture of target and sporting ammunition or for use in muzzle-loading flint or percussion weapons. The exclusions contained in paragraphs (a)-(d) do not apply to the term "explosive" as used in the definition of "firearm" in subsection (6)

(6) "Firearm" means any weapon (including a starter gun) which will, is designed to, or may readily be converted to expel a projectile by the action of an explosive; the frame or receiver of any such weapon; any firearm muffler or firearm silencer; any destructive device; or any machine gun. The term "firearm" does not include an antique firearm unless the antique firearm is used in the commission of a crime.

(7) "Indictment" means an indictment or an information in any court under which a crime punishable by imprisonment for a term exceeding 1 year may be prosecuted.

(8) "Law enforcement officer" means:

    (a) All officers or employees of the United States or the State of Florida, or any agency, commission, department, board, division, municipality, or subdivision thereof, who have authority to make arrests;

    (b) Officers or employees of the United States or the State of Florida, or any agency, commission, department, board, division, municipality, or subdivision thereof, duly authorized to carry a concealed weapon;

    (c) Members of the Armed Forces of the United States, the organized reserves, state militia, or Florida National Guard, when on duty, when preparing themselves for, or going to or from, military duty, or under orders;

    (d) An employee of the state prisons or correctional systems who has been so designated by the Department of Corrections or by a warden of an institution;

    (e) All peace officers;

    (f) All state attorneys and United States attorneys and their respective assistants and investigators.

(9) "Machine gun" means any firearm, as defined herein, which shoots, or is designed to shoot, automatically more than one shot, without manually reloading, by a single function of the trigger.

(10) "Short-barreled shotgun" means a shotgun having one or more barrels less than 18 inches in length and any weapon made from a shotgun (whether by alteration, modification, or otherwise) if such weapon as modified has an overall length of less than 26 inches.

(11) "Short-barreled rifle" means a rifle having one or more barrels less than 16 inches in length and any weapon made from a rifle (whether by alteration, modification, or otherwise) if such weapon as modified has an overall length of less than 26 inches.

(12) "Slungshot" means a small mass of metal, stone, sand, or similar material fixed on a flexible handle, strap, or the like, used as a weapon.

(13) "Weapon" means any dirk, knife, metallic knuckles, slungshot, billie, tear gas gun, chemical weapon or device, or other deadly weapon except a firearm or a common pocketknife, plastic knife, or blunt-bladed table knife.

(14) "Electric weapon or device" means any device which, through the application or use of electrical current, is designed, redesigned, used, or intended to be used for offensive or defensive purposes, the destruction of life, or the infliction of injury.

(15) "Dart-firing stun gun" means any device having one or more darts that are capable of delivering an electrical current.

(16) "Readily accessible for immediate use" means that a firearm or other weapon is carried on the person or within such close proximity and in such a manner that it can be retrieved and used as easily and quickly as if carried on the person.

(17) "Securely encased" means in a glove compartment, whether or not locked; snapped in a holster; in a gun case, whether or not locked; in a zippered gun case; or in a closed box or container which requires a lid or cover to be opened for access.

(18) "Sterile area" means the area of an airport to which access is controlled by the inspection of persons and property in accordance with federally approved airport security programs.

(19) "Ammunition" means an object consisting of all of the following:

(a) A fixed metallic or nonmetallic hull or casing containing a primer.

(b) One or more projectiles, one or more bullets, or shot.

(c) Gunpowder.

All of the specified components must be present for an object to be ammunition.

790.01

Unlicensed carrying of concealed weapons or concealed firearms.–

(1) Except as provided in subsection (3), a person who is not licensed under s. 790.06 and who carries a concealed weapon or electric weapon or device on or about his or her person commits a misdemeanor of the first degree, punishable as provided in s. 775.082 or s. 775.083.

(2) Except as provided in subsection (3), a person who is not licensed under s. 790.06 and who carries a concealed firearm on or about his or her person commits a felony of the third degree, punishable as provided in s. 775.082, s. 775.083, or s. 775.084.

(3) This section does not apply to:

(a) A person who carries a concealed weapon, or a person who may lawfully possess a firearm and who carries a concealed firearm, on or about his or her person while in the act of evacuating during a mandatory evacuation order issued during a state of emergency declared by the Governor pursuant to chapter 252 or declared by a local authority pursuant to chapter 870. As used in this subsection, the term "in the act of evacuating" means the immediate and urgent movement of a person away from the evacuation zone within 48 hours after a mandatory evacuation is ordered. The 48 hours may be extended by an order issued by the Governor.

(b) A person who carries for purposes of lawful self-defense, in a concealed manner:

1. A self-defense chemical spray.

2. A nonlethal stun gun or dart-firing stun gun or other nonlethal electric weapon or device that is designed solely for defensive purposes.

(4) This section does not preclude any prosecution for the use of an electric weapon or device, a dart-firing stun gun, or a self-defense chemical spray during the commission of any criminal offense under s. 790.07, s. 790.10, s. 790.23, or s. 790.235, or for any other criminal offense.

790.015

Nonresidents who are United States citizens and hold a concealed weapons license in another state; reciprocity.–

(1) Notwithstanding s. 790.01, a nonresident of Florida may carry a concealed weapon or concealed firearm while in this state if the nonresident:

(a) Is 21 years of age or older.

(b) Has in his or her immediate possession a valid license to carry a concealed weapon or concealed firearm issued to the nonresident in his or her state of residence.

(c) Is a resident of the United States.

(2) A nonresident is subject to the same laws and restrictions with respect to carrying a concealed weapon or concealed firearm as a resident of Florida who is so licensed.

(3) If the resident of another state who is the holder of a valid license to carry a concealed weapon or concealed firearm issued in another state establishes legal residence in this state by:

(a) Registering to vote;

(b) Making a statement of domicile pursuant to s. 222.17; or

(c) Filing for homestead tax exemption on property in this state, the license shall remain in effect for 90 days following the date on which the holder of the license establishes legal state residence.

(4) This section applies only to nonresident concealed weapon or concealed firearm license holders from states that honor Florida concealed weapon or concealed firearm licenses.

(5) The requirement of paragraph (1)(a) does not apply to a person who:

(a) Is a service member, as defined in s. 250.01; or

(b) Is a veteran of the United States Armed Forces who was discharged under honorable conditions.

790.053
Open carrying of weapons.—

(1) Except as otherwise provided by law and in subsection (2), it is unlawful for any person to openly carry on or about his or her person any firearm or electric weapon or device. It is not a violation of this section for a person licensed to carry a concealed firearm as provided in s. 790.06(1), and who is lawfully carrying a firearm in a concealed manner, to briefly and openly display the firearm to the ordinary sight of another person, unless the firearm is intentionally displayed in an angry or threatening manner, not in necessary self-defense.

(2) A person may openly carry, for purposes of lawful self-defense:

(a) A self-defense chemical spray.

(b) A nonlethal stun gun or dart-firing stun gun or other nonlethal electric weapon or device that is designed solely for defensive purposes.

(3) Any person violating this section commits a misdemeanor of the second degree, punishable as provided in s. 775.082 or s. 775.083.

790.06

License to carry concealed weapon or firearm.–

(1) The Department of Agriculture and Consumer Services is authorized to issue licenses to carry concealed weapons or concealed firearms to persons qualified as provided in this section. Each such license must bear a color photograph of the licensee. For the purposes of this section, concealed weapons or concealed firearms are defined as a handgun, electronic weapon or device, tear gas gun, knife, or billie, but the term does not include a machine gun as defined in s. 790.001(9). Such licenses shall be valid throughout the state for a period of 7 years from the date of issuance. Any person in compliance with the terms of such license may carry a concealed weapon or concealed firearm notwithstanding the provisions of s. 790.01. The licensee must carry the license, together with valid identification, at all times in which the licensee is in actual possession of a concealed weapon or firearm and must display both the license and proper identification upon demand by a law enforcement officer. Violations of the provisions of this subsection shall constitute a noncriminal violation with a penalty of $25, payable to the clerk of the court.

(2) The Department of Agriculture and Consumer Services shall issue a license if the applicant:

    (a) Is a resident of the United States and a citizen of the United States or a permanent resident alien of the United States, as determined by the United States Bureau of Citizenship and Immigration Services, or is a consular security official of a foreign government that maintains diplomatic relations and treaties of commerce, friendship, and navigation with the United States and is certified as such by the foreign government and by the appropriate embassy in this country;

(b) Is 21 years of age or older;

(c) Does not suffer from a physical infirmity which prevents the safe handling of a weapon or firearm;

(d) Is not ineligible to possess a firearm pursuant to s. 790.23 by virtue of having been convicted of a felony;

(e) Has not been committed for the abuse of a controlled substance or been found guilty of a crime under the provisions of chapter 893 or similar laws of any other state relating to controlled substances within a 3-year period immediately preceding the date on which the application is submitted;

(f) Does not chronically and habitually use alcoholic beverages or other substances to the extent that his or her normal faculties are impaired. It shall be presumed that an applicant chronically and habitually uses alcoholic beverages or other substances to the extent that his or her normal faculties are impaired if the applicant has been committed under chapter 397 or under the provisions of former chapter 396 or has been convicted under s. 790.151 or has been deemed a habitual offender under s. 856.011(3), or has had two or more convictions under s. 316.193 or similar laws of any other state, within the 3-year period immediately preceding the date on which the application is submitted;

(g) Desires a legal means to carry a concealed weapon or firearm for lawful self-defense;

(h) Demonstrates competence with a firearm by any one of the following:

1. Completion of any hunter education or hunter safety

course approved by the Fish and Wildlife Conservation Commission or a similar agency of another state;

2. Completion of any National Rifle Association firearms safety or training course;

3. Completion of any firearms safety or training course or class available to the general public offered by a law enforcement, junior college, college, or private or public institution or organization or firearms training school, utilizing instructors certified by the National Rifle Association, Criminal Justice Standards and Training Commission, or the Department of Agriculture and Consumer Services;

4. Completion of any law enforcement firearms safety or training course or class offered for security guards, investigators, special deputies, or any division or subdivision of law enforcement or security enforcement;

5. Presents evidence of equivalent experience with a firearm through participation in organized shooting competition or military service;

6. Is licensed or has been licensed to carry a firearm in this state or a county or municipality of this state, unless such license has been revoked for cause; or

7. Completion of any firearms training or safety course or class conducted by a state-certified or National Rifle Association certified firearms instructor; A photocopy of a certificate of completion of any of the courses or classes; or an affidavit from the instructor, school, club, organization, or group that conducted or taught said course or class attesting to the completion of the course or class by the applicant; or a copy of any document which shows completion of the course or class or evidences participation in firearms competition shall

constitute evidence of qualification under this paragraph; any person who conducts a course pursuant to subparagraph 2., subparagraph 3., or subparagraph 7., or who, as an instructor, attests to the completion of such courses, must maintain records certifying that he or she observed the student safely handle and discharge the firearm;

(i) Has not been adjudicated an incapacitated person under s. 744.331, or similar laws of any other state, unless 5 years have elapsed since the applicant's restoration to capacity by court order;

(j) Has not been committed to a mental institution under chapter 394, or similar laws of any other state, unless the applicant produces a certificate from a licensed psychiatrist that he or she has not suffered from disability for at least 5 years prior to the date of submission of the application;

(k) Has not had adjudication of guilt withheld or imposition of sentence suspended on any felony or misdemeanor crime of domestic violence unless 3 years have elapsed since probation or any other conditions set by the court have been fulfilled, or the record has been sealed or expunged;

(l) Has not been issued an injunction that is currently in force and effect and that restrains the applicant from committing acts of domestic violence or acts of repeat violence; and

(m) Is not prohibited from purchasing or possessing a firearm by any other provision of Florida or federal law.

(3) The Department of Agriculture and Consumer Services shall deny a license if the applicant has been found guilty of, had adjudication of guilt withheld for, or had imposition of sentence suspended for one or more crimes of violence constituting a misdemeanor, unless 3 years have elapsed since probation or any other conditions set by the court have been fulfilled or the record

has been sealed or expunged. The Department of Agriculture and Consumer Services shall revoke a license if the licensee has been found guilty of, had adjudication of guilt withheld for, or had imposition of sentence suspended for one or more crimes of violence within the preceding 3 years. The department shall, upon notification by a law enforcement agency, a court, or the Florida Department of Law Enforcement and subsequent written verification, suspend a license or the processing of an application for a license if the licensee or applicant is arrested or formally charged with a crime that would disqualify such person from having a license under this section, until final disposition of the case. The department shall suspend a license or the processing of an application for a license if the licensee or applicant is issued an injunction that restrains the licensee or applicant from committing acts of domestic violence or acts of repeat violence.

(4) The application shall be completed, under oath, on a form promulgated by the Department of Agriculture and Consumer Services and shall include:

(a) The name, address, place and date of birth, race, and occupation of the applicant;

(b) A statement that the applicant is in compliance with criteria contained within subsections (2) and (3);

(c) A statement that the applicant has been furnished a copy of this chapter and is knowledgeable of its provisions;

(d) A conspicuous warning that the application is executed under oath and that a false answer to any question, or the submission of any false document by the applicant, subjects the applicant to criminal prosecution under s. 837.06; and

(e) A statement that the applicant desires a concealed weapon or firearms license as a means of lawful self-defense.

(5) The applicant shall submit to the Department of Agriculture and Consumer Services or an approved tax collector pursuant to s. 790.0625:

(a) A completed application as described in subsection (4).

(b) A nonrefundable license fee of up to $70 if he or she has not previously been issued a statewide license or of up to $60 for renewal of a statewide license. The cost of processing fingerprints as required in paragraph (c) shall be borne by the applicant. However, an individual holding an active certification from the Criminal Justice Standards and Training Commission as a law enforcement officer, correctional officer, or correctional probation officer as defined in s. 943.10(1), (2), (3), (6), (7), (8), or (9) is exempt from the licensing requirements of this section. If such individual wishes to receive a concealed weapons or firearms license, he or she is exempt from the background investigation and all background investigation fees, but must pay the current license fees regularly required to be paid by nonexempt applicants. Further, a law enforcement officer, a correctional officer, or a correctional probation officer as defined in s. 943.10(1), (2), or (3) is exempt from the required fees and background investigation for a period of 1 year after his or her retirement.

(c) A full set of fingerprints of the applicant administered by a law enforcement agency or the Division of Licensing of the Department of Agriculture and Consumer Services or an approved tax collector pursuant to s. 790.0625.

(d) A photocopy of a certificate, affidavit, or document as described in paragraph (2)(h).

(e) A full frontal view color photograph of the applicant taken within the preceding 30 days, in which the head, including hair, measures 7/8 of an inch wide and 11/8 inches high.

(6)

   (a) The Department of Agriculture and Consumer Services, upon receipt of the items listed in subsection (5), shall forward the full set of fingerprints of the applicant to the Department of Law Enforcement for state and federal processing, provided the federal service is available, to be processed for any criminal justice information as defined in s. 943.045. The cost of processing such fingerprints shall be payable to the Department of Law Enforcement by the Department of Agriculture and Consumer Services.

   (b) The sheriff's office shall provide fingerprinting service if requested by the applicant and may charge a fee not to exceed $5 for this service.

   (c) The Department of Agriculture and Consumer Services shall, within 90 days after the date of receipt of the items listed in subsection (5):

     1. Issue the license; or

     2. Deny the application based solely on the ground that the applicant fails to qualify under the criteria listed in subsection (2) or subsection (3). If the Department of Agriculture and Consumer Services denies the application, it shall notify the applicant in writing, stating the ground for denial and informing the applicant of any right to a hearing pursuant to chapter 120.

     3. In the event the department receives criminal history information with no final disposition on a crime which may disqualify the applicant, the time limitation prescribed by this paragraph may be suspended until receipt of the final disposition or proof of restoration of civil and firearm rights.

   (d) In the event a legible set of fingerprints, as determined by the Department of Agriculture and Consumer Services or the Federal Bureau of Investigation, cannot be obtained after two attempts, the Department of Agriculture and Consumer Services shall determine eligibility based upon the name checks conducted by the Florida Department of Law Enforcement.

(e) A consular security official of a foreign government that maintains diplomatic relations and treaties of commerce, friendship, and navigation with the United States and is certified as such by the foreign government and by the appropriate embassy in this country must be issued a license within 20 days after the date of the receipt of a completed application, certification document, color photograph as specified in paragraph (5)(e), and a nonrefundable license fee of $300. Consular security official licenses shall be valid for 1 year and may be renewed upon completion of the application process as provided in this section.

(7) The Department of Agriculture and Consumer Services shall maintain an automated listing of license holders and pertinent information, and such information shall be available online, upon request, at all times to all law enforcement agencies through the Florida Crime Information Center.

(8) Within 30 days after the changing of a permanent address, or within 30 days after having a license lost or destroyed, the licensee shall notify the Department of Agriculture and Consumer Services of such change. Failure to notify the Department of Agriculture and Consumer Services pursuant to the provisions of this subsection shall constitute a noncriminal violation with a penalty of $25.

(9) In the event that a concealed weapon or firearm license is lost or destroyed, the license shall be automatically invalid, and the

person to whom the same was issued may, upon payment of $15 to the Department of Agriculture and Consumer Services, obtain a duplicate, or substitute thereof, upon furnishing a notarized statement to the Department of Agriculture and Consumer Services that such license has been lost or destroyed.

(10) A license issued under this section shall be suspended or revoked pursuant to chapter 120 if the licensee:

(a) Is found to be ineligible under the criteria set forth in subsection (2);

(b) Develops or sustains a physical infirmity which prevents the safe handling of a weapon or firearm;

(c) Is convicted of a felony which would make the licensee ineligible to possess a firearm pursuant to s. 790.23;

(d) Is found guilty of a crime under the provisions of chapter 893, or similar laws of any other state, relating to controlled substances;

(e) Is committed as a substance abuser under chapter 397, or is deemed a habitual offender under s. 856.011(3), or similar laws of any other state;

(f) Is convicted of a second violation of s. 316.193, or a similar law of another state, within 3 years of a previous conviction of such section, or similar law of another state, even though the first violation may have occurred prior to the date on which the application was submitted;

(g) Is adjudicated an incapacitated person under s. 744.331, or similar laws of any other state; or

(h) Is committed to a mental institution under chapter 394, or similar laws of any other state.

(11)

(a) No less than 90 days before the expiration date of the license, the Department of Agriculture and Consumer Services shall mail to each licensee a written notice of the expiration and a renewal form prescribed by the Department of Agriculture and Consumer Services. The licensee must renew his or her license on or before the expiration date by filing with the Department of Agriculture and Consumer Services the renewal form containing a notarized affidavit stating that the licensee remains qualified pursuant to the criteria specified in subsections (2) and (3), a color photograph as specified in paragraph (5)(e), and the required renewal fee. Out-of-state residents must also submit a complete set of fingerprints and fingerprint processing fee. The license shall be renewed upon receipt of the completed renewal form, color photograph, appropriate payment of fees, and, if applicable, fingerprints. Additionally, a licensee who fails to file a renewal application on or before its expiration date must renew his or her license by paying a late fee of $15. A license may not be renewed 180 days or more after its expiration date, and such a license is deemed to be permanently expired. A person whose license has been permanently expired may reapply for licensure; however, an application for licensure and fees under subsection (5) must be submitted, and a background investigation shall be conducted pursuant to this section. A person who knowingly files false information under this subsection is subject to criminal prosecution under s. 837.06.

(b) A license issued to a service member, as defined in s. 250.01, is subject to paragraph (a); however, such a license does not expire while the service member is serving on military orders that have taken him or her over 35 miles from his or her residence and shall be extended, as provided in this paragraph, for up to 180 days after his or her return to such residence. If the license renewal requirements in paragraph

(a) are met within the 180-day extension period, the service member may not be charged any additional costs, such as, but not limited to, late fees or delinquency fees, above the normal license fees. The service member must present to the Department of Agriculture and Consumer Services a copy of his or her official military orders or a written verification from the member's commanding officer before the end of the 180-day period in order to qualify for the extension.

(12)

(a) A license issued under this section does not authorize any person to openly carry a handgun or carry a concealed weapon or firearm into:

1. Any place of nuisance as defined in s. 823.05;
2. Any police, sheriff, or highway patrol station;
3. Any detention facility, prison, or jail;
4. Any courthouse;
5. Any courtroom, except that nothing in this section would preclude a judge from carrying a concealed weapon or determining who will carry a concealed weapon in his or her courtroom;
6. Any polling place;
7. Any meeting of the governing body of a county, public school district, municipality, or special district;
8. Any meeting of the Legislature or a committee thereof;
9. Any school, college, or professional athletic event not related to firearms;
10. Any elementary or secondary school facility or administration building;
11. Any career center;
12. Any portion of an establishment licensed to dispense alcoholic beverages for consumption on the premises,

which portion of the establishment is primarily devoted to such purpose;

13. Any college or university facility unless the licensee is a registered student, employee, or faculty member of such college or university and the weapon is a stun gun or nonlethal electric weapon or device designed solely for defensive purposes and the weapon does not fire a dart or projectile;

14. The inside of the passenger terminal and sterile area of any airport, provided that no person shall be prohibited from carrying any legal firearm into the terminal, which firearm is encased for shipment for purposes of checking such firearm as baggage to be lawfully transported on any aircraft; or

15. Any place where the carrying of firearms is prohibited by federal law.

(b) A person licensed under this section shall not be prohibited from carrying or storing a firearm in a vehicle for lawful purposes.

(c) This section does not modify the terms or conditions of s. 790.251(7).

(d) Any person who knowingly and willfully violates any provision of this subsection commits a misdemeanor of the second degree, punishable as provided in s. 775.082 or s. 775.083.

(13) All moneys collected by the department pursuant to this section shall be deposited in the Division of Licensing Trust Fund, and the Legislature shall appropriate from the fund those amounts deemed necessary to administer the provisions of this section. All revenues collected, less those costs determined by the Department of Agriculture and Consumer

Services to be nonrecurring or one-time costs, shall be deferred over the 7-year licensure period. Notwithstanding the provisions of s. 493.6117, all moneys collected pursuant to this section shall not revert to the General Revenue Fund; however, this shall not abrogate the requirement for payment of the service charge imposed pursuant to chapter 215.

(14) All funds received by the sheriff pursuant to the provisions of this section shall be deposited into the general revenue fund of the county and shall be budgeted to the sheriff.

(15) The Legislature finds as a matter of public policy and fact that it is necessary to provide statewide uniform standards for issuing licenses to carry concealed weapons and firearms for self-defense and finds it necessary to occupy the field of regulation of the bearing of concealed weapons or firearms for self-defense to ensure that no honest, law-abiding person who qualifies under the provisions of this section is subjectively or arbitrarily denied his or her rights. The Department of Agriculture and Consumer Services shall implement and administer the provisions of this section. The Legislature does not delegate to the Department of Agriculture and Consumer Services the authority to regulate or restrict the issuing of licenses provided for in this section, beyond those provisions contained in this section. Subjective or arbitrary actions or rules which encumber the issuing process by placing burdens on the applicant beyond those sworn statements and specified documents detailed in this section or which create restrictions beyond those specified in this section are in conflict with the intent of this section and are prohibited. This section shall be liberally construed to carry out the constitutional right to bear arms for self-defense. This section is supplemental and additional to existing rights to bear arms, and nothing in this section shall impair or diminish such rights.

(16) The Department of Agriculture and Consumer Services shall maintain statistical information on the number of licenses issued, revoked, suspended, and denied.

(17) As amended by chapter 87-24, Laws of Florida, this section shall be known and may be cited as the "Jack Hagler Self Defense Act."

790.062

Members and veterans of United States Armed Forces; exceptions from licensure provisions.—

(1) Notwithstanding s. 790.06(2)(b), the Department of Agriculture and Consumer Services shall issue a license to carry a concealed weapon or firearm under s. 790.06 if the applicant is otherwise qualified and:

(a) Is a service member, as defined in s. 250.01; or

(b) Is a veteran of the United States Armed Forces who was discharged under honorable conditions.

(2) The Department of Agriculture and Consumer Services shall accept fingerprints of an applicant under this section administered by any law enforcement agency, military provost, or other military unit charged with law enforcement duties or as otherwise provided for in s. 790.06(5)(c).

¹790.065

Sale and delivery of firearms.—

(1)

(a) A licensed importer, licensed manufacturer, or licensed dealer may not sell or deliver from her or his inventory at her or his licensed premises any firearm to another person, other than a licensed importer, licensed manufacturer, licensed dealer, or licensed collector, until she or he has:

1. Obtained a completed form from the potential buyer or transferee, which form shall have been promulgated by the Department of Law Enforcement and provided by the licensed importer, licensed manufacturer, or licensed dealer, which shall include the name, date of birth, gender, race, and social security number or other identification number of such potential buyer or transferee and has inspected proper identification including an identification containing a photograph of the potential buyer or transferee.

[2]2. Collected a fee from the potential buyer for processing the criminal history check of the potential buyer. The fee shall be established by the Department of Law Enforcement and may not exceed $8 per transaction. The Department of Law Enforcement may reduce, or suspend collection of, the fee to reflect payment received from the Federal Government applied to the cost of maintaining the criminal history check system established by this section as a means of facilitating or supplementing the National Instant Criminal Background Check System. The Department of Law Enforcement shall, by rule, establish procedures for the fees to be transmitted by the licensee to the Department of Law Enforcement. All such fees shall be deposited into the Department of Law Enforcement Operating Trust Fund, but shall be segregated from all other funds deposited into such trust fund and must be accounted for separately. Such segregated funds must not be used for any purpose other than the operation of the criminal history checks required by this section. The Department of Law Enforcement, each year prior to

February 1, shall make a full accounting of all receipts and expenditures of such funds to the President of the Senate, the Speaker of the House of Representatives, the majority and minority leaders of each house of the Legislature, and the chairs of the appropriations committees of each house of the Legislature. In the event that the cumulative amount of funds collected exceeds the cumulative amount of expenditures by more than $2.5 million, excess funds may be used for the purpose of purchasing soft body armor for law enforcement officers.

3. Requested, by means of a toll-free telephone call, the Department of Law Enforcement to conduct a check of the information as reported and reflected in the Florida Crime Information Center and National Crime Information Center systems as of the date of the request.

4. Received a unique approval number for that inquiry from the Department of Law Enforcement, and recorded the date and such number on the consent form.

(b) However, if the person purchasing, or receiving delivery of, the firearm is a holder of a valid concealed weapons or firearms license pursuant to the provisions of s. 790.06 or holds an active certification from the Criminal Justice Standards and Training Commission as a "law enforcement officer," a "correctional officer," or a "correctional probation officer" as defined in s. 943.10(1), (2), (3), (6), (7), (8), or (9), this subsection does not apply.

(c) This subsection does not apply to the purchase, trade, or transfer of a rifle or shotgun by a resident of this state when the resident makes such purchase, trade, or transfer from a licensed importer, licensed manufacturer, or licensed dealer in another state.

(2) Upon receipt of a request for a criminal history record check, the Department of Law Enforcement shall, during the licensee's call or by return call, forthwith:

(a) Review any records available to determine if the potential buyer or transferee:

1. Has been convicted of a felony and is prohibited from receipt or possession of a firearm pursuant to s. 790.23;

2. Has been convicted of a misdemeanor crime of domestic violence, and therefore is prohibited from purchasing a firearm;

3. Has had adjudication of guilt withheld or imposition of sentence suspended on any felony or misdemeanor crime of domestic violence unless 3 years have elapsed since probation or any other conditions set by the court have been fulfilled or expunction has occurred; or

4. Has been adjudicated mentally defective or has been committed to a mental institution by a court or as provided in sub-sub-subparagraph b.(II), and as a result is prohibited by state or federal law from purchasing a firearm.

   a. As used in this subparagraph, "adjudicated mentally defective" means a determination by a court that a person, as a result of marked subnormal intelligence, or mental illness, incompetency, condition, or disease, is a danger to himself or herself or to others or lacks the mental capacity to contract or manage his or her own affairs. The phrase includes a judicial finding of incapacity under s. 744.331(6)(a), an acquittal by reason of insanity of a person charged with a criminal offense, and a judicial finding that a criminal defendant is not competent to stand trial.

   b. As used in this subparagraph, "committed to a mental

institution" means:

(I) Involuntary commitment, commitment for mental defectiveness or mental illness, and commitment for substance abuse. The phrase includes involuntary inpatient placement as defined in s. 394.467, involuntary outpatient placement as defined in s. 394.4655, involuntary assessment and stabilization under s. 397.6818, and involuntary substance abuse treatment under s. 397.6957, but does not include a person in a mental institution for observation or discharged from a mental institution based upon the initial review by the physician or a voluntary admission to a mental institution; or

(II) Notwithstanding sub-sub-subparagraph (I), voluntary admission to a mental institution for outpatient or inpatient treatment of a person who had an involuntary examination under s. 394.463, where each of the following conditions have been met:

(A) An examining physician found that the person is an imminent danger to himself or herself or others.

(B) The examining physician certified that if the person did not agree to voluntary treatment, a petition for involuntary outpatient or inpatient treatment would have been filed under s. 394.463(2)(i)4., or the examining physician certified that a petition was filed and the person subsequently agreed to voluntary treatment prior to a court hearing on the petition.

(C) Before agreeing to voluntary treatment, the person received written notice of that finding and certification, and written notice that as a result of such finding, he or she may be prohibited from purchasing a firearm, and may not be eligible to apply for or retain a concealed weapon or firearms license under s. 790.06 and the person acknowledged such notice in writing, in substantially the following form: "I understand that the doctor who examined me believes I am a danger to myself or to others. I understand that if I do not agree to voluntary treatment, a petition will be filed in court to require me to receive involuntary treatment. I understand that if that petition is filed, I have the right to contest it. In the event a petition has been filed, I understand that I can subsequently agree to voluntary treatment prior to a court hearing. I understand that by agreeing to voluntary treatment in either of these situations, I may be prohibited from buying firearms and from applying for or retaining a concealed weapons or firearms license until I apply for and receive relief from that restriction under Florida law."

(D) A judge or a magistrate has, pursuant to sub-sub-subparagraph c.(II), reviewed the record of the finding, certification, notice, and written acknowledgment classifying the person as an imminent danger to himself or herself or others, and ordered that such record be submitted to the department.

c. In order to check for these conditions, the department shall compile and maintain an automated database of persons who are prohibited from purchasing a firearm based on court records of adjudications of mental defectiveness or commitments to mental institutions.

(I) Except as provided in sub-sub-subparagraph (II), clerks of court shall submit these records to the department within 1 month after the rendition of the adjudication or commitment. Reports shall be submitted in an automated format. The reports must, at a minimum, include the name, along with any known alias or former name, the sex, and the date of birth of the subject.

(II) For persons committed to a mental institution pursuant to sub-sub-subparagraph b.(II), within 24 hours after the person's agreement to voluntary admission, a record of the finding, certification, notice, and written acknowledgment must be filed by the administrator of the receiving or treatment facility, as defined in s. 394.455, with the clerk of the court for the county in which the involuntary examination under s. 394.463 occurred. No fee shall be charged for the filing under this sub-sub-subparagraph. The clerk must present the records to a judge or magistrate within 24 hours after receipt of the records. A judge or magistrate is required and has the lawful authority to review the records ex parte and, if the judge or magistrate determines that the record supports the classifying of the person as an imminent danger to himself or herself or others, to order that the record be submitted to the department. If a judge or magistrate orders the submittal of the record to the department, the record must be submitted to the department within 24 hours.

d. A person who has been adjudicated mentally defective

or committed to a mental institution, as those terms are defined in this paragraph, may petition the circuit court that made the adjudication or commitment, or the court that ordered that the record be submitted to the department pursuant to sub-sub-subparagraph c.(II), for relief from the firearm disabilities imposed by such adjudication or commitment. A copy of the petition shall be served on the state attorney for the county in which the person was adjudicated or committed. The state attorney may object to and present evidence relevant to the relief sought by the petition. The hearing on the petition may be open or closed as the petitioner may choose. The petitioner may present evidence and subpoena witnesses to appear at the hearing on the petition. The petitioner may confront and cross-examine witnesses called by the state attorney. A record of the hearing shall be made by a certified court reporter or by court-approved electronic means. The court shall make written findings of fact and conclusions of law on the issues before it and issue a final order. The court shall grant the relief requested in the petition if the court finds, based on the evidence presented with respect to the petitioner's reputation, the petitioner's mental health record and, if applicable, criminal history record, the circumstances surrounding the firearm disability, and any other evidence in the record, that the petitioner will not be likely to act in a manner that is dangerous to public safety and that granting the relief would not be contrary to the public interest. If the final order denies relief, the petitioner may not petition again for relief from firearm disabilities until 1 year after the date of the final order. The petitioner may seek judicial review of a final order denying relief in the district court of appeal having jurisdiction over the court that issued the order. The review shall be conducted de novo. Relief from a firearm disability granted under this sub-subparagraph has no effect on the loss of civil rights, including firearm rights, for any reason other than the particular adjudication of mental defectiveness or commitment to a mental institution from which relief is granted.

e. Upon receipt of proper notice of relief from firearm disabilities granted under sub-subparagraph d., the department shall delete any mental health record of the person granted relief from the automated database of persons who are prohibited from purchasing a firearm based on court records of adjudications of mental defectiveness or commitments to mental institutions.

f. The department is authorized to disclose data collected pursuant to this subparagraph to agencies of the Federal Government and other states for use exclusively in determining the lawfulness of a firearm sale or transfer. The department is also authorized to disclose this data to the Department of Agriculture and Consumer Services for purposes of determining eligibility for issuance of a concealed weapons or concealed firearms license and for determining whether a basis exists for revoking or suspending a previously issued license pursuant to s. 790.06(10). When a potential buyer or transferee appeals a non-approval based on these records, the clerks of court and mental institutions shall, upon request by the department, provide information to help determine whether the potential buyer or transferee is the same person as the subject of the record. Photographs and any other data that could confirm or negate identity must be made available to the department for such purposes, notwithstanding any other provision of state law to the contrary. Any such information that is made confidential or exempt from disclosure by law shall retain such confidential or exempt status when transferred to the department.

(b) Inform the licensee making the inquiry either that records demonstrate that the buyer or transferee is so prohibited and provide the licensee a non-approval number, or provide the licensee with a unique approval number.

(c)

1. Review any records available to it to determine whether the potential buyer or transferee has been indicted or has had an information filed against her or him for an offense that is a felony under either state or federal law, or, as mandated by federal law, has had an injunction for protection against domestic violence entered against the potential buyer or transferee under s. 741.30, has had an injunction for protection against repeat violence entered against the potential buyer or transferee under s. 784.046, or has been arrested for a dangerous crime as specified in s. 907.041(4) (a) or for any of the following enumerated offenses:

   a. Criminal anarchy under ss. 876.01 and 876.02.

   b. Extortion under s. 836.05.

   c. Explosives violations under s. 552.22(1) and (2).

   d. Controlled substances violations under chapter 893.

   e. Resisting an officer with violence under s. 843.01.

   f. Weapons and firearms violations under this chapter.

   g. Treason under s. 876.32.

   h. Assisting self-murder under s. 782.08.

   i. Sabotage under s. 876.38.

j. Stalking or aggravated stalking under s. 784.048.

If the review indicates any such indictment, information, or arrest, the department shall provide to the licensee a conditional non-approval number.

2. Within 24 working hours, the department shall determine the disposition of the indictment, information, or arrest and inform the licensee as to whether the potential buyer is prohibited from receiving or possessing a firearm. For purposes of this paragraph, "working hours" means the hours from 8 a.m. to 5 p.m. Monday through Friday, excluding legal holidays.

3. The office of the clerk of court, at no charge to the department, shall respond to any department request for data on the disposition of the indictment, information, or arrest as soon as possible, but in no event later than 8 working hours.

4. The department shall determine as quickly as possible within the allotted time period whether the potential buyer is prohibited from receiving or possessing a firearm.

5. If the potential buyer is not so prohibited, or if the department cannot determine the disposition information within the allotted time period, the department shall provide the licensee with a conditional approval number.

6. If the buyer is so prohibited, the conditional non-approval number shall become a non-approval number.

7. The department shall continue its attempts to obtain the disposition information and may retain a record of all approval numbers granted without sufficient disposition information. If the department later obtains disposition information which indicates:

a. That the potential buyer is not prohibited from owning

a firearm, it shall treat the record of the transaction in accordance with this section; or

b. That the potential buyer is prohibited from owning a firearm, it shall immediately revoke the conditional approval number and notify local law enforcement.

8. During the time that disposition of the indictment, information, or arrest is pending and until the department is notified by the potential buyer that there has been a final disposition of the indictment, information, or arrest, the conditional non-approval number shall remain in effect.

(3) In the event of scheduled computer downtime, electronic failure, or similar emergency beyond the control of the Department of Law Enforcement, the department shall immediately notify the licensee of the reason for, and estimated length of, such delay. After such notification, the department shall forthwith, and in no event later than the end of the next business day of the licensee, either inform the requesting licensee if its records demonstrate that the buyer or transferee is prohibited from receipt or possession of a firearm pursuant to Florida and Federal law or provide the licensee with a unique approval number. Unless notified by the end of said next business day that the buyer or transferee is so prohibited, and without regard to whether she or he has received a unique approval number, the licensee may complete the sale or transfer and shall not be deemed in violation of this section with respect to such sale or transfer.

(4)

(a) Any records containing any of the information set forth in subsection (1) pertaining to a buyer or transferee who is not found to be prohibited from receipt or transfer of a firearm by reason of Florida and federal law which records are created by the Department of Law Enforcement to conduct the criminal history record check shall be confidential and exempt from the provisions of s. 119.07(1) and may not be disclosed by the Department of Law Enforcement or any officer or employee thereof to any person or to another agency. The Department of Law Enforcement shall destroy any such records forthwith after it communicates the approval and non-approval numbers to the licensee and, in any event, such records shall be destroyed within 48 hours after the day of the response to the licensee's request.

(b) Notwithstanding the provisions of this subsection, the Department of Law Enforcement may maintain records of NCIC transactions to the extent required by the Federal Government, and may maintain a log of dates of requests for criminal history records checks, unique approval and non-approval numbers, license identification numbers, and transaction numbers corresponding to such dates for a period of not longer than 2 years or as otherwise required by law.

(c) Nothing in this chapter shall be construed to allow the State of Florida to maintain records containing the names of purchasers or transferees who receive unique approval numbers or to maintain records of firearm transactions.

(d) Any officer or employee, or former officer or employee of the Department of Law Enforcement or law enforcement agency who intentionally and maliciously violates the provisions of this subsection commits a felony of the third degree punishable as provided in s. 775.082 or s. 775.083.

(5) The Department of Law Enforcement shall establish a toll-free telephone number which shall be operational 7 days a week with the exception of Christmas Day and New Year's Day, for a period of 12 hours a day beginning at 9 a.m. and ending at 9 p.m., for purposes of responding to inquiries as described in this

section from licensed manufacturers, licensed importers, and licensed dealers. The Department of Law Enforcement shall employ and train such personnel as are necessary expeditiously to administer the provisions of this section.

(6) Any person who is denied the right to receive or purchase a firearm as a result of the procedures established by this section may request a criminal history records review and correction in accordance with the rules promulgated by the Department of Law Enforcement.

(7) It shall be unlawful for any licensed dealer, licensed manufacturer, or licensed importer willfully and intentionally to request criminal history record information under false pretenses, or willfully and intentionally to disseminate criminal history record information to any person other than the subject of such information. Any person convicted of a violation of this subsection commits a felony of the third degree punishable as provided in s. 775.082 or s. 775.083.

(8) The Department of Law Enforcement shall promulgate regulations to ensure the identity, confidentiality, and security of all records and data provided pursuant to this section.

(9) This section shall become effective at such time as the Department of Law Enforcement has notified all licensed importers, licensed manufacturers, and licensed dealers in writing that the procedures and toll-free number described in this section are operational. This section shall remain in effect only during such times as the procedures described in subsection (2) remain operational.

(10) A licensed importer, licensed manufacturer, or licensed dealer is not required to comply with the requirements of this section in the event of:

(a) Unavailability of telephone service at the licensed premises due to the failure of the entity which provides telephone service in the state, region, or other geographical area in which the licensee is located to provide telephone service to the premises of the licensee due to the location of said premises; or the interruption of telephone service by reason of hurricane, tornado, flood, natural disaster, or other act of God, war, invasion, insurrection, riot, or other bona fide emergency, or other reason beyond the control of the licensee; or

(b) Failure of the Department of Law Enforcement to comply with the requirements of subsections (2) and (3).

(11) Compliance with the provisions of this chapter shall be a complete defense to any claim or cause of action under the laws of any state for liability for damages arising from the importation or manufacture, or the subsequent sale or transfer to any person who has been convicted in any court of a crime punishable by imprisonment for a term exceeding 1 year, of any firearm which has been shipped or transported in interstate or foreign commerce. The Department of Law Enforcement, its agents and employees shall not be liable for any claim or cause of action under the laws of any state for liability for damages arising from its actions in lawful compliance with this section.

(12)

(a) Any potential buyer or transferee who willfully and knowingly provides false information or false or fraudulent identification commits a felony of the third degree punishable as provided in s. 775.082 or s. 775.083.

(b) Any licensed importer, licensed manufacturer, or licensed dealer who violates the provisions of subsection (1) commits a felony of the third degree punishable as provided in s. 775.082 or s. 775.083.

(c) Any employee or agency of a licensed importer, licensed manufacturer, or licensed dealer who violates the provisions of subsection (1) commits a felony of the third degree punishable as provided in s. 775.082 or s. 775.083.

(d) Any person who knowingly acquires a firearm through purchase or transfer intended for the use of a person who is prohibited by state or federal law from possessing or receiving a firearm commits a felony of the third degree, punishable as provided in s. 775.082 or s. 775.083.

(13) This section does not apply to employees of sheriff's offices, municipal police departments, correctional facilities or agencies, or other criminal justice or governmental agencies when the purchases or transfers are made on behalf of an employing agency for official law enforcement purposes.

[1]Note.—A. Section 1, ch. 89-191, provides that "[t]his section expires on the effective date of federal law which provides access to national criminal history information and requires national criminal history checks on potential buyers or transferees on firearms."
B. Section 3, ch. 90-316, provides that "[t]his act shall not be construed to nullify the expiration of s. 790.065, Florida Statutes, provided for in chapter 89-191, Laws of Florida."

[2]Note.—Section 2, ch. 2009-233, provides that "[s]ection 790.065, Florida Statutes, must be reviewed by the Legislature and approved for continuation before the limit of $8 on the fee established by the Department of Law Enforcement under s. 790.065(1)(b), Florida Statutes, may be increased." Paragraph (1)(b) was redesignated as subparagraph (1)(a)2. by s. 4, ch. 2011-145.

790.0655

Purchase and delivery of handguns; mandatory waiting period; exceptions; penalties.—

(1)

    (a) There shall be a mandatory 3-day waiting period, which shall be 3 days, excluding weekends and legal holidays, between the purchase and the delivery at retail of any handgun. "Purchase" means the transfer of money or other valuable consideration to the retailer. "Handgun" means a firearm capable of being carried and used by one hand, such as a pistol or revolver. "Retailer" means and includes every person engaged in the business of making sales at retail or for distribution, or use, or consumption, or storage to be used or consumed in this state, as defined in s. 212.02(13).

    (b) Records of handgun sales must be available for inspection by any law enforcement agency, as defined in s. 934.02, during normal business hours.

(2) The 3-day waiting period shall not apply in the following circumstances:

    (a) When a handgun is being purchased by a holder of a concealed weapons permit as defined in s. 790.06.

    (b) To a trade-in of another handgun.

(3) It is a felony of the third degree, punishable as provided in s. 775.082, s. 775.083, or s. 775.084:

    (a) For any retailer, or any employee or agent of a retailer, to deliver a handgun before the expiration of the 3-day waiting period, subject to the exceptions provided in subsection (2).

    (b) For a purchaser to obtain delivery of a handgun by fraud, false pretense, or false representation.

790.07

Persons engaged in criminal offense, having weapons.–

(1) Whoever, while committing or attempting to commit any felony or while under indictment, displays, uses, threatens, or attempts to use any weapon or electric weapon or device or carries a concealed weapon is guilty of a felony of the third degree, punishable as provided in s. 775.082, s. 775.083, or s. 775.084.

(2) Whoever, while committing or attempting to commit any felony, displays, uses, threatens, or attempts to use any firearm or carries a concealed firearm is guilty of a felony of the second degree, punishable as provided in s. 775.082, s. 775.083, and s. 775.084.

(3) The following crimes are excluded from application of this section: Antitrust violations, unfair trade practices, restraints of trade, nonsupport of dependents, bigamy, or other similar offenses.

(4) Whoever, having previously been convicted of a violation of subsection (1) or subsection (2) and, subsequent to such conviction, displays, uses, threatens, or attempts to use any weapon, firearm, or electric weapon or device, carries a concealed weapon, or carries a concealed firearm while committing or attempting to commit any felony or while under indictment is guilty of a felony of the first degree, punishable as provided in s. 775.082, s. 775.083, or s. 775.084. Sentence shall not be suspended or deferred under the provisions of this subsection.

790.09

Manufacturing or selling slungshot

Whoever manufactures or causes to be manufactured, or sells or exposes for sale any instrument or weapon of the kind usually known as slungshot, or metallic knuckles, shall be guilty of a misdemeanor of the second degree, punishable as provided in s. 775.082 or s. 775.083.

790.10

Improper exhibition of dangerous weapons or firearms

If any person having or carrying any dirk, sword, sword cane, firearm, electric weapon or device, or other weapon shall, in the presence of one or more persons, exhibit the same in a rude, careless, angry, or threatening manner, not in necessary self-defense, the person so offending shall be guilty of a misdemeanor of the first degree, punishable as provided in s. 775.082 or s. 775.083.

790.115

Possessing or discharging weapons or firearms at a school-sponsored event or on school property prohibited; penalties; exceptions.

(1) A person who exhibits any sword, sword cane, firearm, electric weapon or device, destructive device, or other weapon as defined in s. 790.001(13), including a razor blade, box cutter, or common pocketknife, except as authorized in support of school-sanctioned activities, in the presence of one or more persons in a rude, careless, angry, or threatening manner and not in lawful self-defense, at a school-sponsored event or on the grounds or facilities of any school, school bus, or school bus stop, or within 1,000 feet of the real property that comprises a public or private elementary school, middle school, or secondary school, during school hours or during the time of a sanctioned school activity, commits a felony of the third degree, punishable as provided

in s. 775.082, s. 775.083, or s. 775.084. This subsection does not apply to the exhibition of a firearm or weapon on private real property within 1,000 feet of a school by the owner of such property or by a person whose presence on such property has been authorized, licensed, or invited by the owner.

(2)

(a) A person shall not possess any firearm, electric weapon or device, destructive device, or other weapon as defined in s. 790.001(13), including a razor blade or box cutter, except as authorized in support of school-sanctioned activities, at a school-sponsored event or on the property of any school, school bus, or school bus stop; however, a person may carry a firearm:

1. In a case to a firearms program, class or function which has been approved in advance by the principal or chief administrative officer of the school as a program or class to which firearms could be carried;

2. In a case to a career center having a firearms training range; or

3. In a vehicle pursuant to s. 790.25(5); except that school districts may adopt written and published policies that waive the exception in this subparagraph for purposes of student and campus parking privileges.

For the purposes of this section, "school" means any preschool, elementary school, middle school, junior high school, secondary school, career center, or postsecondary school, whether public or nonpublic.

(b) A person who willfully and knowingly possesses any electric weapon or device, destructive device, or other weapon as defined in s. 790.001(13), including a razor blade or box cutter, except as authorized in support of school-sanctioned activities, in violation of this subsection commits a felony of the third degree, punishable as provided in s. 775.082, s. 775.083, or s. 775.084.

(c)

1. A person who willfully and knowingly possesses any firearm in violation of this subsection commits a felony of the third degree, punishable as provided in s. 775.082, s. 775.083, or s. 775.084.

2. A person who stores or leaves a loaded firearm within the reach or easy access of a minor who obtains the firearm and commits a violation of subparagraph 1. commits a misdemeanor of the second degree, punishable as provided in s. 775.082 or s. 775.083; except that this does not apply if the firearm was stored or left in a securely locked box or container or in a location which a reasonable person would have believed to be secure, or was securely locked with a firearm-mounted push-button combination lock or a trigger lock; if the minor obtains the firearm as a result of an unlawful entry by any person; or to members of the Armed Forces, National Guard, or State Militia, or to police or other law enforcement officers, with respect to firearm possession by a minor which occurs during or incidental to the performance of their official duties.

(d) A person who discharges any weapon or firearm while in violation of paragraph (a), unless discharged for lawful defense of himself or herself or another or for a lawful purpose, commits a felony of the second degree, punishable as provided in s. 775.082, s. 775.083, or s. 775.084.

(e) The penalties of this subsection shall not apply to persons licensed under s. 790.06. Persons licensed under s. 790.06 shall be punished as provided in s. 790.06(12), except that a license holder who unlawfully discharges a weapon or firearm on school property as prohibited by this subsection commits a felony of the second degree, punishable as provided in s. 775.082, s. 775.083, or s. 775.084.

(3) This section does not apply to any law enforcement officer as defined in s. 943.10(1), (2), (3), (4), (6), (7), (8), (9), or (14).

(4) Notwithstanding s. 985.24, s. 985.245, or s. 985.25(1), any minor under 18 years of age who is charged under this section with possessing or discharging a firearm on school property shall be detained in secure detention, unless the state attorney authorizes the release of the minor, and shall be given a probable cause hearing within 24 hours after being taken into custody. At the hearing, the court may order that the minor continue to be held in secure detention for a period of 21 days, during which time the minor shall receive medical, psychiatric, psychological, or substance abuse examinations pursuant to s. 985.18, and a written report shall be completed.

790.15

Discharging firearm in public or on residential property.

(1) Except as provided in subsection (2) or subsection (3), any person who knowingly discharges a firearm in any public place or on the right-of-way of any paved public road, highway, or street, who knowingly discharges any firearm over the right-of-way of any paved public road, highway, or street or over any occupied premises, or who recklessly or negligently discharges a firearm outdoors on any property used primarily as the site of a dwelling as defined in s. 776.013 or zoned exclusively for residential use commits a misdemeanor of the first degree, punishable as provided in s. 775.082 or s. 775.083. This section does not apply to a person lawfully defending life or property

or performing official duties requiring the discharge of a firearm or to a person discharging a firearm on public roads or properties expressly approved for hunting by the Fish and Wildlife Conservation Commission or Florida Forest Service.

(2) Any occupant of any vehicle who knowingly and willfully discharges any firearm from the vehicle within 1,000 feet of any person commits a felony of the second degree, punishable as provided in s. 775.082, s. 775.083, or s. 775.084.

(3) Any driver or owner of any vehicle, whether or not the owner of the vehicle is occupying the vehicle, who knowingly directs any other person to discharge any firearm from the vehicle commits a felony of the third degree, punishable as provided in s. 775.082, s. 775.083, or s. 775.084.

790.151

Using firearm while under the influence of alcoholic beverages, chemical substances, or controlled substances; penalties.

(1) As used in ss. 790.151-790.157, to "use a firearm" means to discharge a firearm or to have a firearm readily accessible for immediate discharge.

(2) For the purposes of this section, "readily accessible for immediate discharge" means loaded and in a person's hand.

(3) It is unlawful and punishable as provided in subsection (4) for any person who is under the influence of alcoholic beverages, any chemical substance set forth in s. 877.111, or any substance controlled under chapter 893, when affected to the extent that his or her normal faculties are impaired, to use a firearm in this state.

(4) Any person who violates subsection (3) commits a misdemeanor of the second degree, punishable as provided in s. 775.082 or s. 775.083.

(5) This section does not apply to persons exercising lawful self-defense or defense of one's property.

790.161

Making, possessing, throwing, projecting, placing, or discharging any destructive device or attempt so to do, felony; penalties.

A person who willfully and unlawfully makes, possesses, throws, projects, places, discharges, or attempts to make, possess, throw, project, place, or discharge any destructive device:

(1) Commits a felony of the third degree, punishable as provided in s. 775.082 or s. 775.084.

(2) If the act is perpetrated with the intent to do bodily harm to any person, or with the intent to do property damage, or if the act results in a disruption of governmental operations, commerce, or the private affairs of another person, commits a felony of the second degree, punishable as provided in s. 775.082 or s. 775.084.

(3) If the act results in bodily harm to another person or in property damage, commits a felony of the first degree, punishable as provided in s. 775.082 or s. 775.084.

(4) If the act results in the death of another person, commits a capital felony, punishable as provided in s. 775.082. In the event the death penalty in a capital felony is held to be unconstitutional by the Florida Supreme Court or the United States Supreme Court, the court having jurisdiction over a person previously sentenced to death for a capital felony shall cause such person to be brought before the court, and the court shall sentence such person to life imprisonment if convicted of murder in the first degree or of a capital felony under this subsection, and such

person shall be ineligible for parole. No sentence of death shall be reduced as a result of a determination that a method of execution is held to be unconstitutional under the State Constitution or the Constitution of the United States.

790.1612
Authorization for governmental manufacture, possession, and use of destructive devices.

The governing body of any municipality or county and the Division of State Fire Marshal of the Department of Financial Services have the power to authorize the manufacture, possession, and use of destructive devices as defined in s. 790.001(4).

790.17
Furnishing weapons to minors under 18 years of age or persons of unsound mind and furnishing firearms to minors under 18 years of age prohibited.

(1) A person who sells, hires, barters, lends, transfers, or gives any minor under 18 years of age any dirk, electric weapon or device, or other weapon, other than an ordinary pocketknife, without permission of the minor's parent or guardian, or sells, hires, barters, lends, transfers, or gives to any person of unsound mind an electric weapon or device or any dangerous weapon, other than an ordinary pocketknife, commits a misdemeanor of the first degree, punishable as provided in s. 775.082 or s. 775.083.

(2)

    (a) A person may not knowingly or willfully sell or transfer a firearm to a minor under 18 years of age, except that a person may transfer ownership of a firearm to a minor with permission of the parent or guardian. A person who violates this paragraph commits a felony of the third degree, punishable as provided in s. 775.082, s. 775.083, or s. 775.084.

(b) The parent or guardian must maintain possession of the firearm except pursuant to s. 790.22.

790.174

Safe storage of firearms required.

(1) A person who stores or leaves, on a premise under his or her control, a loaded firearm, as defined in s. 790.001, and who knows or reasonably should know that a minor is likely to gain access to the firearm without the lawful permission of the minor's parent or the person having charge of the minor, or without the supervision required by law, shall keep the firearm in a securely locked box or container or in a location which a reasonable person would believe to be secure or shall secure it with a trigger lock, except when the person is carrying the firearm on his or her body or within such close proximity thereto that he or she can retrieve and use it as easily and quickly as if he or she carried it on his or her body.

(2) It is a misdemeanor of the second degree, punishable as provided in s. 775.082 or s. 775.083, if a person violates subsection (1) by failing to store or leave a firearm in the required manner and as a result thereof a minor gains access to the firearm, without the lawful permission of the minor's parent or the person having charge of the minor, and possesses or exhibits it, without the supervision required by law:

(a) In a public place; or

(b) In a rude, careless, angry, or threatening manner in violation of s. 790.10.

This subsection does not apply if the minor obtains the firearm as a result of an unlawful entry by any person.

(3) As used in this act, the term "minor" means any person under the age of 16.

790.175

Transfer or sale of firearms; required warnings; penalties.

(1) Upon the retail commercial sale or retail transfer of any firearm, the seller or transferor shall deliver a written warning to the purchaser or transferee, which warning states, in block letters not less than 1/4 inch in height:

"IT IS UNLAWFUL, AND PUNISHABLE BY IMPRISONMENT AND FINE, FOR ANY ADULT TO STORE OR LEAVE A FIREARM IN ANY PLACE WITHIN THE REACH OR EASY ACCESS OF A MINOR UNDER 18 YEARS OF AGE OR TO KNOWINGLY SELL OR OTHERWISE TRANSFER OWNERSHIP OR POSSESSION OF A FIREARM TO A MINOR OR A PERSON OF UNSOUND MIND."

(2) Any retail or wholesale store, shop, or sales outlet which sells firearms must conspicuously post at each purchase counter the following warning in block letters not less than 1 inch in height:

"IT IS UNLAWFUL TO STORE OR LEAVE A FIREARM IN ANY PLACE WITHIN THE REACH OR EASY ACCESS OF A MINOR UNDER 18 YEARS OF AGE OR TO KNOWINGLY SELL OR OTHERWISE TRANSFER OWNERSHIP OR POSSESSION OF A FIREARM TO A MINOR OR A PERSON OF UNSOUND MIND."

(3) Any person or business knowingly violating a requirement to provide warning under this section commits a misdemeanor of the second degree, punishable as provided in s. 775.082 or s. 775.083.

790.22

Use of BB guns, air or gas-operated guns, or electric weapons or devices by minor under 16; limitation; possession of firearms by minor under 18 prohibited; penalties.

(1) The use for any purpose whatsoever of BB guns, air or gas-operated guns, or electric weapons or devices, by any minor under the age of 16 years is prohibited unless such use is under the supervision and in the presence of an adult who is acting with the consent of the minor's parent.

(2) Any adult responsible for the welfare of any child under the age of 16 years who knowingly permits such child to use or have in his or her possession any BB gun, air or gas-operated gun, electric weapon or device, or firearm in violation of the provisions of subsection (1) of this section commits a misdemeanor of the second degree, punishable as provided in s. 775.082 or s. 775.083.

(3) A minor under 18 years of age may not possess a firearm, other than an unloaded firearm at his or her home, unless:

(a) The minor is engaged in a lawful hunting activity and is:

1. At least 16 years of age; or

2. Under 16 years of age and supervised by an adult.

(b) The minor is engaged in a lawful marksmanship competition or practice or other lawful recreational shooting activity and is:

1. At least 16 years of age; or

2. Under 16 years of age and supervised by an adult who is acting with the consent of the minor's parent or guardian.

(c) The firearm is unloaded and is being transported by the minor directly to or from an event authorized in paragraph (a) or paragraph (b).

(4)

(a) Any parent or guardian of a minor, or other adult responsible for the welfare of a minor, who knowingly and willfully permits the minor to possess a firearm in violation of subsection (3) commits a felony of the third degree, punishable as provided in s. 775.082, s. 775.083, or s. 775.084.

(b) Any natural parent or adoptive parent, whether custodial or noncustodial, or any legal guardian or legal custodian of a minor, if that minor possesses a firearm in violation of subsection (3) may, if the court finds it appropriate, be required to participate in classes on parenting education which are approved by the Department of Juvenile Justice, upon the first conviction of the minor. Upon any subsequent conviction of the minor, the court may, if the court finds it appropriate, require the parent to attend further parent education classes or render community service hours together with the child.

(c) The juvenile justice circuit advisory boards or the Department of Juvenile Justice shall establish appropriate community service programs to be available to the alternative sanctions coordinators of the circuit courts in implementing this subsection. The boards or department shall propose the implementation of a community service program in each circuit, and may submit a circuit plan, to be implemented upon approval of the circuit alternative sanctions coordinator.

(d) For the purposes of this section, community service may be provided on public property as well as on private property with the expressed permission of the property owner. Any community service provided on private property is limited to such things as removal of graffiti and restoration of vandalized property.

(5)

(a) A minor who violates subsection (3) commits a misdemeanor of the first degree; for a first offense, may serve a period of detention of up to 3 days in a secure detention facility; and, in addition to any other penalty provided by law, shall be required to perform 100 hours of community service; and:

1. If the minor is eligible by reason of age for a driver license or driving privilege, the court shall direct the Department of Highway Safety and Motor Vehicles to revoke or to withhold issuance of the minor's driver license or driving privilege for up to 1 year.

2. If the minor's driver license or driving privilege is under suspension or revocation for any reason, the court shall direct the Department of Highway Safety and Motor Vehicles to extend the period of suspension or revocation by an additional period of up to 1 year.

3. If the minor is ineligible by reason of age for a driver license or driving privilege, the court shall direct the Department of Highway Safety and Motor Vehicles to withhold issuance of the minor's driver license or driving privilege for up to 1 year after the date on which the minor would otherwise have become eligible.

(b) For a second or subsequent offense, a minor who violates subsection (3) commits a felony of the third degree and shall serve a period of detention of up to 15 days in a secure detention facility and shall be required to perform not less than 100 nor more than 250 hours of community service, and:

1. If the minor is eligible by reason of age for a driver license or driving privilege, the court shall direct the Department of Highway Safety and Motor Vehicles to revoke or to withhold issuance of the minor's driver license or driving privilege for up to 2 years.

2. If the minor's driver license or driving privilege is under suspension or revocation for any reason, the court shall

direct the Department of Highway Safety and Motor Vehicles to extend the period of suspension or revocation by an additional period of up to 2 years.

3. If the minor is ineligible by reason of age for a driver license or driving privilege, the court shall direct the Department of Highway Safety and Motor Vehicles to withhold issuance of the minor's driver license or driving privilege for up to 2 years after the date on which the minor would otherwise have become eligible.

For the purposes of this subsection, community service shall be performed, if possible, in a manner involving a hospital emergency room or other medical environment that deals on a regular basis with trauma patients and gunshot wounds.

(6) Any firearm that is possessed or used by a minor in violation of this section shall be promptly seized by a law enforcement officer and disposed of in accordance with s. 790.08(1)-(6).

(7) The provisions of this section are supplemental to all other provisions of law relating to the possession, use, or exhibition of a firearm.

(8) Notwithstanding s. 985.24 or s. 985.25(1), if a minor is charged with an offense that involves the use or possession of a firearm, including a violation of subsection (3), or is charged for any offense during the commission of which the minor possessed a firearm, the minor shall be detained in secure detention, unless the state attorney authorizes the release of the minor, and shall be given a hearing within 24 hours after being taken into custody. At the hearing, the court may order that the minor continue to be held in secure detention in accordance with the applicable time periods specified in s. 985.26(1)-(5), if the court finds that the minor meets the criteria specified in s. 985.255, or if the court finds by clear and convincing evidence that the minor is a

clear and present danger to himself or herself or the community. The Department of Juvenile Justice shall prepare a form for all minors charged under this subsection which states the period of detention and the relevant demographic information, including, but not limited to, the gender, age, and race of the minor; whether or not the minor was represented by private counsel or a public defender; the current offense; and the minor's complete prior record, including any pending cases. The form shall be provided to the judge for determining whether the minor should be continued in secure detention under this subsection. An order placing a minor in secure detention because the minor is a clear and present danger to himself or herself or the community must be in writing, must specify the need for detention and the benefits derived by the minor or the community by placing the minor in secure detention, and must include a copy of the form provided by the department.

(9) Notwithstanding s. 985.245, if the minor is found to have committed an offense that involves the use or possession of a firearm, as defined in s. 790.001, other than a violation of subsection (3), or an offense during the commission of which the minor possessed a firearm, and the minor is not committed to a residential commitment program of the Department of Juvenile Justice, in addition to any other punishment provided by law, the court shall order:

(a) For a first offense, that the minor shall serve a minimum period of detention of 15 days in a secure detention facility; and

1. Perform 100 hours of community service; and may

2. Be placed on community control or in a nonresidential commitment program.

(b) For a second or subsequent offense, that the minor shall serve a mandatory period of detention of at least 21 days in a secure detention facility; and

1. Perform not less than 100 nor more than 250 hours of community service; and may

2. Be placed on community control or in a nonresidential commitment program.

The minor shall not receive credit for time served before adjudication. For the purposes of this subsection, community service shall be performed, if possible, in a manner involving a hospital emergency room or other medical environment that deals on a regular basis with trauma patients and gunshot wounds.

(10) If a minor is found to have committed an offense under subsection (9), the court shall impose the following penalties in addition to any penalty imposed under paragraph (9)(a) or paragraph (9)(b):

(a) For a first offense:

1. If the minor is eligible by reason of age for a driver license or driving privilege, the court shall direct the Department of Highway Safety and Motor Vehicles to revoke or to withhold issuance of the minor's driver license or driving privilege for up to 1 year.

2. If the minor's driver license or driving privilege is under suspension or revocation for any reason, the court shall direct the Department of Highway Safety and Motor Vehicles to extend the period of suspension or revocation by an additional period for up to 1 year.

3. If the minor is ineligible by reason of age for a driver license or driving privilege, the court shall direct the Department of Highway Safety and Motor Vehicles to withhold issuance of the minor's driver license or driving privilege for up to 1 year after the date on which the minor would otherwise have become eligible.

(b) For a second or subsequent offense:

    1. If the minor is eligible by reason of age for a driver license or driving privilege, the court shall direct the Department of Highway Safety and Motor Vehicles to revoke or to withhold issuance of the minor's driver license or driving privilege for up to 2 years.

    2. If the minor's driver license or driving privilege is under suspension or revocation for any reason, the court shall direct the Department of Highway Safety and Motor Vehicles to extend the period of suspension or revocation by an additional period for up to 2 years.

    3. If the minor is ineligible by reason of age for a driver license or driving privilege, the court shall direct the Department of Highway Safety and Motor Vehicles to withhold issuance of the minor's driver license or driving privilege for up to 2 years after the date on which the minor would otherwise have become eligible.

790.221

Possession of short-barreled rifle, short-barreled shotgun, or machine gun; penalty.

(1) It is unlawful for any person to own or to have in his or her care, custody, possession, or control any short-barreled rifle, short-barreled shotgun, or machine gun which is, or may readily be made, operable; but this section shall not apply to antique firearms.

(2) A person who violates this section commits a felony of the second degree, punishable as provided in s. 775.082, s. 775.083, or s. 775.084.

(3) Firearms in violation hereof which are lawfully owned and possessed under provisions of federal law are excepted.

790.225

Ballistic self-propelled knives; unlawful to manufacture, sell, or possess; forfeiture; penalty.

(1) It is unlawful for any person to manufacture, display, sell, own, possess, or use a ballistic self-propelled knife which is a device that propels a knifelike blade as a projectile and which physically separates the blade from the device by means of a coil spring, elastic material, or compressed gas. A ballistic self-propelled knife is declared to be a dangerous or deadly weapon and a contraband item. It shall be subject to seizure and shall be disposed of as provided in s. 790.08(1) and (6).

(2) This section shall not apply to:

(a) Any device from which a knifelike blade opens, where such blade remains physically integrated with the device when open.

(b) Any device which propels an arrow, a bolt, or a dart by means of any common bow, compound bow, crossbow, or underwater spear gun.

(3) Any person violating the provisions of subsection (1) is guilty of a misdemeanor of the first degree, punishable as provided in s. 775.082 or s. 775.083.

790.23

Felons and delinquents; possession of firearms, ammunition, or electric weapons or devices unlawful.

(1) It is unlawful for any person to own or to have in his or her care, custody, possession, or control any firearm, ammunition, or electric weapon or device, or to carry a concealed weapon, including a tear gas gun or chemical weapon or device, if that person has been:

(a) Convicted of a felony in the courts of this state;

(b) Found, in the courts of this state, to have committed a delinquent act that would be a felony if committed by an adult and such person is under 24 years of age;

(c) Convicted of or found to have committed a crime against the United States which is designated as a felony;

(d) Found to have committed a delinquent act in another state, territory, or country that would be a felony if committed by an adult and which was punishable by imprisonment for a term exceeding 1 year and such person is under 24 years of age; or

(e) Found guilty of an offense that is a felony in another state, territory, or country and which was punishable by imprisonment for a term exceeding 1 year.

(2) This section shall not apply to a person convicted of a felony whose civil rights and firearm authority have been restored.

(3) Except as otherwise provided in subsection (4), any person who violates this section commits a felony of the second degree, punishable as provided in s. 775.082, s. 775.083, or s. 775.084.

(4) Notwithstanding the provisions of s. 874.04, if the offense described in subsection (1) has been committed by a person who has previously qualified or currently qualifies for the penalty enhancements provided for in s. 874.04, the offense is a felony of the first degree, punishable by a term of years not exceeding life or as provided in s. 775.082, s. 775.083, or s. 775.084.

790.233

Possession of firearm or ammunition prohibited when person is subject to an injunction against committing acts of domestic violence, stalking, or cyberstalking; penalties.

(1) A person may not have in his or her care, custody, possession, or control any firearm or ammunition if the person has been issued

a final injunction that is currently in force and effect, restraining that person from committing acts of domestic violence, as issued under s. 741.30 or from committing acts of stalking or cyberstalking, as issued under s. 784.0485.

(2) A person who violates subsection (1) commits a misdemeanor of the first degree, punishable as provided in s. 775.082 or s. 775.083

(3) It is the intent of the Legislature that the disabilities regarding possession of firearms and ammunition are consistent with federal law. Accordingly, this section does not apply to a state or local officer as defined in s. 943.10(14), holding an active certification, who receives or possesses a firearm or ammunition for use in performing official duties on behalf of the officer's employing agency, unless otherwise prohibited by the employing agency.

790.235

Possession of firearm or ammunition by violent career criminal unlawful; penalty.

(1) Any person who meets the violent career criminal criteria under s. 775.084(1)(d), regardless of whether such person is or has previously been sentenced as a violent career criminal, who owns or has in his or her care, custody, possession, or control any firearm, ammunition, or electric weapon or device, or carries a concealed weapon, including a tear gas gun or chemical weapon or device, commits a felony of the first degree, punishable as provided in s. 775.082, s. 775.083, or s. 775.084. A person convicted of a violation of this section shall be sentenced to a mandatory minimum of 15 years' imprisonment; however, if the person would be sentenced to a longer term of imprisonment

under s. 775.084(4)(d), the person must be sentenced under that provision. A person convicted of a violation of this section is not eligible for any form of discretionary early release, other than pardon, executive clemency, or conditional medical release under s. 947.149.

(2) For purposes of this section, the previous felony convictions necessary to meet the violent career criminal criteria under s. 775.084(1)(d) may be convictions for felonies committed as an adult or adjudications of delinquency for felonies committed as a juvenile. In order to be counted as a prior felony for purposes of this section, the felony must have resulted in a conviction sentenced separately, or an adjudication of delinquency entered separately, prior to the current offense, and sentenced or adjudicated separately from any other felony that is to be counted as a prior felony.

(3) This section shall not apply to a person whose civil rights and firearm authority have been restored.

790.24

Report of medical treatment of certain wounds; penalty for failure to report.

Any physician, nurse, or employee thereof and any employee of a hospital, sanitarium, clinic, or nursing home knowingly treating any person suffering from a gunshot wound or life-threatening injury indicating an act of violence, or receiving a request for such treatment, shall report the same immediately to the sheriff's department of the county in which said treatment is administered or request therefor received. This section does not affect any requirement that a person has to report abuse pursuant to chapter 39 or chapter 415. Any such person willfully failing to report such treatment or request therefor is guilty of a misdemeanor of the first degree, punishable as provided in s. 775.082 or s. 775.083.

790.25

Lawful ownership, possession, and use of firearms and other weapons.

(1) DECLARATION OF POLICY.

The Legislature finds as a matter of public policy and fact that it is necessary to promote firearms safety and to curb and prevent the use of firearms and other weapons in crime and by incompetent persons without prohibiting the lawful use in defense of life, home, and property, and the use by United States or state military organizations, and as otherwise now authorized by law, including the right to use and own firearms for target practice and marksmanship on target practice ranges or other lawful places, and lawful hunting and other lawful purposes.

(2) USES NOT AUTHORIZED.

(a) This section does not authorize carrying a concealed weapon without a permit, as prohibited by ss. 790.01 and 790.02.

(b) The protections of this section do not apply to the following:

1. A person who has been adjudged mentally incompetent, who is addicted to the use of narcotics or any similar drug, or who is a habitual or chronic alcoholic, or a person using weapons or firearms in violation of ss. 790.07-790.115, 790.145-790.19, 790.22-790.24;

2. Vagrants and other undesirable persons as defined in 1s. 856.02;

3. A person in or about a place of nuisance as defined in s. 823.05, unless such person is there for law enforcement or some other lawful purpose.

(3) LAWFUL USES.

The provisions of ss. 790.053 and 790.06 do not apply in the following instances, and, despite such sections, it is lawful for the following persons to own, possess, and lawfully use firearms and other weapons, ammunition, and supplies for lawful purposes:

(a) Members of the Militia, National Guard, Florida State Defense Force, Army, Navy, Air Force, Marine Corps, Coast Guard, organized reserves, and other armed forces of the state and of the United States, when on duty, when training or preparing themselves for military duty, or while subject to recall or mobilization;

(b) Citizens of this state subject to duty in the Armed Forces under s. 2, Art. X of the State Constitution, under chapters 250 and 251, and under federal laws, when on duty or when training or preparing themselves for military duty;

(c) Persons carrying out or training for emergency management duties under chapter 252;

(d) Sheriffs, marshals, prison or jail wardens, police officers, Florida highway patrol officers, game wardens, revenue officers, forest officials, special officers appointed under the provisions of chapter 354, and other peace and law enforcement officers and their deputies and assistants and full-time paid peace officers of other states and of the Federal Government who are carrying out official duties while in this state;

(e) Officers or employees of the state or United States duly authorized to carry a concealed weapon;

(f) Guards or messengers of common carriers, express companies, armored car carriers, mail carriers, banks, and other financial institutions, while actually employed in and about the shipment, transportation, or delivery of any money, treasure, bullion, bonds, or other thing of value within this state;

(g) Regularly enrolled members of any organization duly authorized to purchase or receive weapons from the United States or from this state, or regularly enrolled members of clubs organized for target, skeet, or trap shooting, while at or going to or from shooting practice; or regularly enrolled members of clubs organized for modern or antique firearms collecting, while such members are at or going to or from their collectors' gun shows, conventions, or exhibits;

(h) A person engaged in fishing, camping, or lawful hunting or going to or returning from a fishing, camping, or lawful hunting expedition;

(i) A person engaged in the business of manufacturing, repairing, or dealing in firearms, or the agent or representative of any such person while engaged in the lawful course of such business;

(j) A person firing weapons for testing or target practice under safe conditions and in a safe place not prohibited by law or going to or from such place;

(k) A person firing weapons in a safe and secure indoor range for testing and target practice;

(l) A person traveling by private conveyance when the weapon is securely encased or in a public conveyance when the weapon is securely encased and not in the person's manual possession;

(m) A person while carrying a pistol unloaded and in a secure wrapper, concealed or otherwise, from the place of purchase to his or her home or place of business or to a place of repair or back to his or her home or place of business;

(n) A person possessing arms at his or her home or place of business;

(o) Investigators employed by the several public defenders of the state, while actually carrying out official duties, provided such investigators:

1. Are employed full time;

2. Meet the official training standards for firearms established by the Criminal Justice Standards and Training Commission as provided in s. 943.12(5) and the requirements of ss. 493.6108(1)(a) and 943.13(1)-(4); and

3. Are individually designated by an affidavit of consent signed by the employing public defender and filed with the clerk of the circuit court in the county in which the employing public defender resides.

(p) Investigators employed by the capital collateral regional counsel, while actually carrying out official duties, provided such investigators:

1. Are employed full time;

2. Meet the official training standards for firearms as established by the Criminal Justice Standards and Training Commission as provided in s. 943.12(1) and the requirements of ss. 493.6108(1)(a) and 943.13(1)-(4); and

3. Are individually designated by an affidavit of consent signed by the capital collateral regional counsel and filed with the clerk of the circuit court in the county in which the investigator is headquartered.

(4) CONSTRUCTION.

This act shall be liberally construed to carry out the declaration of policy herein and in favor of the constitutional right to keep and bear arms for lawful purposes. This act is supplemental and additional to existing rights to bear arms now guaranteed by law and decisions of the courts of Florida, and nothing herein shall impair or diminish any of such rights. This act shall supersede any law, ordinance, or regulation in conflict herewith.

(5) POSSESSION IN PRIVATE CONVEYANCE.

Notwithstanding subsection (2), it is lawful and is not a violation of

s. 790.01 for a person 18 years of age or older to possess a concealed firearm or other weapon for self-defense or other lawful purpose within the interior of a private conveyance, without a license, if the firearm or other weapon is securely encased or is otherwise not readily accessible for immediate use. Nothing herein contained prohibits the carrying of a legal firearm other than a handgun anywhere in a private conveyance when such firearm is being carried for a lawful use. Nothing herein contained shall be construed to authorize the carrying of a concealed firearm or other weapon on the person. This subsection shall be liberally construed in favor of the lawful use, ownership, and possession of firearms and other weapons, including lawful self-defense as provided in s. 776.012.

---

[1]790.251

Protection of the right to keep and bear arms in motor vehicles for self-defense and other lawful purposes; prohibited acts; duty of public and private employers; immunity from liability; enforcement.

(1) SHORT TITLE.

This section may be cited as the "Preservation and Protection of the Right to Keep and Bear Arms in Motor Vehicles Act of 2008."

(2) DEFINITIONS.

As used in this section, the term:

  (a) "Parking lot" means any property that is used for parking motor vehicles and is available to customers, employees, or invitees for temporary or long-term parking or storage of motor vehicles.

  (b) "Motor vehicle" means any automobile, truck, minivan, sports utility vehicle, motor home, recreational vehicle, motorcycle, motor scooter, or any other vehicle operated on the roads of this state and required to be registered under state law.

(c) "Employee" means any person who possesses a valid license issued pursuant to s. 790.06 and:

1. Works for salary, wages, or other remuneration;

2. Is an independent contractor; or

3. Is a volunteer, intern, or other similar individual for an employer.

(d) "Employer" means any business that is a sole proprietorship, partnership, corporation, limited liability company, professional association, cooperative, joint venture, trust, firm, institution, or association, or public sector entity, that has employees.

(e) "Invitee" means any business invitee, including a customer or visitor, who is lawfully on the premises of a public or private employer.

As used in this section, the term "firearm" includes ammunition and accoutrements attendant to the lawful possession and use of a firearm.

(3) LEGISLATIVE INTENT; FINDINGS.

This act is intended to codify the long-standing legislative policy of the state that individual citizens have a constitutional right to keep and bear arms, that they have a constitutional right to possess and keep legally owned firearms within their motor vehicles for self-defense and other lawful purposes, and that these rights are not abrogated by virtue of a citizen becoming a customer, employee, or invitee of a business entity. It is the finding of the Legislature that a citizen's lawful possession, transportation, and secure keeping of firearms and ammunition within his or her motor vehicle is essential to the exercise of the fundamental constitutional right to keep and bear arms and the constitutional right of self-defense. The Legislature finds that protecting and preserving these rights is essential to the exercise of freedom and individual responsibility. The Legislature further finds that no citizen can or should be required to waive or abrogate his or her right to possess and securely keep firearms and ammunition locked within his or her motor vehicle by virtue of becoming a customer, employee, or invitee of any employer or business establishment within the state, unless specifically required by state or federal law.

(4) PROHIBITED ACTS.

No public or private employer may violate the constitutional rights of any customer, employee, or invitee as provided in paragraphs (a)-(e):

(a) No public or private employer may prohibit any customer, employee, or invitee from possessing any legally owned firearm when such firearm is lawfully possessed and locked inside or locked to a private motor vehicle in a parking lot and when the customer, employee, or invitee is lawfully in such area.

(b) No public or private employer may violate the privacy rights of a customer, employee, or invitee by verbal or written inquiry regarding the presence of a firearm inside or locked to a private motor vehicle in a parking lot or by an actual search of a private motor vehicle in a parking lot to ascertain the presence of a firearm within the vehicle. Further, no public or private employer may take any action against a customer, employee, or invitee based upon verbal or written statements of any party concerning possession of a firearm stored inside a private motor vehicle in a parking lot for lawful purposes. A search of a private motor vehicle in the parking lot of a public or private employer to ascertain the presence of a firearm within the vehicle may only be conducted by on-duty law enforcement personnel, based upon due process and must comply with constitutional protections.

(c) No public or private employer shall condition employment upon either:

1. The fact that an employee or prospective employee holds or does not hold a license issued pursuant to s. 790.06; or

2. Any agreement by an employee or a prospective employee that prohibits an employee from keeping a legal firearm locked inside or locked to a private motor vehicle in a parking lot when such firearm is kept for lawful purposes.

(d) No public or private employer shall prohibit or attempt to prevent any customer, employee, or invitee from entering the parking lot of the employer's place of business because the customer's, employee's, or invitee's private motor vehicle contains a legal firearm being carried for lawful purposes, that is out of sight within the customer's, employee's, or invitee's private motor vehicle.

(e) No public or private employer may terminate the employment of or otherwise discriminate against an employee, or expel a customer or invitee for exercising his or her constitutional right to keep and bear arms or for exercising the right of self-defense as long as a firearm is never exhibited on company property for any reason other than lawful defensive purposes.

This subsection applies to all public sector employers, including those already prohibited from regulating firearms under the provisions of s. 790.33.

(5) DUTY OF CARE OF PUBLIC AND PRIVATE EMPLOYERS; IMMUNITY FROM LIABILITY.

(a) When subject to the provisions of subsection (4), a public or private employer has no duty of care related to the actions prohibited under such subsection.

(b) A public or private employer is not liable in a civil action based on actions or inactions taken in compliance with this section. The immunity provided in this subsection does not apply to civil actions based on actions or inactions of public or private employers that are unrelated to compliance with this section.

(c) Nothing contained in this section shall be interpreted to expand any existing duty, or create any additional duty, on the part of a public or private employer, property owner, or property owner's agent.

(6) ENFORCEMENT.

The Attorney General shall enforce the protections of this act on behalf of any customer, employee, or invitee aggrieved under this act. If there is reasonable cause to believe that the aggrieved person's rights under this act have been violated by a public or private employer, the Attorney General shall commence a civil or administrative action for damages, injunctive relief and civil penalties, and such other relief as may be appropriate under the provisions of s. 760.51, or may negotiate a settlement with any employer on behalf of any person aggrieved under the act. However, nothing in this act shall prohibit the right of a person aggrieved under this act to bring a civil action for violation of rights protected under the act. In any successful action brought by a customer, employee, or invitee aggrieved under this act, the court shall award all reasonable personal costs and losses suffered by the aggrieved person as a result of the violation of rights under this act. In any action brought pursuant to this act, the court shall award all court costs and attorney's fees to the prevailing party.

(7) EXCEPTIONS.

The prohibitions in subsection (4) do not apply to:

(a) Any school property as defined and regulated under s. 790.115.

(b) Any correctional institution regulated under s. 944.47 or chapter 957.

(c) Any property where a nuclear-powered electricity generation facility is located.

(d) Property owned or leased by a public or private employer or the landlord of a public or private employer upon which are conducted substantial activities involving national defense, aerospace, or homeland security.

(e) Property owned or leased by a public or private employer or the landlord of a public or private employer upon which the primary business conducted is the manufacture, use, storage, or transportation of combustible or explosive materials regulated under state or federal law, or property owned or leased by an employer who has obtained a permit required under 18 U.S.C. s. 842 to engage in the business of importing, manufacturing, or dealing in explosive materials on such property.

(f) A motor vehicle owned, leased, or rented by a public or private employer or the landlord of a public or private employer.

(g) Any other property owned or leased by a public or private employer or the landlord of a public or private employer upon which possession of a firearm or other legal product by a customer, employee, or invitee is prohibited pursuant to any federal law, contract with a federal government entity, or general law of this state.

[1]Note—Section 15, ch. 2011-119, provides that "[t]he amendments made to ss. 509.144 and 932.701, Florida Statutes, and the creation of s. 901.1503, Florida Statutes, by this act do not affect or impede the provisions of s. 790.251, Florida Statutes, or any other protection or right guaranteed by the Second Amendment to the United States Constitution."

790.27

Alteration or removal of firearm serial number or possession, sale, or delivery of firearm with serial number altered or removed prohibited; penalties.

(1)

    (a) It is unlawful for any person to knowingly alter or remove the manufacturer's or importer's serial number from a firearm with intent to disguise the true identity thereof.

    (b) Any person violating paragraph (a) is guilty of a felony of the third degree, punishable as provided in s. 775.082, s. 775.083, or s. 775.084.

(2)

    (a) It is unlawful for any person to knowingly sell, deliver, or possess any firearm on which the manufacturer's or importer's serial number has been unlawfully altered or removed.

    (b) Any person violating paragraph (a) is guilty of a misdemeanor of the first degree, punishable as provided in s. 775.082 or s. 775.083.

(3) This section shall not apply to antique firearms.

790.31

Armor-piercing or exploding ammunition or dragon's breath shotgun shells, bolo shells, or flechette shells prohibited.–

(1) As used in this section, the term:

    (a) "Armor-piercing bullet" means any bullet which has a steel inner core or core of equivalent hardness and a truncated cone and which is designed for use in a handgun as an armor-piercing or metal-piercing bullet.

    (b) "Exploding bullet" means any bullet that can be fired from any firearm, if such bullet is designed or altered so as to detonate or forcibly break up through the use of an explosive or deflagrant contained wholly or partially within or attached to such bullet. The term does not include any bullet designed to expand or break up through the mechanical forces of impact alone or any signaling device or pest control device not designed to impact on any target.

(c) "Handgun" means a firearm capable of being carried and used by one hand, such as a pistol or revolver.

(d) "Dragon's breath shotgun shell" means any shotgun shell that contains exothermic pyrophoric misch metal as the projectile and that is designed for the sole purpose of throwing or spewing a flame or fireball to simulate a flamethrower.

(e) "Bolo shell" means any shell that can be fired in a firearm and that expels as projectiles two or more metal balls connected by solid metal wire.

(f) "Flechette shell" means any shell that can be fired in a firearm and that expels two or more pieces of fin-stabilized solid metal wire or two or more solid dart-type projectiles.

(2)

(a) Any person who manufactures, sells, offers for sale, or delivers any armor-piercing bullet or exploding bullet, or dragon's breath shotgun shell, bolo shell, or flechette shell is guilty of a felony of the third degree, punishable as provided in s. 775.082, s. 775.083, or s. 775.084.

(b) Any person who possesses an armor-piercing bullet or exploding bullet with knowledge of its armor-piercing or exploding capabilities loaded in a handgun, or who possesses a dragon's breath shotgun shell, bolo shell, or flechette shell with knowledge of its capabilities loaded in a firearm, is guilty of a felony of the third degree, punishable as provided in s. 775.082, s. 775.083, or s. 775.084.

(c) Any person who possesses with intent to use an armor-piercing bullet or exploding bullet or dragon's breath shotgun shell, bolo shell, or flechette shell to assist in the commission of a criminal act is guilty of a felony of the second degree, punishable as provided in s. 775.082, s. 775.083, or s. 775.084.

(3) This section does not apply to:

(a) The possession of any item described in subsection (1) by any law enforcement officer, when possessed in connection with the performance of his or her duty as a law enforcement officer, or law enforcement agency.

(b) The manufacture of items described in subsection (1) exclusively for sale or delivery to law enforcement agencies.

(c) The sale or delivery of items described in subsection (1) to law enforcement agencies.

790.33

Field of regulation of firearms and ammunition preempted.

(1) PREEMPTION.

Except as expressly provided by the State Constitution or general law, the Legislature hereby declares that it is occupying the whole field of regulation of firearms and ammunition, including the purchase, sale, transfer, taxation, manufacture, ownership, possession, storage, and transportation thereof, to the exclusion of all existing and future county, city, town, or municipal ordinances or any administrative regulations or rules adopted by local or state government relating thereto. Any such existing ordinances, rules, or regulations are hereby declared null and void.

(2) POLICY AND INTENT.

(a) It is the intent of this section to provide uniform firearms laws in the state; to declare all ordinances and regulations null and void which have been enacted by any jurisdictions other than state and federal, which regulate firearms, ammunition, or components thereof; to prohibit the enactment of any future ordinances or regulations relating to firearms, ammunition, or components thereof unless specifically authorized by this section or general law; and to require local jurisdictions to enforce state firearms laws.

(b) It is further the intent of this section to deter and prevent the violation of this section and the violation of rights protected under the constitution and laws of this state related to firearms, ammunition, or components thereof, by the abuse of official authority that occurs when enactments are passed in violation of state law or under color of local or state authority.

(3) PROHIBITIONS; PENALTIES.

(a) Any person, county, agency, municipality, district, or other entity that violates the Legislature's occupation of the whole field of regulation of firearms and ammunition, as declared in subsection (1), by enacting or causing to be enforced any local ordinance or administrative rule or regulation impinging upon such exclusive occupation of the field shall be liable as set forth herein.

(b) If any county, city, town, or other local government violates this section, the court shall declare the improper ordinance, regulation, or rule invalid and issue a permanent injunction against the local government prohibiting it from enforcing such ordinance, regulation, or rule. It is no defense that in enacting the ordinance, regulation, or rule the local government was acting in good faith or upon advice of counsel.

(c) If the court determines that a violation was knowing and willful, the court shall assess a civil fine of up to $5,000 against the elected or appointed local government official or officials or administrative agency head under whose jurisdiction the violation occurred.

(d) Except as required by applicable law, public funds may not be used to defend or reimburse the unlawful conduct of any person found to have knowingly and willfully violated this section.

(e) A knowing and willful violation of any provision of this section by a person acting in an official capacity for any entity enacting or causing to be enforced a local ordinance or administrative rule or regulation prohibited under paragraph (a) or otherwise under color of law shall be cause for termination of employment or contract or removal from office by the Governor.

(f) A person or an organization whose membership is adversely affected by any ordinance, regulation, measure, directive, rule, enactment, order, or policy promulgated or caused to be enforced in violation of this section may file suit against any county, agency, municipality, district, or other entity in any court of this state having jurisdiction over any defendant to the suit for declaratory and injunctive relief and for actual damages, as limited herein, caused by the violation. A court shall award the prevailing plaintiff in any such suit:

1. Reasonable attorney's fees and costs in accordance with the laws of this state, including a contingency fee multiplier, as authorized by law; and

2. The actual damages incurred, but not more than $100,000. Interest on the sums awarded pursuant to this subsection shall accrue at the legal rate from the date on which suit was filed.

(4) EXCEPTIONS.

This section does not prohibit:

(a) Zoning ordinances that encompass firearms businesses along with other businesses, except that zoning ordinances that are designed for the purpose of restricting or prohibiting the sale, purchase, transfer, or manufacture of firearms or ammunition as a method of regulating firearms or ammunition are in conflict with this subsection and are prohibited;

(b) A duly organized law enforcement agency from enacting and enforcing regulations pertaining to firearms, ammunition, or firearm accessories issued to or used by peace officers in the course of their official duties;

(c) Except as provided in s. 790.251, any entity subject to the prohibitions of this section from regulating or prohibiting the carrying of firearms and ammunition by an employee of the entity during and in the course of the employee's official duties;

(d) A court or administrative law judge from hearing and resolving any case or controversy or issuing any opinion or order on a matter within the jurisdiction of that court or judge; or

(e) The Florida Fish and Wildlife Conservation Commission from regulating the use of firearms or ammunition as a method of taking wildlife and regulating the shooting ranges managed by the commission.

(5) SHORT TITLE.

As created by chapter 87-23, Laws of Florida, this section may be cited as the "Joe Carlucci Uniform Firearms Act."

➢ APPENDICES ◂

FORMS
APPENDIX B
Selected Federal Forms

ATF Form 4473 Page 1

OMB No. 1140-0020

U.S. Department of Justice
Bureau of Alcohol, Tobacco, Firearms and Explosives

Firearms Transaction Record

	Transferor's/Seller's Transaction Serial Number *(If any)*

WARNING: You may not receive a firearm if prohibited by Federal or State law. The information you provide will be used to determine whether you are prohibited from receiving a firearm. Certain violations of the Gun Control Act, 18 U.S.C. 921 et. seq., are punishable by up to 10 years imprisonment and/or up to a $250,000 fine.

Read the Notices, Instructions, and Definitions on this form. Prepare in original only at the licensed premises *("licensed premises" includes business temporarily conducted from a qualifying gun show or event in the same State in which the licensed premises is located)* unless the transaction qualifies under 18 U.S.C. 922(c). All entries must be handwritten in ink. "PLEASE PRINT."

Section A - Must Be Completed Personally By Transferee/Buyer

1. Transferee's/Buyer's Full Name *(If legal name contains an initial only, record "IO" after the initial. If no middle initial or name, record "NMN".)*

Last Name *(Including suffix (e.g., Jr, Sr, II, III))*	First Name	Middle Name

2. Current State of Residence and Address (U.S. Postal abbreviations are acceptable. Cannot be a post office box.)

Number and Street Address	City	County	State	ZIP Code

3. Place of Birth U.S. City and State -OR- Foreign Country	4. Height Ft. In.	5. Weight *(Lbs.)*	6. Sex ☐ Male ☐ Female	7. Birth Date Month Day Year

8. Social Security Number *(Optional, but will help prevent misidentification)*	9. Unique Personal Identification Number *(UPIN)* if applicable *(See Instructions for Question 9.)*

10.a. Ethnicity ☐ Hispanic or Latino ☐ Not Hispanic or Latino	10.b. Race *(In addition to ethnicity, select one or more race in 10.b. Both 10.a. and 10.b. must be answered.)* ☐ American Indian or Alaska Native ☐ Black or African American ☐ White ☐ Asian ☐ Native Hawaiian or Other Pacific Islander

11. Answer the following questions by checking or marking "yes" or "no" in the boxes to the right of the questions.	Yes	No
a. Are you the actual transferee/buyer of the firearm(s) listed on this form? **Warning: You are not the actual transferee/buyer if you are acquiring the firearm(s) on behalf of another person. If you are not the actual transferee/buyer, the licensee cannot transfer the firearm(s) to you.** *Exception: If you are picking up a repaired firearm(s) for another person, you are not required to answer 11.a. and may proceed to question 11.b. (See Instructions for Question 11.a.)*	☐	☐
b. Are you under indictment or information in any court for a **felony**, or any other crime for which the judge could imprison you for more than one year? *(See Instructions for Question 11.b.)*	☐	☐
c. Have you ever been convicted in any court of a **felony**, or any other crime for which the judge could have imprisoned you for more than one year, even if you received a shorter sentence including probation? *(See Instructions for Question 11.c.)*	☐	☐
d. Are you a fugitive from justice? *(See Instructions for Question 11.d.)*	☐	☐
e. Are you an unlawful user of, or addicted to, marijuana or any depressant, stimulant, narcotic drug, or any other controlled substance? **Warning: The use or possession of marijuana remains unlawful under Federal law regardless of whether it has been legalized or decriminalized for medicinal or recreational purposes in the state where you reside.**	☐	☐
f. Have you ever been adjudicated as a mental defective **OR** have you ever been committed to a mental institution? *(See Instructions for Question 11.f.)*	☐	☐
g. Have you been discharged from the Armed Forces under **dishonorable** conditions?	☐	☐
h. Are you subject to a court order restraining you from harassing, stalking, or threatening your child or an intimate partner or child of such partner? *(See Instructions for Question 11.h.)*	☐	☐
i. Have you ever been **convicted** in any court of a misdemeanor crime of domestic violence? *(See Instructions for Question 11.i.)*	☐	☐

12.a. Country of Citizenship: *(Check/List more than one, if applicable. Nationals of the United States may check U.S.A.)*
☐ United States of America *(U.S.A.)*   ☐ Other Country/Countries *(Specify)*

	Yes	No
12.b. Have you ever renounced your United States citizenship?	☐	☐
12.c. Are you an alien **illegally** or **unlawfully** in the United States?	☐	☐
12.d.1. Are you an alien who has been admitted to the United States under a nonimmigrant visa? *(See Instructions for Question 12.d.)*	☐	☐
12.d.2. If "yes", do you fall within any of the exceptions stated in the instructions? ☐ N/A	☐	☐

13. If you are an alien, record your U.S.-Issued Alien or Admission number *(AR#, USCIS#, or I94#)*:

Previous Editions Are Obsolete

Transferee/Buyer Continue to Next Page
STAPLE IF PAGES BECOME SEPARATED

ATF E-Form 4473 (5300.9)
Revised October 2016

ATF Form 4473 Page 2

I certify that my answers in Section A are true, correct, and complete. I have read and understand the Notices, Instructions, and Definitions on ATF Form 4473. I understand that answering "yes" to question 11.a. if I am not the actual transferee/buyer is a crime punishable as a felony under Federal law, and may also violate State and/or local law. I understand that a person who answers "yes" to question 11.b. through 11.i and/or 12.b. through 12.c. is prohibited from purchasing or receiving a firearm. I understand that a person who answers "yes" to question 12.d.1. is prohibited from receiving or possessing a firearm, unless the person answers "yes" to question 12.d.2. and provides the documentation required in 18.c. I also understand that making any false oral or written statement, or exhibiting any false or misrepresented identification with respect to this transaction, is a crime punishable as a felony under Federal law, and may also violate State and/or local law. I further understand that the repetitive purchase of firearms for the purpose of resale for livelihood and profit without a Federal firearms license is a violation of Federal law. *(See Instructions for Question 14.)*

14. Transferee's/Buyer's Signature	15. Certification Date

Section B - Must Be Completed By Transferor/Seller

16. Type of firearm(s) to be transferred *(check or mark all that apply):*	17. If transfer is at a qualifying gun show or event:
☐ Handgun ☐ Long Gun *(rifles or shotguns)* ☐ Other Firearm *(frame, receiver, etc. See Instructions for Question 16.)*	Name of Function: _____ City, State: _____

18.a. Identification *(e.g., Virginia Driver's license (VA DL) or other valid government-issued photo identification.)* *(See Instructions for Question 18.a.)*

Issuing Authority and Type of Identification	Number on Identification	Expiration Date of Identification *(if any)*		
		Month	Day	Year

18.b. Supplemental Government Issued Documentation *(if identification document does not show current residence address) (See Instructions for Question 18.b.)*

18.c. Exception to the Nonimmigrant Alien Prohibition: If the transferee/buyer answered "YES" to 12.d.2. the transferor/seller must record the type of documentation showing the exception to the prohibition and attach a copy to this ATF Form 4473. *(See Instructions for Question 18.c.)*

Questions 19, 20, or 21 Must Be Completed Prior To The Transfer Of The Firearm(s) *(See Instructions for Questions 19, 20 and 21.)*

19.a. Date the transferee's/buyer's identifying information in Section A was transmitted to NICS or the appropriate State agency:	19.b. The NICS or State transaction number *(if provided)* was:
Month / Day / Year	

19.c. The response initially (first) provided by NICS or the appropriate State agency was:	19.d. The following response(s) was/were later received from NICS or the appropriate State agency:
☐ Proceed ☐ Delayed ☐ Denied *[The firearm(s) may be transferred on* ☐ Cancelled _____ *if State law permits (optional)]*	☐ Proceed _____ *(date)* ☐ Overturned ☐ Denied _____ *(date)* ☐ Cancelled _____ *(date)* ☐ No response was provided within 3 business days.

19.e. *(Complete if applicable.)* After the firearm was transferred, the following response was received from NICS or the appropriate State agency on:

_____ *(date).* ☐ Proceed ☐ Denied ☐ Cancelled

19.f. The name and Brady identification number of the NICS examiner. *(Optional)*	19.g. Name of FFL Employee Completing NICS check. *(Optional)*
_____ *(name)* _____ *(number)*	

20. ☐ No NICS check was required because a background check was completed during the NFA approval process on the individual who will receive the NFA firearm(s), as reflected on the approved NFA application. *(See Instructions for Question 20.)*

21. ☐ No NICS check was required because the transferee/buyer has a valid permit from the State where the transfer is to take place, which qualifies as an exemption to NICS. *(See Instructions for Question 21.)*

Issuing State and Permit Type	Date of Issuance *(if any)*	Expiration Date *(if any)*	Permit Number *(if any)*

Section C - Must Be Completed Personally By Transferee/Buyer

If the transfer of the firearm(s) takes place on a different day from the date that the transferee/buyer signed Section A, the transferee/buyer must complete Section C immediately prior to the transfer of the firearm(s). *(See Instructions for Question 22 and 23.)*

I certify that my answers to the questions in Section A of this form are still true, correct, and complete.

22. Transferee's/Buyer's Signature	23. Recertification Date

Transferor/Seller Continue to Next Page
STAPLE IF PAGES BECOME SEPARATED

ATF E-Form 4473 (5300.9)
Revised October 2016

ATF Form 4473 Page 3

Section D - Must Be Completed By Transferor/Seller Even If The Firearm(s) is Not Transferred

24. Manufacturer and Importer *(If any) (If the manufacturer and importer are different, the FFL must include both.)*	25. Model *(If Designated)*	26. Serial Number	27. Type *(See Instructions for Question 27.)*	28. Caliber or Gauge
1.				
2.				
3.				
4.				

REMINDER - By the Close of Business Complete ATF Form 3310.4 For Multiple Purchases of Handguns Within 5 Consecutive Business Days

29. Total Number of Firearms Transferred *(Please handwrite by printing e.g., zero, one, two, three, etc. Do not use numerals.)*	30. Check if any part of this transaction is a pawn redemption. ☐ Line Number(s) From Question 24 Above:
31. For Use by Licensee *(See Instructions for Question 31.)*	32. Check if this transaction is to facilitate a private party transfer. ☐ *(See Instructions for Question 32.)*

33. Trade/corporate name and address of transferor/seller and Federal Firearm License Number *(Must contain at least first three and last five digits of FFL Number X-XX-XXXXX.) (Hand stamp may be used.)*

The Person Transferring The Firearm(s) Must Complete Questions 34-37.
For Denied/Cancelled Transactions, the Person Who Completed Section B Must Complete Questions 34-36.

I certify that: (1) I have read and understand the Notices, Instructions, and Definitions on this ATF Form 4473; (2) the information recorded in Sections B and D is true, correct, and complete; and (3) this entire transaction record has been completed at my licensed business premises ("licensed premises" includes business temporarily conducted from a qualifying gun show or event in the same State in which the licensed premises is located) unless this transaction has met the requirements of 18 U.S.C. 922(c). Unless this transaction has been denied or cancelled, I further certify on the basis of — (1) the transferee's/buyer's responses in Section A (and Section C, if applicable); (2) my verification of the identification recorded in question 18 (and my re-verification at the time of transfer, *if Section C was completed);* and (3) State or local law applicable to the firearms business — it is my belief that it is not unlawful for me to sell, deliver, transport, or otherwise dispose of the firearm(s) listed on this form to the person identified in Section A.

34. Transferor's/Seller's Name *(Please print)*	35. Transferor's/Seller's Signature	36. Transferor's/Seller's Title	37. Date Transferred

NOTICES, INSTRUCTIONS, AND DEFINITIONS

Purpose of the Form: The information and certification on this form are designed so that a person licensed under 18 U.S.C. 923 may determine if he/she may lawfully sell or deliver a firearm to the person identified in Section A, and to alert the transferee/buyer of certain restrictions on the receipt and possession of firearms. The transferor/seller of a firearm must determine the lawfulness of the transaction and maintain proper records of the transaction. Consequently, the transferor/seller must be familiar with the provisions of 18 U.S.C. 921-931 and the regulations in 27 CFR Parts 478 and 479. In determining the lawfulness of the sale or delivery of a rifle or shotgun to a resident of another State, the transferor/seller is presumed to know the applicable State laws and published ordinances in both the transferor's/seller's State and the transferee's/buyer's State. *(See ATF Publication 5300.5, State Laws and Published Ordinances.)*

Generally, ATF Form 4473 must be completed on the licensed business premises when a firearm is transferred over-the-counter. Federal law, 18 U.S.C. 922(c), allows a licensed importer, manufacturer, or dealer to sell a firearm to a nonlicensee who does not appear in person at the licensee's business premises only if the transferee/buyer meets certain requirements. These requirements are set forth in section 922(c), 27 CFR 478.96(b), and ATF Procedure 2013-2.

After the transferor/seller has completed the firearms transaction, he/she must make the completed, original ATF Form 4473 *(which includes the Notices, General Instructions, and Definitions),* and any supporting documents, part of his/her permanent records. Such Forms 4473 must be retained for at least 20 years and after that period may be submitted to ATF. Filing may be chronological *(by date of disposition),* alphabetical *(by name of purchaser),* or numerical *(by transaction serial number),* as long as all of the transferor's/seller's completed Forms 4473 are filed in the same manner.

FORMS 4473 FOR DENIED/CANCELLED TRANSFERS MUST BE RETAINED: If the transfer of a firearm is denied/cancelled by NICS, or if for any other reason the transfer is not completed after a NICS check is initiated, the licensee must retain the ATF Form 4473 in his/her records for at least 5 years. Forms 4473 with respect to which a sale, delivery, or transfer did not take place shall be separately retained in alphabetical *(by name of transferee)* or chronological *(by date of transferee's certification)* order.

If the transferor/seller or the transferee/buyer discovers that an ATF Form 4473 is incomplete or improperly completed after the firearm has been transferred, and the transferor/seller or the transferee/buyer wishes to correct the omission(s) or error(s), photocopy the inaccurate form and make any necessary additions or revisions to the photocopy. The transferor/seller should only make changes to Sections B and D. The transferee/buyer should only make changes to Section A and C. Whoever made the changes should initial and date the changes. The corrected photocopy should be attached to the original Form 4473 and retained as part of the transferor's/seller's permanent records.

Exportation of Firearms: The State or Commerce Departments may require a firearms exporter to obtain a license prior to export. **Warning:** Any person who exports a firearm without proper authorization may be fined not more than $1,000,000 and/or imprisoned for not more than 20 years. See 22 U.S.C. 2778(c).

Section A

The transferee/buyer must personally complete Section A of this form and certify *(sign)* that the answers are true, correct, and complete. However, if the transferee/buyer is unable to read and/or write, the answers *(other than the signature)* may be completed by another person, excluding the transferor/seller. Two persons *(other than the transferor/seller)* must then sign as witnesses to the transferee's/buyer's answers and signature/certification in question 14.

ATF E-Form 4473 (5300.9)
Revised October 2016

ATF Form 1 Page 1

U.S. Department of Justice
Bureau of Alcohol, Tobacco, Firearms and Explosives

OMB No. 1140-0011 (06/30/2019)

Application to Make and Register a Firearm

ATF Control Number

To: National Firearms Act Division, Bureau of Alcohol, Tobacco, Firearms and Explosives, P.O. Box 530298, Atlanta, GA 30353-0298

(Submit in duplicate. See Instructions attached.)

As required by Sections 5821 (b), 5822, and 5841 of the National Firearms Act, Title 26 U.S.C., Chapter 53, the undersigned hereby submits application to make and register the firearm described below.

1. Type of Application *(check one)*

2. Application is made by:

☐ INDIVIDUAL ☐ TRUST or LEGAL ENTITY ☐ GOVERNMENT ENTITY

3a. Trade name *(If any)*

a. Tax Paid. Submit your tax payment of $200 with the application. The tax may be paid by credit or debit card, check, or money order. Please complete item 17. Upon approval of the application, we will affix and cancel the required National Firearms Act Stamp. *(See Instruction 2c and 3)*

3b. Applicant's name and mailing address *(Type or print below and between the dots) (see Instruction 2d)*

b. Tax Exempt because firearm is being made on behalf of the United States, or any department, independent establishment, or agency thereof.

3c. If P.O. Box is shown above, street address must be given here

c. Tax Exempt because firearm is being made by or on behalf of any State or possession of the United States, or any political subdivision thereof, or any official police organization of such a government entity engaged in criminal investigations.

3d. County | 3e. Telephone (area code and number) | 3f. e-mail address (optional)

4. Description of Firearm *(complete items a through k) (See Instruction 2j)*

a. Name and Address of Original Manufacturer and/or Importer of Firearm *(if any)*

b. Type of Firearm to be made *(See definition 1c)* If a destructive device, complete item 4j

c. Caliber or Gauge *(Specify one)*

d. Model

Length *(Inches)* | e. Of Barrel: | f. Overall:

g. Serial Number

h. Additional Description *(Include all numbers and other identifying data to include maker's name, city and state which will appear on the firearm) (use additional sheet if necessary)*

i. State Why You Intend To Make Firearm *(Use additional sheet if necessary)*

j. Type of destructive device (check one box): ☐ Firearm ☐ Explosives *(if the Explosives box is checked, complete item 5 and see Instruction 2l)*

If an explosive type destructive device, identify the type of explosive(s): _____

k. Is this firearm being reactivated? ☐ Yes ☐ No *(See definition 1k)*

5. Applicant's Federal Firearms License *(If any)* or Explosives License or Permit Number

(Give complete 15-digit Number)

6. Special *(Occupational)* Tax Status *(if applicable) (See definitions)*

a. Employer Identification Number | b. Class

Under Penalties of Perjury, I Declare that I have examined this application, including accompanying documents, and to the best of my knowledge and belief it is true, accurate and complete and the making and possession of the firearm described above would not constitute a violation of Title 18, U.S.C., Chapter 44, Title 26, U.S.C., Chapter 53; or any provisions of State or local law.

7. Signature of Applicant | 8. Name and Title of Authorized Official | 9. Date

The space below is for the use of the Bureau of Alcohol, Tobacco, Firearms and Explosives

By authority of the Director, Bureau of Alcohol, Tobacco, Firearms and Explosives, this application has been examined and the applicant's making and registration of the firearm described above is:

☐ Approved *(With the following conditions, if any)*

☐ Disapproved *(For the following reasons)*

Authorized ATF Official | Date

Previous Editions Are Obsolete

ATF Copy

ATF E-Form 1 (5320.1)
Revised August 2017

ATF Form 1 Page 2

10. Law Enforcement Notification *(See instruction 2g)*

Each applicant is to provide notification of the proposed making and possession of the firearm described on this Form 1 by providing a copy of the completed form to the chief law enforcement officer in the agency identified below:

Agency or Department Name   Name and Title of Official

Address (Street address or P.O. Box, City, State and Zip Code) to which sent (mailed or delivered)

Information for the Chief Law Enforcement Officer

This form provides notification of the applicant's intent to make and register a National Firearms Act (NFA) firearm. No action on your part is required. However, should you have information that may disqualify this person from making or possessing a firearm, please contact the NFA Division at (304) 616-4500 or NFA@atf.gov. A "Yes" answer to items 11.a. through 11.h. or 13.b. or 13.c. could disqualify a person from acquiring or possessing a firearm. Also, ATF will not approve an application if the making or possession of the firearm is in violation of State or local law.

Maker's Questions *(complete only when the maker is an individual)*

A maker who is an individual must complete this Section.

11. Answer questions 11.a. through 11.h. Answer questions 13 and 14, if applicable. For any "Yes" answer the applicant shall provide details on a separate sheet. *(See instruction 7c and definitions)*

	Yes	No	12. Photograph
a. Are you under indictment or information in any court for a felony, or any other crime, for which the judge could imprison you for more than one year? *(See definition 1n)*			
b. Have you ever been convicted in any court for a felony, or any other crime, for which the judge could have imprisoned you for more than one year, even if you received a shorter sentence including probation? *(See definition 1n)*			Affix Recent Photograph Here *(Approximately 2" x 2")* *(See instruction 2e)*
c. Are you a fugitive from justice? *(See definition 1t)*			
d. Are you an unlawful user of, or addicted to, marijuana or any depressant, stimulant, narcotic drug, or any other controlled substance? **Warning: The use or possession of marijuana remains unlawful under Federal law regardless of whether it has been legalized or decriminalized for medicinal or recreational purposes in the state where you reside.**			
e. Have you ever been adjudicated as a mental defective OR have you ever been committed to a mental institution? *(See definition 1o and 1p)*			
f. Have you been discharged from the Armed Forces under **dishonorable** conditions?			
g. Are you subject to a court order restraining you from harassing, stalking, or threatening your child or an intimate partner or child of such partner? *(See definition 1q)*			
h. Have you ever been convicted in any court of a misdemeanor crime of domestic violence? *(See definition 1r)*			

13a. Country of Citizenship: *(Check/List more than one, if applicable. Nationals of the United States may check U.S.A.) (See definition 1s)*

☐ United States of America   ☐ Other Country/Countries *(specify)*: _____

	Yes	No
b. Have you ever renounced your United States citizenship?		
c. Are you an alien illegally or unlawfully in the United States?		
d.1. Are you an alien who has been admitted to the United States under a nonimmigrant visa?		
d.2. If "yes", do you fall within any of the exceptions stated in the instructions? Attach the documentation to the application ☐ N/A		

14. If you are an alien, record your U.S.-Issued Alien or Admission number (AR#, USCIS#, or 194#): _____

CERTIFICATION: Under penalties imposed by 18 U.S.C. § 924 and 26 U.S.C. § 5861, I certify that, upon submission of this form to ATF, a completed copy of this form will be directed to the chief law enforcement officer (CLEO) shown in item 10, that the statements, as applicable, contained in this certification, and any attached documents in support thereof, are true and correct to the best of my knowledge and belief. NOTE: See instructions 2.d(2) and 2.d(3) for the items to be completed depending on the type of applicant.

Signature of Maker   Date

ATF Form 1 Page 3

15. Number of Responsible Persons *(see definitions)* associated with the applicant trust or legal entity _____

16. Provide the full name (printed or typed) below for each Responsible Person associated with the applicant trust or legal entity *(if there are more Responsible Persons than can be listed on the form, attach a separate sheet listing the additional Responsible Person(s))*. Please note that a completed Form 5320.23, National Firearms Act (NFA) Responsible Person Questionnaire, must be submitted with the Form 1 application for each Responsible Person.

Full Name   Full Name

_____   _____

_____   _____

_____   _____

---

17. Method of Payment *(Check one) (See Instruction 2h) (if paying by credit/debit card, complete the sections below)*

☐ Check *(Enclosed)*   ☐ Cashier's Check or Money Order *(Enclosed)*   ☐ Visa   ☐ Mastercard   ☐ American Express   ☐ Discover   ☐ Diners Club

Credit/Debit Card Number *(No dashes)*	Name as Printed on the Credit/Debit Card	Expiration Date *(Month & year)*

Credit/Debit Card Billing Address:	Address:		
	City:	State:	Zip Code:

Tax Amount: $

I Authorize ATF to Charge my Credit/Debit Card the Above Amount.

_____   _____
Signature of Cardholder   Date

Your credit/debit card will be charged the above stated amount upon receipt of your application. The charge will be reflected on your credit/debit card statement. In the event your application is NOT approved, the above amount will be credited to the credit/debit card noted above.

Important Information for Currently Registered Firearms

If you are the current registrant of the firearm described on this form, please note the following information.

Estate Procedures: For procedures regarding the transfer of firearms in an estate resulting from the death of the registrant identified in item 3b, the executor should contact the NFA Division, Bureau of ATF, 244 Needy Road, Martinsburg, WV 25405.

Interstate Movement: If the firearm identified in item 4 is a **machinegun, short-barreled rifle, short-barreled shotgun,** or **destructive device,** the registrant may be required by 18 U.S.C. § 922(a)(4) to obtain permission from ATF prior to any transportation in interstate or foreign commerce. ATF Form 5320.20 can be used to request this permission.

Change of Description or Address: The registrant shall notify the NFA Division, Bureau of Alcohol, Tobacco, Firearms and Explosives, 244 Needy Road, Martinsburg, WV 25405, in writing, of any change to the description of the firearm in item 4, or any change to the address of the registrant.

Restrictions on Possession: Any restriction *(see approval block on face of form)* on the possession of the firearm identified in item 4 continues with the further transfer of the firearm.

Persons Prohibited from Possessing Firearms: If the registrant becomes prohibited from possessing a firearm, please contact the NFA Division for procedures on how to dispose of the firearm.

Proof of Registration: A person possessing a firearm registered as required by the NFA shall retain proof of registration which shall be made available to any ATF officer upon request.

Paperwork Reduction Act Notice

This form is in accordance with the Paperwork Reduction Act of 1995. The information you provide is used to establish that the applicant's making and possession of the firearm would be in conformance with Federal, State, and local law. The data is used as proof of lawful registration of a firearm to the manufacturer. The furnishing of this information is mandatory *(26 U.S.C. § 5822)*.

The estimated average burden associated with this collection of information is 4.0 hours per respondent or recordkeeper, depending on individual circumstances. Comments concerning the accuracy of this burden estimate and suggestion for reducing this burden should be addressed to Reports Management Officer, Information Technology Coordination Staff, Bureau of Alcohol, Tobacco, Firearms and Explosives, Washington, DC 20226.

An agency may not conduct or sponsor, and a person is not required to respond to, a collection of information unless it displays a currently valid OMB control number.

ATF Copy

ATF E-Form 1 (5320.1)
Revised August 2017

ATF Form 4 Page 1

U.S. Department of Justice
Bureau of Alcohol, Tobacco, Firearms and Explosives

OMB No. 1140-0014 (06/30/2019)

Application for Tax Paid Transfer and Registration of Firearm

ATF Control Number

SUBMIT in DUPLICATE to: National Firearms Act Branch
Bureau of Alcohol, Tobacco, Firearms and Explosives, P.O. Box 530298, Atlanta, GA 30353-0298

1. Type of Transfer *(Check one)*

☐ $5   ☐ $200

Submit the appropriate tax payment with the application. The tax may be paid by credit or debit card, check, or money order. Please complete item 20. Upon approval of the application, we will affix and cancel the required National Firearms Act stamp. *(See instructions 2b, 2i and 3)*

2a. Transferee's Name and Address *(Include trade name, if any) (See Instruction 2d)*

☐ INDIVIDUAL   ☐ TRUST or LEGAL ENTITY

2b. County

3a. Transferor's Name and Address *(Include trade name, if any) (Executors: see instruction 2k)*

3b. e-mail address *(optional)*

3c. Transferor's Telephone *(Area Code and Number)*

3d. If Applicable: Decedent's Name, Address, and Date of Death

3e. Number, Street, City, State and Zip Code of Residence *(or Firearms Business Premises)* If Different from Item 3a.

The above-named and undersigned transferor hereby makes application as required by Section 5812 of the National Firearms Act to transfer and register the firearm described below to the transferee.

4. Description of Firearm *(Complete items a through h) (See instruction 2m)*

a. Name and Address of Maker, Manufacturer and/or Importer of Firearm	b. Type of Firearm *(See definitions)*	c. Caliber or Gauge	d. Model
			e. Of Barrel: / f. Overall: — Length *(Inches)*
			g. Serial Number

h. Additional Description or Data Appearing on Firearm *(Attach additional sheet if necessary)*

5. Transferee's Federal Firearms License *(If any)*				6. Transferee's Special (Occupational) Tax Status *(If any)*	
(Give complete 15-digit number) (See instruction 2c)				a. Employer Identification Number	b. Class
First 6 digits	2 digits	2 digits	5 digits		

7. Transferor's Federal Firearms License *(If any)*				8. Transferor's Special (Occupational) Tax Status *(If any)*	
First 6 digits	2 digits	2 digits	5 digits	a. Employer Identification Number	b. Class

Under Penalties of Perjury, I Declare that I have examined this application, and to the best of my knowledge and belief it is true, correct and complete, and that the transfer of the described firearm to the transferee and receipt and possession of it by the transferee are not prohibited by the provisions of Title 18, United States Code; Chap 44; Title 26, United States Code; Chap 53; or any provisions of State or local law.

9. Signature of Transferor *(Or authorized official)*

10. Name and Title of Authorized Official *(Print or type)*

11. Date

The Space Below is for the use of the Bureau of Alcohol, Tobacco, Firearms and Explosives

By Authority of The Director, This Application Has Been Examined, and the Transfer and Registration of the Firearm Described Herein and the Interstate Movement of that Firearm, When Applicable to the Transferee are:

Stamp Denomination

☐ Approved *(With the following conditions, if any)*

☐ Disapproved *(For the following reasons)*

Signature of Authorized ATF Official

Date

Previous Editions are Obsolete

ATF Copy

ATF E-Form 4 (5320.4)
Revised May 2016

ATF Form 4 Page 2

Transferee Certification

12. Law Enforcement Notification *(See instruction 2f)*

The transferee is to provide notification of the proposed acquisition and possession of the firearm described on this Form 4 by providing a copy of the completed form to the chief law enforcement officer in the agency identified below:

Agency or Department Name　　　　　　　　　　　　　　　Name and Title of Official

---

Address (Street address or P.O. Box, City, State and Zip Code) to which sent (mailed or delivered))

Information for the Chief Law Enforcement Officer

This form provides notification of the transferee's intent to acquire and possess the National Firearms Act (NFA) firearm. No action on your part is required. However, should you have information that may disqualify this person from acquiring or possessing a firearm, please contact the NFA Branch at (304) 616-4500 or NFA@atf.gov. A "Yes" answer to items 14.a through 14.h or 16.b or 16.c could disqualify a person from acquiring or possessing a firearm. Also, ATF will not approve an application if the transfer or possession of the firearm is in violation of State or local law.

13. **Transferee Necessity Statement** *(See instruction 2e)*

I, _____ , have a reasonable necessity to possess the machinegun, short-barreled rifle,
(Name and Title of Transferee)

short-barreled shotgun, or destructive device described on this application for the following reason(s) _____

and my possession of the device or weapon would be consistent with public safety (18 U.S.C. § 922(b) (4) and 27 CFR § 478.98).

Transferee Questions (Complete Only When Transferee is An Individual)

14. Answer questions 14.a. through 14.h. Answer questions 16 and 17, if applicable. For any "Yes" answer the transferee shall provide details on a separate sheet. *(See instruction 7b and definitions)*

		Yes	No	15. Photograph
a.	Are you under indictment or information in any court for a felony, or any other crime, for which the judge could imprison you for more than one year? *(See definition 1m)*			
b.	Have you ever been convicted in any court for a felony, or any other crime, for which the judge could have imprisoned you for more than one year, even if you received a shorter sentence including probation? *(See definition 1n)*			Affix Recent Photograph Here *(Approximately 2" x 2")* *(See instruction 2g)*
c.	Are you a fugitive from justice? *(See definitions 1s)*			
d.	Are you an unlawful user of, or addicted to, marijuana or any depressant, stimulant, narcotic drug, or any other controlled substance? **Warning: The use or possession of marijuana remains unlawful under Federal law regardless of whether it has been legalized or decriminalized for medicinal or recreational purposes in the state where you reside.**			
e.	Have you ever been adjudicated as a mental defective OR have you ever been committed to a mental institution? *(See definitions 1n and 1o)*			
f.	Have you been discharged from the Armed Forces under **dishonorable** conditions?			
g.	Are you subject to a court order restraining you from harassing, stalking, or threatening your child or an intimate partner or child of such partner? *(See definition 1p)*			
h.	Have you ever been convicted in any court of a misdemeanor crime of domestic violence? *(See definition 1q)*			

16a. Country of Citizenship *(Check/List more than one, if applicable. Nationals of the United States may check U.S.A.) (See definition 1r)*

☐ United States of America　　　☐ Other Country/Countries (specify): _____

		Yes	No
b.	Have you ever renounced your United States citizenship?		
c.	Are you an alien illegally or unlawfully in the United States?		
d.1.	Are you an alien who has been admitted to the United States under a nonimmigrant visa?		
d.2.	If "yes", do you fall within any of the exceptions stated in the instructions? Attach the documentation to the application ☐ N/A		

17. If you are an alien. record your U.S.-Issued Alien or Admission number (AR#, USCIS#, or I94#):

CERTIFICATION: Under penalties imposed by 18 U.S.C. § 924 and 26 U.S.C. § 5861, I certify that, upon submission of this form to ATF, a completed copy of this form will be directed to the chief law enforcement officer (CLEO) shown in item 12, that the statements, as applicable, contained in this certification, and any attached documents in support thereof, are true and correct to the best of my knowledge and belief. NOTE: See Instructions 2.d(2) and 2.d(3) for the items to be completed depending on the type of transferee.

Signature of Transferee　　　　　　　　　　　　Date

ATF Copy

ATF E-Form 4 (5320.4)
Revised May 2016

ATF Form 4 Page 3

18. Number of Responsible Persons *(see definitions)* associated with the transferee trust or legal entity _____

19. Provide the full name (printed or typed) below for each Responsible Person associated with the applicant trust or legal entity (if there are more Responsible Persons than can be listed on the form, attach a separate sheet listing the additional Responsible Person(s)). Please note that a completed Form 5320.23, National Firearms Act (NFA) Responsible Person Questionnaire, must be submitted with the Form 4 application for each Responsible Person.

Full Name   Full Name

---

20. **Method of Payment** *(Check one) (See instruction 21)* (if paying by credit/debit card, complete the sections below)

☐ Check *(Enclosed)*   ☐ Cashier's Check or Money Order *(Enclosed)*   ☐ Visa   ☐ Mastercard   ☐ American Express   ☐ Discover   ☐ Diners Club

Credit/Debit Card Number *(No dashes)*	Name as Printed on the Credit/Debit Card	Expiration Date *(Month & year)*

Credit/Debit Card Billing Address:	Address:		
	City:	State:	Zip Code:

Total Amount:
$

I Authorize ATF to Charge my Credit/Debit Card the Tax Amount.

_____   _____
Signature of Cardholder   Date

Your credit/debit card will be charged the above stated amount upon receipt of the application. The charge will be reflected on your credit/debit card statement. In the event your application is NOT approved, the above amount will be credited to the credit/debit card noted above.

Important Information for Currently Registered Firearms
If you are the current registrant of the firearm described on this form, please note the following information.

Estate Procedures: For procedures regarding the transfer of firearms in an estate resulting from the death of the registrant identified in item 2a, the executor should contact the NFA Branch, Bureau of Alcohol, Tobacco, Firearms and Explosives, 244 Needy Road, Martinsburg, WV 25405.

Change of Address: Unless currently licensed under the Gun Control Act, the registrant shall notify the NFA Branch, Bureau of Alcohol, Tobacco, Firearms, and Explosives, 244 Needy Road, Martinsburg, WV 25405, in writing, of any change to the address in item 2a.

Change of Description: The registrant shall notify the NFA Branch, Bureau of Alcohol, Tobacco, Firearms and Explosives, 244 Needy Road, Martinsburg, WV 25405, in writing, of any change to the description of the firearm(s) in item 4.

Interstate Movement: If the firearm identified in item 4 is a **machinegun, short-barreled rifle, short-barreled shotgun, or destructive device**, the registrant may be required by 18 U.S.C. § 922(a)(4) to obtain permission from ATF prior to any transportation in interstate or foreign commerce. ATF E-Form 5320.20 can be used to request this permission.

Restrictions on Possession: Any restriction *(see approval block on face of form)* on the possession of the firearm identified in item 4 continues with the further transfer of the firearm.

Persons Prohibited from Possessing Firearms: If the registrant becomes prohibited from possessing a firearm, please contact the NFA Branch for procedures on how to dispose of the firearm.

Proof of Registration: A person possessing a firearm registered as required by the NFA shall retain proof of registration which shall be made available to any ATF officer upon request.

Paperwork Reduction Act Notice
This form meets the clearance requirements of the Paperwork Reduction Act of 1995. The information you provide is used in applying to transfer serviceable firearms taxpaid. Data is used to identify transferor, transferee, and firearm, and to ensure legality for transfer under Federal, State and local laws. The furnishing of this information is mandatory (26 U.S.C. § 5812).

The estimated average burden associated with this collection of information is 3.78 hours per respondent or recordkeeper, depending on individual circumstances. Comments concerning the accuracy of this burden estimate and suggestion for reducing this burden should be addressed to Reports Management Officer, Information Technology Coordination Staff, Bureau of Alcohol, Tobacco, Firearms and Explosives, Washington, DC 20226.

An agency may not conduct or sponsor, and a person is not required to respond to, a collection of information unless it displays a currently valid OMB control number.

ATF Copy

ATF E-Form 4 (5320.4)
Revised May 2016

ATF Form 5320.23 Page 1

U.S. Department of Justice
Bureau of Alcohol, Tobacco, Firearms and Explosives

OMB No. 1140-0107 (06/30/2019)

National Firearms Act *(NFA)*
Responsible Person Questionnaire

Complete the form in duplicate. The ATF copy of the form, with fingerprints on Form FD-258 and photograph, will be submitted with the ATF Form 1, 4, or 5 (to the address shown on the specific form) and the other copy will be directed to the responsible person's chief law enforcement officer. *(See Instructions)*

1. Please check the appropriate box to indicate with which ATF form this questionnaire will be submitted.

☐ ATF Form 1 ☐ ATF Form 4 ☐ ATF Form 5

2. Name and Address of Applicant or Transferee *(as shown on the ATF Form 1, 4 or 5) (see instruction 2)*

3a. Name and Home Address of Responsible Person	3b. Telephone *(Area code and Number)*
	3c. e-mail address *(optional)*
	3d. Other names used *(including maiden name)*

4a. Type of Firearm *(see definition 5)*	3e. Photograph
4b. Name and Address of Maker, Manufacturer and/or Importer of Firearm	Affix recent Photograph Here *(Approximately 2" x 2")* *(See instruction 3b)*

4c. Firearm Model	4d. Caliber or Gauge	4e. Firearm Serial Number	

5. Law Enforcement Notification *(See instruction 5)*

As a responsible person (see definition 4) of the trust or legal entity identified in Item 2 of this form, I am required to provide notification of the proposed making or acquisition and possession of the firearm described in item 4 of this form by providing a copy of the completed form to the chief law enforcement officer (CLEO) in the agency identified below:

Agency or Department Name   Name and Title of Official

Address (Street address or P.O. Box, City, State and Zip Code) to which sent (mailed or delivered)

Information for the Chief Law Enforcement Officer

This form provides notification of the maker or transferee's intent to make or acquire and possess a National Firearms Act (NFA) firearm. No action on your part is required. However, should you have information that may disqualify this person from making or possessing a firearm, please contact the NFA Branch at (304) 616-4500 or NFA@atf.gov. A "Yes" answer to items 6h or item 7b or 7c could disqualify a person from acquiring or possessing a firearm. Also, ATF may not approve an application if the transfer or possession of the firearm would be in violation of State or local law.

ATF Copy

ATF E-Form 5320.23
Revised May 2016

ATF Form 5320.23 Page 2

6. Answer questions 6.a through 6.h. Answer questions 7 and 8 if applicable. For any "Yes" answer the transferee shall provide details on a separate sheet. *(See definitions 8-12)*

	Yes	No
a. Are you under indictment or information in any court for a felony, or any other crime, for which the judge could imprison you for more than one year? *(See definition 8)*		
b. Have you ever been convicted in any court for a felony, or any other crime, for which the judge could have imprisoned you for more than one year, even if you received a shorter sentence including probation? *(See definition 8)*		
c. Are you a fugitive from justice? *(See definition 13)*		
d. Are you an unlawful user of, or addicted to, marijuana or any depressant, stimulant, narcotic drug, or any other controlled substance? **Warning: The use or possession of marijuana remains unlawful under Federal law regardless of whether is has been legalized or decriminalized for medicinal or recreational purposes in the state where you reside.**		
e. Have you ever been adjudicated as a mental defective **OR** have you ever been committed to a mental institution? *(See definitions 9 and 10)*		
f. Have you been discharged from the Armed Forces under **dishonorable** conditions?		
g. Are you subject to a court order restraining you from harassing, stalking, or threatening your child or an intimate partner or child of such partner? *(See definition 11)*		
h. Have you ever been convicted in any court of a misdemeanor crime of domestic violence? *(See definition 14)*		

7a. Country of Citizenship: *(Check/List more than one, if applicable. Nationals of the United States may check U.S.A.) (See definition 12)*

☐ United States of America   ☐ Other Country/Countries (specify): _____

	Yes	No
b. Have you ever renounced your United States citizenship?		
c. Are you an alien illegally or unlawfully in the United States?		
d.1. Are you an alien who has been admitted to the United States under a nonimmigrant visa?		
d.2. If "yes", do you fall within any of the exceptions stated in the instructions? Attach the documentation to the questionnaire ☐ N/A		

8. If you are an alien, record your U.S.-Issued Alien or Admission number (AR#, USCIS#, or 194#): _____

CERTIFICATION: Under penalties imposed by 18 U.S.C. § 924 and 26 U.S.C. § 5861, I certify that, upon submission of this form to ATF, a completed copy of this form will be directed to the chief law enforcement officer (CLEO) shown in item 5, that the statements contained in this certification, and any attached documents in support thereof, are true and correct to the best of my knowledge and belief.

_____   _____
Signature of Responsible Person   Date

Instructions

1. Completion: Each responsible person (see definition 4) of a trust or legal entity seeking to make or acquire a National Firearms Act *(NFA)* firearm shall complete this form in duplicate. (see instruction 9)
   a. Each responsible person must submit his/her fingerprints and photograph with this form *(see below)*.
   b. Please note that this form is not required when the applicant on Form 1, 4 or 5 is an individual.
2. Item 2- Enter the name, trade name *(if any)* and address of the trust or legal entity identified on the Form 1 (items 3a and b); Form 4 *(item 2a)*; or Form 5 *(item 2a)*
3. Item 3- Responsible Person information
   a. Provide the information for the responsible person in items 3a through 3e.
   b. Item 3e - Photograph: The responsible person shall attach, in item 3e on the ATF copy of the form only, a 2-inch by 2-inch frontal view photograph taken within one year prior to the date of the filing of the form. Item 3e is obscured on the CLEO copy.
4. Firearm information
   a. Type of NFA firearm: see definition 5 and as identified in item 4b of Form 1, 4, or 5
   b. Name of maker, manufacturer and/or importer: as identified in item 4a of Form 1, 4, or 5
   c. Firearm Model: identified in item 4d of Form 1, 4, or 5
   d. Caliber or Gauge: identified in item 4c of Form 1, 4 or 5
   e. Firearm Serial Number: identified in item 4g of Form 1, 4 or 5. Item 4e is obscured on the CLEO copy.
5. Item 5- Law Enforcement Notification: Each responsible person must provide a notification on this form of the proposed making or acquisition of an NFA firearm to his/her chief law enforcement officer having jurisdiction where the responsible person is located. The chief law enforcement officer is considered to be the Chief of Police; the Sheriff; the Head of the State Police; or a State or local district attorney or prosecutor.
6. Complete items 6 through 8
7. Fingerprints: The responsible person shall submit, in duplicate with the ATF copy of this form, his or her fingerprints on FBI Form FD-258 and the fingerprints must be clear for accurate classification and taken by someone properly equipped to take them. No fingerprints are required with the copy of the form sent to the chief law enforcement officer.
8. State or Local Permit: If the State in which the responsible person resides requires the responsible person to have a State or Local permit or licensee, a copy of the permit or license must be submitted with this form.
9. Disposition: The ATF copy of the form, with the fingerprints and photograph, shall be submitted with the ATF Form 1, 4 or 5. The other copy shall be directed to the responsible person's chief law enforcement officer identified in item 5 of this form.
10. Sign and date the form. The signature must be original.

ATF Copy

ATF E-Form 5320.23
Revised May 2016

ATF Form 5320.23 Page 3

U.S. Department of Justice
Bureau of Alcohol, Tobacco, Firearms and Explosives

OMB No. 1140-0107 (06/30/2019)

National Firearms Act *(NFA)*
Responsible Person Questionnaire

Complete the form in duplicate. The ATF copy of the form, with fingerprints on Form FD-258 and photograph, will be submitted with the ATF Form 1, 4, or 5 (to the address shown on the specific form) and the other copy will be directed to the responsible person's chief law enforcement officer. *(See Instructions)*

1. Please check the appropriate box to indicate with which ATF form this questionnaire will be submitted.

☐ ATF Form 1   ☐ ATF Form 4   ☐ ATF Form 5

2. Name and Address of Applicant or Transferee *(as shown on the ATF Form 1, 4 or 5) (see instruction 2)*

3a. Name and Home Address of Responsible Person	3b. Telephone *(Area code and Number)*
	3c. e-mail address *(optional)*
	3d. Other names used *(including maiden name)*

4a. Type of Firearm *(see definition 5)*

4b. Name and Address of Maker, Manufacturer and/or Importer of Firearm

4c. Firearm Model	4d. Caliber or Gauge

5. Law Enforcement Notification *(See instruction 5)*

As a responsible person (see definition 4) of the trust or legal entity identified in Item 2 of this form, I am required to provide notification of the proposed making or acquisition and possession of the firearm described in item 4 of this form by providing a copy of the completed form to the chief law enforcement officer (CLEO) in the agency identified below:

Agency or Department Name   Name and Title of Official

Address (Street address or P.O. Box, City, State and Zip Code) to which sent (mailed or delivered)

Information for the Chief Law Enforcement Officer

This form provides notification of the maker or transferee's intent to make or acquire and possess a National Firearms Act (NFA) firearm. No action on your part is required. However, should you have information that may disqualify this person from making or possessing a firearm, please contact the NFA Branch at (304) 616-4500 or NFA@atf.gov. A "Yes" answer to items 6h or item 7b or 7c could disqualify a person from acquiring or possessing a firearm. Also, ATF may not approve an application if the transfer or possession of the firearm would be in violation of State or local law.

CLEO Copy

ATF E-Form 5320.23
Revised May 2016

6. Answer questions 6.a through 6.h. Answer questions 7 and 8 if applicable. For any "Yes" answer the transferee shall provide details on a separate sheet. *(See definitions 8-12)*

	Yes	No
a. Are you under indictment or information in any court for a felony, or any other crime, for which the judge could imprison you for more than one year? *(See definition 8)*		
b. Have you ever been convicted in any court for a felony, or any other crime, for which the judge could have imprisoned you for more than one year, even if you received a shorter sentence including probation? *(See definition 8)*		
c. Are you a fugitive from justice? *(See definition 13)*		
d. Are you an unlawful user of, or addicted to, marijuana or any depressant, stimulant, narcotic drug, or any other controlled substance? **Warning: The use or possession of marijuana remains unlawful under Federal law regardless of whether is has been legalized or decriminalized for medicinal or recreational purposes in the state where you reside.**		
e. Have you ever been adjudicated as a mental defective OR have you ever been committed to a mental institution? *(See definitions 9 and 10)*		
f. Have you been discharged from the Armed Forces under **dishonorable** conditions?		
g. Are you subject to a court order restraining you from harassing, stalking, or threatening your child or an intimate partner or child of such partner? *(See definition 11)*		
h. Have you ever been convicted in any court of a misdemeanor crime of domestic violence? *(See definition 14)*		

7a. Country of Citizenship: *(Check/List more than one, if applicable. Nationals of the United States may check U.S.A.) (See definition 12)*

☐ United States of America ☐ Other Country/Countries (specify): _____

	Yes	No
b. Have you ever renounced your United States citizenship?		
c. Are you an alien illegally or unlawfully in the United States?		
d.1. Are you an alien who has been admitted to the United States under a nonimmigrant visa?		
d.2. If "yes", do you fall within any of the exceptions stated in the instructions? Attach the documentation to the questionnaire ☐ N/A		

8. If you are an alien, record your U.S.-Issued Alien or Admission number (AR#, USCIS#, or 194#): _____

CERTIFICATION: Under penalties imposed by 18 U.S.C. § 924 and 26 U.S.C. § 5861, I certify that, upon submission of this form to ATF, a completed copy of this form will be directed to the chief law enforcement officer (CLEO) shown in item 5, that the statements contained in this certification, and any attached documents in support thereof, are true and correct to the best of my knowledge and belief.

_____   _____
Signature of Responsible Person   Date

Instructions

1. Completion: Each responsible person (see definition 4) of a trust or legal entity seeking to make or acquire a National Firearms Act *(NFA)* firearm shall complete this form in duplicate. (see instruction 9)
   a. Each responsible person must submit his/her fingerprints and photograph with this form *(see below)*.
   b. Please note that this form is not required when the applicant on Form 1, 4 or 5 is an individual.
2. Item 2- Enter the name, trade name *(if any)* and address of the trust or legal entity identified on the Form 1 (items 3a and b); Form 4 *(item 2a)*; or Form 5 *(item 2a)*
3. Item 3- Responsible Person information
   a. Provide the information for the responsible person in items 3a through 3e.
   b. Item 3e - Photograph: The responsible person shall attach, in item 3e on the ATF copy of the form only, a 2-inch by 2-inch frontal view photograph taken within one year prior to the date of the filing of the form. Item 3c is obscured on the CLEO copy.
4. Firearm information
   a. Type of NFA firearm: see definition 5 and as identified in item 4b of Form 1, 4 or 5
   b. Name of maker, manufacturer and/or importer: as identified in item 4a of Form 1, 4 or 5
   c. Firearm Model: identified in item 4d of Form 1, 4 or 5
   d. Caliber or Gauge: identified in item 4c of Form 1, 4 or 5
   e. Firearm Serial Number: identified in item 4g of Form 1, 4 or 5. Item 4e is obscured on the CLEO copy.
5. Item 5- Law Enforcement Notification: Each responsible person must provide a notification on this form of the proposed making or acquisition of an NFA firearm to his/her chief law enforcement officer having jurisdiction where the responsible person is located. The chief law enforcement officer is considered to be the Chief of Police; the Sheriff; the Head of the State Police; or a State or local district attorney or prosecutor.
6. Complete items 6 through 8
7. Fingerprints: The responsible person shall submit, in duplicate with the ATF copy of this form, his or her fingerprints on FBI Form FD-258 and the fingerprints must be clear for accurate classification and taken by someone properly equipped to take them. No fingerprints are required with the copy of the form sent to the chief law enforcement officer.
8. State or Local Permit: If the State in which the responsible person resides requires the responsible person to have a State or Local permit or licensee, a copy of the permit or license must be submitted with this form.
9. Disposition: The ATF copy of the form, with the fingerprints and photograph, shall be submitted with the ATF Form 1, 4 or 5. The other copy shall be directed to the responsible person's chief law enforcement officer identified in item 5 of this form.
10. Sign and date the form. The signature must be original.

CLEO Copy

ATF E-Form 5320.23
Revised May 2016

➤ ABOUT THE ◄

AUTHORS

DAVID S. KATZ CO-AUTHOR

David Katz strongly believes that the Founding Fathers of our country knew that only by allowing law abiding citizens to keep and bear arms could the people of this country be free. David has been practicing criminal law as a defense attorney since first becoming licensed to practice law. He has handled thousands of cases defending the constitutional rights of the citizens of Florida. David has earned a reputation as a top criminal defense lawyer nationally and is frequently invited to speak at continuing legal education seminars in Florida and throughout the country. At these seminars, David helps to teach defense trial skills to other criminal defense lawyers. Additionally, David has lectured on firearms laws hundreds of times throughout the State of Florida. David has previously authored or co-authored eight books on criminal defense and trial skills, including several manuals used to train other lawyers in the art of criminal defense.

David has earned numerous awards throughout his legal career including a Superb rating and Client Choice Award from Avvo and the Client Distinction Award from Martindale-Hubble. David has also been chosen as a Top 100 Trial Lawyer in Florida by the National Trial Lawyers and awarded the status of Rising Star by Super Lawyers Magazine.

David and his partner James Phillips stand ready to defend the rights of the thousands of U.S. Law Shield members in Florida against charges that may be brought against them if they are ever forced to use their firearm or other CWFL weapon in self-defense.

JAMES D. PHILLIPS CO-AUTHOR

Mr. Phillips is an aggressive trial attorney, who uses his knowledge and experience as a former prosecutor to zealously advocate for his clients. Mr. Phillips has defended individuals charged with misdemeanors, felonies, sex crimes, firearms crimes, internet crimes, felonies punishable by life and murder in State and Federal courts.

Mr. Phillips has been the featured speaker at seminars throughout the State of Florida, lecturing on Self-Defense, Use of Deadly Force, Castle Doctrine and Stand Your Ground. Also, Mr. Phillips has been the key speaker at various seminars throughout the country where he has taught and trained other attorneys on jury selection, cross examination and trial strategies in criminal trials. Mr. Phillips is a published author on topics regarding DUI Defense, Jury Selection, Plea Bargaining, and Trial Strategy.

Based on his experience, peer-reviews and client reviews, Mr. Phillips has received Superb rating since 2011 from AVVO, the highest level an attorney can obtain, and has been rated Preeminent (5 out of 5) by Martindale-Hubbell Client Review as of May 2013. Furthermore, Martindale-Hubbell has presented Mr. Phillips with the Client's Distinction award for 2013 through 2015. He has received recognition for his demonstrated leadership and achievement in the legal profession by being selected for inclusion in Strathmore's Who's Who for 2013. Since 2013, Mr. Phillips has been selected every year as a Rising Star by Super Lawyers (less than 2.5% of all attorneys receive this honor) and was selected as one of Central Florida's Top 100 Trial Lawyers, and as one of Florida's Top 40 Trial Lawyers Under 40 by The National Trial Lawyers for the past three years. Mr. Phillips was featured in Orlando Style Magazine's September 2014 edition as one of Central Florida's Legal Elite.